Pitching Championship Horseshoes

OTTIE W. RENO

The Author

The author is a common pleas judge who pitches horseshoes for a hobby.

Pitching Championship Horseshoes

Second Edition, Revised

Ottie W. Reno

South Brunswick and New York: A. S. Barnes and Company
London: Thomas Yoseloff Ltd

© 1971 by A. S. Barnes and Co., Inc.
New Material © 1975 by A. S. Barnes and Co., Inc.
Library of Congress Catalogue Card Number: 73-5328

A. S. Barnes and Co., Inc.
Cranbury, New Jersey 08512

Thomas Yoseloff Ltd
108 New Bond Street
London W1Y 0QX, England

ISBN 0-498-01408-8 (cloth)
ISBN 0-498-01410-X (paper)
Printed in the United States of America

Dedicated to the recognition
of horseshoe pitching as a sport.
This game is as
American as banjo
and is part and parcel
of American history.

Contents

	Preface	9
	Acknowledgments	12
1	In the Beginning	15
2	A Pastime Becomes a Science	18
3	Construction and Care of Playing Courts	25
4	Tools of the Trade	38
5	Official Playing Rules and Constitution	42
6	How to Pitch Ringers	63
7	Your Local Club and Its Pitching Program	122
8	Useful Charts and Tables	144
9	Methods of Scoring	173
10	The National Horseshoe Pitchers' Association	187
11	Horseshoe Pitching's Hall of Fame	191
12	State Champions	204
13	World Tournament Records	262
14	Canadian Records	290
15	The Women	298
16	The Juniors	327
17	Advantages of Horseshoe Pitching	325
18	Horseshoe Pitching Goes to South Africa	351
	Index	358

Preface

In 1963 I published *The Story of Horseshoes* because there was no book on the open market on the sport of horseshoe pitching. This 169-page book contained all of the information that a new local horseshoe pitching club or a beginning pitcher would need to get started in the game. It was distributed in all 50 states, most of the provinces of Canada and some foreign countries. The book is now out of print, but it has served its purpose.

In the eleven years that have since come and gone, horseshoe pitching has shown a tremendous growth: membership in the NHPA has constantly grown; new clubs have sprung up everywhere; state chapters have become active in the states where play had been at a standstill; playing courts both inside and outside have been built; and game-related items such as scoreboards, pitching shoes, awards, and scoring aids are being manufactured.

Between 1963 and 1970 many letters came to me concerning the first book and I spent many relaxing hours talking with pitchers about its contents. They expressed the greatest interest in "How to Pitch," "How to Run Club Activities," and "Statistics on the Champions" in that order.

In 1971 the first edition of this book was published.

In it a conscious effort was made to enlarge and clarify those areas of interest as well as to include much new material so as to make a more useful item for both individual pitchers and new clubs.

A player who knows little or nothing about the game can find inside everything he will need to get started. Pitching tips from Ted Allen, John Monasmith, Harold Reno, Curt Day, Elmer Hohl, Dan Kuchcinski, Paul Focht, and Don Titcomb—all eight World Champions—as well as other state and open tournament champions will benefit beginners and veterans alike. Those interested in organizing a local club, promoting league and tournament play, or polishing various aspects of their own game can find here the necessary aids.

For the women we included pitching tips from three women's World Champions, Vicki Chappelle Winston, Ruth Hangen, and Sue Gillespie Kuchcinski. Women will find that horseshoe pitching holds much for them. So will juniors under 17 years of age and the old-timers who have passed retirement age.

Indications are that some 30 million Americans pitch horseshoes and that most of them pitch less than 30 percent ringers. These players are the principal targets of my book. Only a small percentage of them compete regularly in league or tournament play.

In this revision I have brought the lists of champions and records up to date, rearranged and improved some of the chapters, and added a new one about horseshoe pitching in South Africa and its sister game of Jukskei. Some of the pictures have been replaced and some new ones have been added.

Many ingredients go into the making of a champion; reading this book will not transform the reader into one. However, some basic instruction and familiarity with the game can start him in the right direction and save him a lot of time. It has been my experience that beginners get too little help from experienced players. Those already in the game are reluctant to help: some are unable; others are unwilling. Too often a beginner's plea for help will be met with a reply as vague as "Each pitcher just about has to work it out for himself. Keep trying and your problems will work themselves out." This kind of advice is of little help.

Anyone can play the game. No one has ever mastered it. The challenge is there for players of all degrees of ability, all ages and both sexes.

My hope is simply to provide those interested in pitching horseshoes with a chance to get into the game. Each player will have to decide for himself how much time and effort he will put into the game. His efficiency at pitching ringers, his enjoyment of the sport, and his ability to deliver under fire will increase in direct relation to the work he puts into the game.

OTTIE W. RENO

Acknowledgments

The author gratefully acknowledges the help given by all the state and provincial secretaries listed in chapter 10 in compiling information for the lists of champions, and the permission to quote from the champions in chapters 6, 15, and 17, and particularly to the National Secretaries Robert G. Pence and W. Ray Williams for making their records available.

Pitching Championship Horseshoes

1

In the Beginning

The origin of horseshoe pitching is shrouded in mystery. Looking back into antiquity, using a few facts and a lot of personal supposition, different writers have given different versions of its beginning.

The most likely origin of the game is that it started as a substitute for the Olympic game of discus throwing. The Greeks idolized the athletes who competed in the Olympic games and sought to imitate them.

The type of equipment used in the Olympic contests, including the discus, was too expensive for the average person to afford. It seems likely that poor people began to fashion substitutes for the discus and to hurl them for a distance. They eventually hammered out metal rings, shaped a great deal like a discus, and developed a game similar to quoits. The accent soon shifted from distance to accuracy, with pegs being placed in the ground as targets. They tried to encircle the peg for ringers, and thus was born a new game that was the predecessor of the game of horseshoes.

This game was being played before the birth of Christ. A few centuries after the dawn of the Christian era Greek and Roman armies began to attach metal strips to the feet of their horses to prevent the hoofs from being torn to pieces on the rough terrain over which they moved. As these first horseshoes were discarded, they were gathered up by soldiers and camp followers and pitched. These shoes were thought to have weighed nearly four pounds.

The open side of the shoe brought out another interesting possibility. In addition to going over the peg as the quoit or metal ring had done, there would be occasional ringers when the peg slipped through the open side.

It is very questionable, however, whether the use of horseshoes instead of metal rings became popular because of more ringers. It seems more likely that their use was more a matter of convenience. It was much easier to use them as they were than to hammer them into closed rings. As we shall see, it was a long time before any emphasis was placed on the open side of the shoe.

The Norman soldiers are said to have brought the game to England when they invaded that country. Both horseshoes and quoits were played in England, with quoits being much preferred by the English. The nobles and aristocrats of England and many other nations played quoits for centuries. There are indications that horseshoes were first pitched in England by the women and children because they were lighter than quoits. Eventually, the men began to pitch them, too. Both games were played in Europe through the eighteenth century.

The early settlers in America brought along the game of quoits and horseshoes. By the time the Revolutionary War was fought, the game of horseshoes was played almost exclusively. Quoits was on its way to becoming extinct, and is now played almost nowhere. A link between the game of horseshoes and our early history is the often quoted observation of the Duke of Wellington that "the Colonial War of Liberation was won on the village

IN THE BEGINNING 17

greens by pitchers of horse hardware." Our forefathers were ardent players of the horseshoe game, and nearly every person in America today has played the game at some time or other in his life.

Horseshoe pitching has been played continuously from that time to the present in all parts of the United States. Our soldiers have played horseshoes in their leisure time in every war. And in spite of this widespread playing of the game, there is no trace of organized play in the United States until an active local club was formed at Meadville, Pennsylvania, in 1899.

The game as we know it today is a very recent one. It came into its own about 1920, at which time pitching the open shoe became a deliberate scientific attempt, instead of a blind toss with merely a hope that it would be a ringer. Around this time many things happened that dramatically changed horseshoe pitching from a haphazard game with no standard rules to a well organized game, which can take its place alongside bowling, golf and other individual sports.

A few landmark changes were:

(a) The formation of an organization or governing body;
(b) Adoption of standard rules;
(c) Development of the open shoe;
(d) Manufacture of standard pitching shoes with better hooks and balance.

2
A Pastime Becomes a Science

About 1900 and shortly thereafter horseshoe pitching began to flourish in different sections of the United States. Kansas, Missouri, Pennsylvania, Iowa, Florida, New York, Ohio and California were among the busiest states. There are records of local clubs and local tournaments in all of these states prior to 1915, and indications that matches were held with players from other states.

One of the things that kept the game from progressing more rapidly was the great variation in playing rules. The pitching distance ranged from 25 feet in some localities to 45 feet in others. Stakes were two inches high in some states, eight inches high in others. A few players had shoes specially made by blacksmiths, but most of them used shoes that had previously been worn by horses. Ringers were scored as five points in some spots and three in others. Leaners were scored as one, two or three points in different communities. In most places the top ringer claimed all ringers under it.

There was no organized body to govern the game, and no set of rules by which to play it. As teams from the different localities began to play matches against each other, it became apparent that a uniform set of rules and a governing body were needed. It was obviously unfair to ask either team to play by the other's rules, particularly if the distance between the stakes varied.

Formation of the Grand League

The first record of an attempt to adopt uniform rules was in 1913, when several Kansas and Missouri players sat down and drafted a set of playing rules. To arrive at the best rules, they pitched a given number of games under each of the different versions of the rules and adopted the one they felt was best.

They then went a step further and set up a ruling body by whose authority these rules were adopted.

In the courtroom of the First District Court, Kansas City, Kansas, on May 16, 1914, the Grand League of the American Horseshoe Pitchers Association became the first ruling body of the horseshoe pitching game. Officers were elected, and a constitution and bylaws were adopted.

Under this parent organization local charters were granted, and the uniform rules were spread into other states and adopted.

Among the rules adopted by the Grand League were some very significant ones. One of the important ones was that equals cancelled equals. One ringer by the second pitcher that landed on top of two ringers by the first pitcher had counted as three ringers for the second pitcher in the past. Now it would cancel one of the first pitcher's ringers but the first pitcher would still score one live ringer. This gave the pitcher who threw two ringers the advantage he had earned.

Another rule, which helped all players by giving them a bigger target, raised the stake to eight inches. The possibility of getting more ringers made the game immediately more attractive. Since that time the height of the stake has been raised to 12 inches and finally to 14. This higher stake, along with a three-inch incline toward the other stake, has made it possible for the players to pitch more ringers. The adoption of the moist clay for a pitching surface has kept ringers from bouncing off the stake after they were pitched.

The league set the rule that shoes should not weigh less than two pounds and not more than two pounds and three ounces. This served to standardize the pitching shoe not too far from the present weight, as set out in the rules elsewhere in this book.

Leaners were set at three points, ringers at five points and shoes within six inches of the stake at one point. The box was three feet on either side and six feet behind the stake. Pitchers were permitted to stand anywhere in the box, and the pitching distance was set at 38½ feet.

The Open Shoe

The advent of the open shoe came about some time between 1905 and 1920. The open shoe, more than any other single innovation, made horseshoe pitching the game it is today. It completely revolutionized the sport. Concentration had been on getting close to the stake in the past, with an occasional ringer. Ringers were so difficult to throw that pitchers did not expect to hit many. There was not enough reward to justify long hours of practice. The open shoe made ringers easier to get, and they became the object of every pitch.

Several persons claim to have discovered the open shoe. One example is the story of Dr. F. M. Robinson of Poughkeepsie, New York, who in 1909 is said to have been playing a game near the Allison Hotel in St. Petersburg, Flor-

A PASTIME BECOMES A SCIENCE

ida, with O. T. Battles of Chardon, Ohio, Frank Elliot of Rochester, New York, and another man whose name is no longer remembered. Battles noticed that Dr. Robinson's shoes were landing "fork to"—his expression for open. This was a surprise, even to the doctor, and upon taking a closer look he found that he was throwing a natural one and three-quarters turn by holding his forefinger around the heel caulk of the shoe.

This story may or may not be true. If it is true, Dr. Robinson may or may not have been the first to pitch the open shoe. It is at least likely that he was the first in St. Petersburg, and that his discovery set that colony of pitchers to practicing the open shoe.

Similar incidents occurred in other parts of the country, and other pitchers began to throw the open shoe, until it finally became commonplace.

The full impact of the open shoe was not felt until the National Tournament of 1920. George W. May, a fireman from Akron, Ohio, came to that tournament, which was held in St. Petersburg, Florida, without any prior record. When he left, he was National Champion, having swept through 24 games without a loss, averaging a little more than 50 per cent ringers. An unbelievable feat at the time, this changed the game over night into a quest for ringers that grows more heated with every passing year. Three men, who had practiced the open shoe with May and had perfected it to a lesser degree, accompanied May to Florida in that historic year, and they took the top four spots in the tournament. Behind May in the final standings were Joe Wilkinson, Scotty Rowan and Huey Palmer.

May is another who claims to have discovered the open shoe. There are no records to answer that question, but the records do establish that he was the first man to make it work in a major tournament. We must leave it to the members of the hot stove league to decide who really discovered it. One thing we can agree on; the open shoe is here to stay.

Manufacturers soon began to make shoes and other pitching equipment in sufficient quantities to supply the demand, and horseshoes containing nail holes were on their way out. The subject of equipment is treated more thoroughly in a later chapter.

The National Horseshoe Pitchers' Association of America

On May 10, 1921, the National Horseshoe Pitchers' Association of the United States was organized. It was incorporated under the laws of the state of Ohio as a nonprofit organization. On February 26, 1925, its name was changed to the National Horseshoe Pitchers' Association of America, the name it still bears. It is the only governing body of national scope today, and it has for its objects the promotion and protection of the game and the maintenance of standard rules throughout the country.

The NHPA has chapters in nearly every state in the United States. The Canadian Horseshoe Pitchers' Association operates in conjunction with the NHPA, and some of the finest Canadian pitchers play in NHPA tournaments. Elmer Hohl of Wellesley, Ontario, won the world championship in 1965, 1968, 1972, and 1973. His mark of 88.5 percent ringers in the 1968 tournament stands as the world record. Ross Stevenson won the 1965 Junior world championship and the 1972 Class B championship.

In addition to holding a World Championship tournament each year, the National Horseshoe Pitchers' Association sanctions and issues Certificates of Championship for state, district, county and open tournaments wherever local clubs bid for those tournaments.

Another venture of the National Horseshoe Pitchers' Association, whose value to the game cannot be estimated, is the monthly magazine, *The Horseshoe Pitchers News Digest,* edited by Ellis Cobb of 1307 Solfisburg Avenue, Aurora, Illinois. This magazine carries horseshoe news from all parts of the country including notices of coming events, results of meets after they are concluded, and manufacturers' ads.

The practice of having a magazine as an instrument of the national association can be credited to the founders of the Grand League in 1914. They originated the Horseshoe Guide, the first publication of its kind, which contained playing rules, a report of the annual convention, officers, the annual world tournament, and other contests. Shortly after the formation of the National Horseshoe Pitchers' Association, R. B. Howard of London, Ohio, began to publish *The Horseshoe World* as the voice of the National Horseshoe Pitchers' Association. It continued until World War II. Between his publication and Cobb's magazines, Byron Jaskulek of New York edited *The Horseshoe Pitcher* for several years. All of them were the same in essence and served to bind the different sections of the horseshoe world together.

The center of the National Horseshoe Pitchers' Association's program is naturally the World Tournament. We will treat that subject in a later chapter. Suffice it to say here that the framework exists on which can be built a much bigger and better game than presently exists. What must be done to get the game of horseshoes on the list of activities of more sportsmen is the chief concern of our national officers at the present time.

Since 1959 a determined and successful effort has been made to move the National Tournament to different parts of the country. By bringing the big event to the back doors of pitchers all over the country the national association has succeeded in building up both the interest and the participation of local clubs. South Gate, California; Murray, Utah; Muncie, Indiana; Greenville, Ohio; Erie, Pennsylvania; Fargo, North Dakota; and Middlesex, New Jersey, have hosted the annual event. The Keene, New Hampshire, club will be the host for the 1974 tournament.

A Class D has been added to increase the number of participants, and greater emphasis has been placed on the women's division as well as that of juniors, seniors and intermediates.

The news media has taken increasing interest in the game. Dan Kuchcinski, a three-time World Champion, appeared on the Johnny Carson "Tonight" show, *Sports Illustrated* covered the 1969 tournament at Erie, Hal Porter has written a successful column for the *Bradenton Herald* for several years and Will Gullickson of the *Fargo Forum* has gained great coverage for the game in many parts of the country. The *New York Times* and the *Los Angeles Times* have given good coverage to the 1971 and 1973 tournaments respectively. Charles Kuralt of CBS News gave excellant coverage on television for the 1973 tournament at Eureka, California. Jennifer Reno, 1971 and 1972 Junior Girls world champion appeared on "What's My Line." News networks, newspapers, radio and television stations carry more and more results of big horseshoe tournaments.

One other area where efforts are being made to increase interest is that of spectator interest. Neatly dressed players have their names and home towns lettered on their shirts. Scoreboards with large and easy to read numbers appear on each court. Round robin schedules are made available so that fans can tell where and when the players meet.

Growth is inevitable.

3

Construction and Care of Playing Courts

A regulation court is essential. Naturally it is possible to play on inferior courts and on occasions might be necessary. But a first-class performance requires first-class playing conditions.

The crudest of all courts and the easiest to build can be a very effective one on which to start practicing.

All you need to do is to find a level plot of ground about 10 feet wide and 50 feet long, free of obstacles such as trees, clothes lines and electric wires. In the middle of this strip drive two stakes in the ground exactly 40 feet apart at the base of the stakes and lean the stakes slightly toward each other. These stakes should be of one-inch steel and should stand 14 inches above the level of the ground. It is preferable to run the court in a north and south direction, so that you will not be pitching into the sun at any time. This court will suffice for practice and for some friendly neighborhood games, particularly if you are only casually interested in pitching or lack either the time or the means to construct an accurate, regulation court.

Now let us assume that you want to build a court that is regulation in all respects. Such a court is not expensive, and if you can do so, it is better to build one in the beginning. In the accompanying diagram you will find all the dimensions for your court. The hard surface on which you will stand may be of concrete, asphalt, lumber or any other material you wish to use. Concrete seems to be the best and most durable.

There are a number of ways to secure your stake. If you have a very long stake, you may merely drive it into the ground. This is not the best way, because shoes striking the top of the stake will drive it farther into the ground or work it loose. A better and most frequently used method is to drive the stake into a piece of cross tie, as shown in the diagram, and bury it in the clay. It may be easily replaced, if the stake breaks.

Possibly the best method is to buy a ready-built box that has a stake on a welded base, already attached to the box. These can be bought from the Diamond Caulk Horseshoe Company and probably others. It involves a little more expense, but it saves a lot of work. If you happen to have a welder in your club, he can easily make these stakes.

The stakes themselves should be of one-inch rolled steel, and the block in which the stake is to be inserted should be treated with creosote or some other substance that will protect it against rot. The hole into which the stake is to be driven should be a 15/16 inch hole, and the bottom of the stake should be dipped in motor oil before being driven. This will insure a snug fit.

The lumber used in building the frames should be two-inch material, so that it will have enough strength to hold the wet concrete in place. How wide it should be will depend on the depth to which you want to pour your con-

CONSTRUCTION AND CARE 27

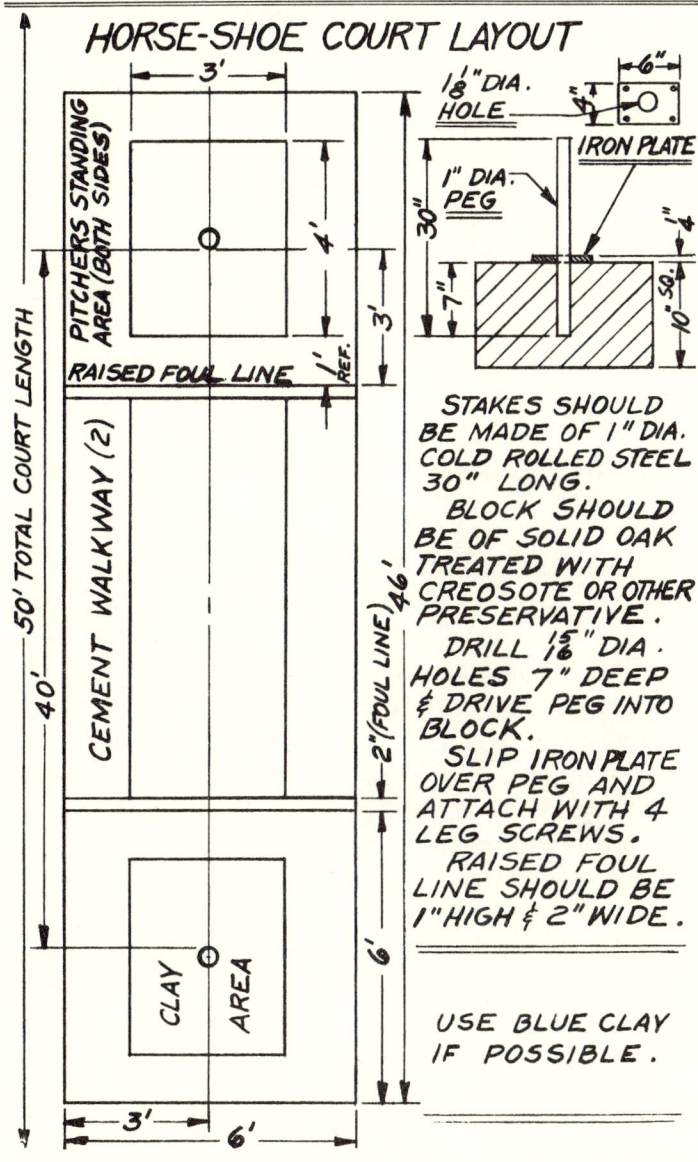

STAKES SHOULD BE MADE OF 1" DIA. COLD ROLLED STEEL 30" LONG.

BLOCK SHOULD BE OF SOLID OAK TREATED WITH CREOSOTE OR OTHER PRESERVATIVE.

DRILL $\frac{15}{16}$" DIA. HOLES 7" DEEP & DRIVE PEG INTO BLOCK.

SLIP IRON PLATE OVER PEG AND ATTACH WITH 4 LEG SCREWS.

RAISED FOUL LINE SHOULD BE 1" HIGH & 2" WIDE.

USE BLUE CLAY IF POSSIBLE.

crete. Four inches should be enough under ordinary circumstances.

The portion marked clay area should be filled with clay, preferably blue clay.

The diagram for building a court shown here will conform to all tournament requirements. On the theory that one picture is worth ten thousand words I have included seven photographs. The first shows a single court in a back yard. The second shows a single court in the basement of a private home. The third picture shows a battery of indoor courts and the others are batteries of outdoor courts.

Care of the Clay

The clay is at its best when it reaches a putty-like consistency that will stop the shoe where it hits without sticking to the shoe. The secret is to keep the right amount of moisture on the clay. After a long day of pitching in the hot sun, a pit will dry out to a point at which it will be necessary to punch holes in the clay and pour water in them. On other occasions, it may be necessary to wet only the surface. A little bit of experience will enable you to gauge the right amount. After wetting down the clay, the next step is to cover it with damp burlap sacks and place a cover over the sacks. This cover should be a solid strip of metal, exterior plywood or hard rubber with a hole in the middle for the stake. This will keep the sunlight, the wind and the rain from ruining the clay for pitching.

Backstops

It is advisable to build some kind of backstop behind

CONSTRUCTION AND CARE 29

Mark Seibold of Huntington, Indiana, is shown practicing on his backyard court a few years ago. Mark was the Junior World Champion in both 1966 and 1969. In 1973 at age 19 Mark tied Elmer Hohl for the Men's World Championship at Eureka, California, losing the title in a playoff.

each stake to stop shoes that bound out of the playing area. This is a safety measure for the protection of persons off the court, and it will save the beginner a lot of steps. This backstop may be made of heavy mesh wire, two-inch lumber, heavy belting, or any other material strong enough to stand up under the pounding of the shoes. Wire seems to be the best, because it does not obstruct the view of the spectators.

This beautiful court lies in the basement of Marvin May's home in Lynchburg, Virginia. Marvin, who is a building contractor by profession, included the court in his house plans and estimates that it added about $250 to the cost of his home. The set-up is complete with scoring devices, comfortable chairs and even a coffee maker.

Lighting

Courts can be lighted for night pitching very easily. The best plan for a single court seems to be to hang a flood lamp with a protective cover directly over each stake at a height of eight to 12 feet. In addition to the

CONSTRUCTION AND CARE 31

This three-court layout at New Rome, Ohio, is a converted school house. The artistry at the back of the playing area was done by Tom Pearce and Larry Mathews. The upper left shows a blower unit that is part of a gas furnace used to heat the building. Handicap leagues and open tournaments keep over 100 pitchers active and make the cost to each man very small. Players in the picture are Tom Pearce, Don Peterson, Frank Griffeth, Columbus Brickles, Ted Harris, and Verlon Kelley (left to right).

flood lamps that light the immediate pitching area, the surrounding area may be lighted with any suitable arrangement of ordinary bulbs out of the line of vision of

These courts are located at Piney Flats, Tennessee. The close view shows an inexpensive but effective lighting arrangement.

The championship division of 36 men is shown here as the 1963 World Tournament got underway at South Gate, California. The 1970 tournament was played on these courts. The equipment here includes palm trees and a gentle ocean breeze coming in from the Pacific.

CONSTRUCTION AND CARE 33

the pitchers to prevent glare. Where a battery of courts is being lighted, it is best to consult an electrician and to use 1500 watt bulbs or larger, fastened to poles at the corners of your court area.

More Than One Court

As your group of pitchers grows, you will want more than one court. Additional courts may be laid alongside the first. Be sure to allow twelve feet between the courts,

This daytime scene at Wheelock Park in Keene, New Hampshire, was taken during the competition for the 1965 Women and Juniors titles. These courts were the home of the 1965, 1968, and 1973 World Tournaments.

This picture was taken on the Heekin Park Courts at Muncie, Indiana, where the 1960 and 1961 World Tournaments were played. This intimate scene really takes you "inside the fence." One is torn between the mounting pressure as the scorekeeper rolls up the score on the one hand and the complete serenity of the setting on the other. The two participants are two veterans of many years of competition, Clarence Giles of Utah on the left and Stan Manker of Ohio.

so as to leave plenty of room. This is not only for reasons of safety, but for reasons of concentration as well. Crowding of courts will make your players uncomfortable and will hurt their game. It is well to look ahead, when you build your first court, to the time when you will need others, and to allow room for expansion.

Wearing Apparel

As far as wearing apparel is concerned, there are no requirements specified in the rules. One should keep both comfort and appearance in mind, however. Comfort is a must in practice and in competition. The two most important areas to consider in this respect are the sleeves of the shirt and the shoes. The shirt must allow plenty of freedom for the pitching arm to extend above the pitcher's head at the end of his follow-through without binding and irritating the skin. Most bowling shirts are excellent, because they are intended to accommodate much the same swing. Tee shirts or light sports shirts are also good. As to footwear, it is important to have shoes with soles that have traction on hard surfaces, as well as shoes that are comfortable. Leather soles are not good, because they get very slippery. Without good traction a pitcher loses his follow-through and sometimes his confidence. As to appearance, it matters most when you play in competition. Anything that is satisfactory to you in practice is all right. In tournament play, however, it lends a great deal to the game of horseshoes if the pitchers are neatly dressed. The custom now is pretty much toward white trousers and white shirts or shirt and slack combinations on which are lettered the name, town and state of the contestants. Any neat outfit is permissible, and there is room in this phase of the game for a lot of experimentation.

Indoor Pitching

More and more indoor courts are appearing around the country. They take the same amount of space as do outdoor courts. The rules require that the ceiling must be at least 12 feet high. Certain problems arise in the preparation of indoor courts, but most of them are easy enough to work out. One of these problems is heating. Another is locating a building of this size in a spot where pitching

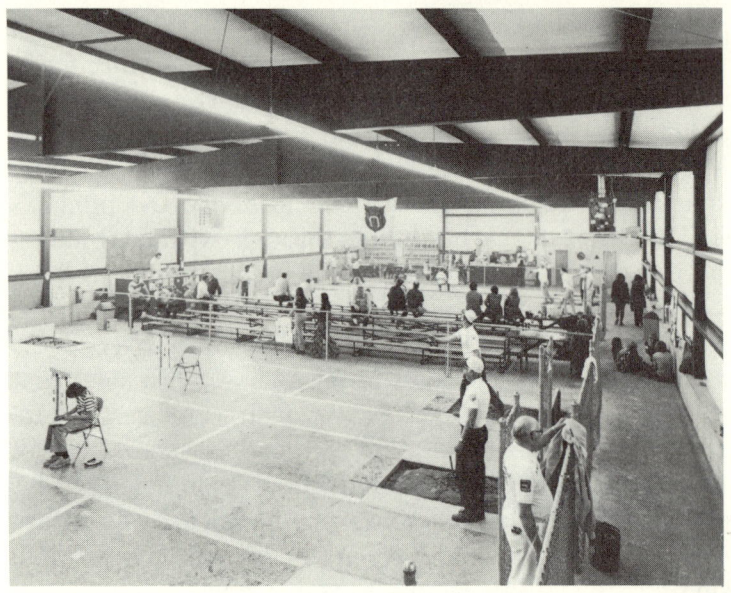

This is the inside of Heritage Recreation Center, Sutton, Massachusetts, unquestionably the finest indoor pitching facility in the world. Built by Ed Domey, this is rapidly transforming some New England pitchers into national championship caliber.

will be permissible. If the floor has to be left in its present condition, it may be necessary to build a six or seven inch platform and lower it in a metal box big enough to hold the clay. Using stakes with a welded base will become a necessity in most instances. If other problems arise on which clubs need advice, they can write to the nearest regional director, listed elsewhere in this book, and receive help based on the similar experience of other local clubs that have built indoor courts.

CONSTRUCTION AND CARE 37

There are many indoor courts worthy of mention, but a few that have provided the most activity are the Redwood Acres "Little Cow Palace" on the fairgrounds at Eureka, California, where the 1973 World Championships were played; Heritage Recreation Center, built by Ed Domey in Sutton, Massachusetts; the Day-bel Courts, built by Don Moore in Dayton, Kentucky; the Rush Indoor Horseshoe Courts, built by Robert Sheppard at Rushville, Indiana; and the Horseshoe Palace, built by Archie Johnson at Sussex, Wisconsin.

4

Tools of the Trade

All that is really necessary to have a horseshoe game is a pair of shoes and a set of stakes driven in the ground. The kind and amount of equipment each player has beyond this is determined by his interest, his financial means, the availability of a market for horseshoe equipment and other factors.

A player will ordinarily want two or more pairs of pitching shoes. The logical move then is to get a carrying case which can be obtained in wood, metal or handcrafted leather.

There are files for removing metal burrs as they appear on the shoes, rulers for measuring close shoes, shop cloths for drying the shoes, and calipers and straight edges for determining points. Pocket notebooks, ringer percentage charts and sweat bands appear everywhere.

Some pitchers take great pride in their dress. Extras include western hats, string ties with horseshoe emblems, belt buckles, and insignias designating titles held.

There are horseshoe courts inside homes, in backyards and in automobile trunks in portable form suitable for pitching anywhere at anytime. Various types of scoreboards exist, as well as qualifying devices and individual name plates.

Many pitchers who travel to different states have campers, trailers and various kinds of sleeping or living quarters.

The object of any hobby is enjoyment, so my advice would be to equip yourself to enjoy the game. One pair of battered old shoes on the back porch might do the trick. You might wind up equipping a house trailer so that you can hit the tournament trail in style. What you finally get will likely correspond closely with the success you have in playing the game.

There are many kinds of pitching shoes available. A few people are still pitching the genuine shoes from horses, but they cannot acquire with these shoes the degree of precision that is needed to compete in the game as it is now played. Shoes made with longer hooks and better balance have greatly increased the number of ringers, as well as interest in the game. This is, I am sure, one of the reasons why horseshoe pitching crowded out the game of quoits. Pitching ringers with quoits was such an infrequent and difficult occurrence that it lost its appeal. Every contestant wants to achieve some success in his game, and if he is willing to practice a few fundamental steps, he can pitch some ringers.

Most of the shoes with which beginners learn to play are cheap brands of "picnic" shoes bought in sets of four at the local hardware store. If you already have these shoes, they can be used all right in the beginning. But if you have no shoes or have mastered the first stages of the game and want to improve, I would recommend that you buy one of the brands listed below. These are the shoes presently being manufactured that have been approved for use in sanctioned NHPA play. My reason for saying this is not to try to affiliate you with that group because they will benefit from your using these shoes. My reason is simply that these shoes have been precision-tested for weight, size and balance. You will be able to select one

PITCHING CHAMPIONSHIP HORSESHOES 40

of these brands and to continue to pitch them as long as you play the game. If you start with an unofficial brand, there will be a period of adjustment when you make the change to an official shoe. Here are the shoes I recommend, listed alphabetically rather than in any order of priority:

Brand Name of Shoe	Manufacturer	Address
Allen	Ted Allen	1045 Linden Avenue Boulder, Colo. 80302
American	St. Pierre Mfg. Co.	317 E. Mountain Street Worcester, Mass. 01606
Detroit Flyer	Detroit Flyer Co.	37015 Charter Oaks Mt. Clemens, Mich. 48043
Diamond Super Ringer	Diamond Tool & Horseshoe Co.	Duluth, Minn. and Toronto, Canada
Dixon Victory	Dale Dixon	2616 49th Street Des Moines, Iowa 50310
Gordon	Gordon Horseshoe Co.	235 Tennyson Cincinnati, Ohio 45226
Imperial	Clyde Martz	3233 Arapahoe Road Pittsburgh, Pa. 15241
Lee	Lee Bennett	4920 Eck Road West Middletown, Ohio 45042
Ohio	Ohio Horseshoe Co.	P.O. Box 5801 Columbus, Ohio 43221

It is worthy of mention here that ready built courts with the stakes mounted in place can be had through the Diamond Tool and Horseshoe Company and that Dale

TOOLS OF THE TRADE 41

Dixon can supply portable courts at a reasonable price. Both addresses are listed above.

Other game-related items can be found at hardware stores, clothing stores and jewelers. Any NHPA official will steer you to the right person if you have trouble locating suitable tools with which to carry on the trade.

Here is a leather carrying case with three compartments. Two compartments will hold two pairs of shoes and the third will hold the file, ruler, ringer percentage book, pen and shop cloth. It makes a compact and clean way to carry your equipment and is not out of place in the living room or on the seat of a new car.

5

Official Playing Rules and NHPA Constitution

In 1971 President Ralph Dykes appointed a Constitution and By-Laws Committee to revise and update the constitution and by-laws and the playing rules including any changes made in recent conventions as well as to correct any errors if they were found to exist. The committee was composed of Ottie Reno, Chairman; Ralph Dykes, Robert Pence, and Ellis Cobb. This committee made the revision and presented the completed version to the 1972 Annual Convention in Greenville, Ohio, where it was adopted. It appears here as adopted by the NHPA in 1972:

CONSTITUTION AND BY-LAWS OF THE NATIONAL HORSESHOE PITCHERS' ASSOCIATION OF AMERICA

PREAMBLE

Inasmuch as the art of horseshoe pitching affords a healthy, scientific, pleasant, and competitive sport, suitable to all persons, at a cost comparable to other sports, and with a desire to unify its adherents, standardize its rules, authorize and conduct tournaments of State, Sectional, National and World scope, promote establishment of leagues and associations and encourage the development of the game in foreign countries, we the horseshoe pitchers of America in convention assembled, do hereby establish the following Constitution and By-Laws for the Association, which henceforth shall be known as the National Horseshoe Pitchers' Association of America, hereafter referred to as the NHPA.

ARTICLE I (NAME)

Section 1. The name of this Association shall be the National Horseshoe Pitchers' Association of America.

ARTICLE II (ADMINISTRATION)

Section 1. All legislative power herein granted shall be vested in an assembly of delegates, chosen by the organizations and/or Associations officially affiliated and in good standing with the NHPA.

The word State in this Constitution applies to all political and geographical divisions commonly known as States, to all Territories and possessions of the United States, and all Provinces and Territories of Canada.

Section 2. Any State may acquire a Charter from the NHPA by obtaining ten (10) members. If a State acquires ten (10) members it shall be entitled to one delegate in the National Convention. If a State acquires twenty-five (25) members it shall be entitled to two (2) delegates. Thereafter a State shall be entitled to one additional delegate for each additional twenty-five (25) members up to a maximum of six (6) delegates.

In no case shall a state be granted more than two charters, or more than twelve (12) delegates to the National Convention. Further, when a state has two charters, the number of delegates who can be seated in the National Convention shall be in proportion to the number of members in each organization at the time of the National Convention.

A list of the names of members and their addresses must be in the hands of the Secretary-Treasurer before the charter will be issued.

Section 3. Any State without a charter may, if it has even one member of the NHPA have that member present at the National Convention with the proviso that that delegate shall not have a vote, but shall, in every other way, be a representative of his State.

The President shall also have the authority to seat as a voting delegate, one NHPA member from a state without a charter as a representative of the members in all such states.

Section 4. Delegates to the National Convention representing State Associations shall present certificates of election or appointment signed by the President of the affiliated and chartered State Associations he or she is delegated to represent.

Section 5. Should the aforementioned methods fail to produce the full quota of a State's delegates the deficiency may be made up by individual members in good standing, chosen in such a manner as the State's members elect. In case of failure of a State to agree or produce its alloted delegation, the Executive Council of the NHPA shall select from the State's members those delegates necessary to fill the vacancies.

Section 6. Members of the Executive Council shall have no voting power at the Convention unless they are also seated as delegates, except in case of a tie vote on a motion before the convention in which case the Executive Council members not seated as delegates have the right to vote on the motion.

Section 7. Twenty (20) delegates shall constitute a quorum and have authority to transact the business of the NHPA when seated in Convention.

Section 8. Voting shall be by ballot, secret ballot, rising vote or ayes and nays according to the discretion of the Chairman. Voting by proxy or mail will not be allowed, nor shall substitution for a delegate representing a State as an individual be allowed. State Associations may substitute a member in good standing if a vacancy in the delegation arises. A delegate must be present in person to have voting power.

Section 9. The officers of the NHPA shall consist of a President, Secretary-Treasurer, First Vice-President, Second Vice-President, Third Vice-President, and Fourth Vice-President.

OFFICIAL PLAYING RULES 45

At least one of the Vice-Presidents must be a woman. These officers shall constitute the Executive Council and have voting power as National Officials. In National Convention sessions the President shall have the power to appoint an administrative assistant and a sergeant at arms.

Section 10. The officials consisting of the President, Secretary-Treasurer, and four Vice-Presidents shall be the Executive Council of the NHPA and shall be in charge of its affairs. They shall be empowered to transact such business, in the interest of the game and the NHPA as they deem advisable, providing such action is not contrary to the Constitution and the By-Laws of the NHPA.

Section 11. The officers shall be elected at the first Convention after the first day of January of the current year and the length of their terms of office shall be defined in Article III, Sections 2–6. The officers may call a meeting in Convention any time they deem advisable.

Section 12. Roberts' Rules of Order, revised and reading as follows shall govern the order of conducting all meetings.

1. Reading of the minutes of the previous meeting.
2. Approval, addition or corrections of the minutes.
3. Reading of the financial report.
4. Reports of officers, boards and standing committees.
5. Reports of special committees.
6. Memorandum of the President.
7. Unfinished business.
8. New business.
9. Report of good and welfare work.
10. Election of officers.
11. Adjournment.

Section 13. In event of the death, resignation or removal of an officer or Committeeman between conventions, the President is empowered to make appointments to fill the unexpired terms, said appointments to be subject to a unanimous vote of the Executive Council within thirty (30) days.

Should the office of the presidency become vacant due to death, resignation, or removal, the first Vice-President shall become President and the Second, Third, and Fourth Vice-

Presidents shall become the First, Second and Third Vice-Presidents respectively and the new President shall appoint a new Fourth Vice-President to fill the unexpired term, said appointment to be subject to the unanimous vote of the Executive Council within thirty (30) days.

Section 14. Any officers of the Executive Council may be removed from their position upon failure to perform the duties of their office, or for any reason or action that tends to reduce or bring discredit to the efficiency of the NHPA. Said removal shall be affected only by a unanimous vote of the Executive Council remaining. Voting may be by registered mail or telegram.

Section 15. The following committees may be appointed by the President from the members of the NHPA; Constitution and By-Laws, Membership, Auditing and Finance, Grievance, Credentials, Publicity, Hall of Fame, Resolutions or any committee the President deems advisable for the good of the NHPA. These Committeemen shall be under the direction of the President, and their duties defined by him. It is necessary that a majority of the members of a special committee be actually in Convention only if a problem or problems arise which necessitate action by that particular committee. No committee may decide an issue without at least a majority of the members present. Should an occasion arise in which immediate action by a committee is necessary when a majority is not present, the President of the NHPA shall have the power to dissolve the existing committee and appoint a new committee. It shall be the duties of all committees to serve willingly and in the best interests of the NHPA.

Any committeeman may be removed from office by the President at his discretion.

ARTICLE III (JUDICIARY)

Section 1. The National Convention shall be held the morning of the first scheduled day of the Men's Championship Class of the World's Tournament. The newly elected officers shall take office at the completion of the Tournament.

Section 2. The President shall be the chief executive officer of the NHPA elected for a term of two years, said election to be held on odd numbered years. He is to preside at all meetings, when able. He is to sign warrants for payment of all accounts, sign all State and Club Charters, as prepared and signed by the Secretary-Treasurer. He has the power to assign specific duties to the other members of the Executive Council.

Section 3. The first Vice-President shall perform the duties of the President in event of the absence or disability of the President.

Section 4. The First, Second, Third and Fourth Vice-Presidents shall at all times perform whatever duties their offices imply, and shall be ready and willing to cooperate with the other members of the Executive Council on any matter which may arise. All, working together, shall continuously strive to encourage, promote and advance the game of horseshoes, the NHPA and the harmony of the members and fulfill any duties assigned them by the President.

Section 5. The First, Second, Third and Fourth Vice-Presidents shall be elected for a term of two (2) years. The First and Third Vice-Presidents shall be elected on odd numbered years and the Second and Fourth Vice-Presidents shall be elected on even numbered years.

Section 6. The Secretary-Treasurer shall be elected for a term of two years, said election to be held on even numbered years. This staggering of the election dates of the officers is for the purpose of enabling each of these officers to have a year's help by the other officer upon assuming office for the first time.

The Secretary-Treasurer shall be the custodian of the records, property, correspondence books, accounts, printing materials and other documents belonging to the Association, and shall turn over, on demand, by the Executive Council, to it, or the authorized representative of the bonding company holding bond on the Secretary-Treasurer, and books or records of the Association in his possession. He shall prepare and transmit to the President warrants for payments of NHPA funds. He shall at all times endeavor to promote harmony and good will within the NHPA.

The Secretary-Treasurer, in his capacity of Treasurer, shall be the custodian of the funds of the NHPA. He shall furnish a complete statement of monies received and paid out at each Convention, and/or anytime the Executive Council demands.

Section 7. Any bill of account or expense against the NHPA except for routine supplies, shall be submitted to the Executive Council, and paid when approved by as many as four of the six members of said Council. If not approved in this manner, amounts contested shall be brought before delegates assembled in Convention and submitted for approval by the majority of those present.

Section 8. The Secretary-Treasurer shall be bonded. A four-fifths majority of the other officers of the Executive Council shall determine the amount of the bond which shall at no time be less than five thousand dollars ($5,000.00). The cost of said bond shall be paid by the NHPA.

Section 9. The President shall receive a travel and expense allowance to cover his actual expenses incurred in attending the World Tournament, subject to approval of the Executive Council.

Section 10. The Secretary-Treasurer shall receive an annual travel and expense allowance of eight hundred dollars ($800.00) per year plus 10¢ per member to compensate for personal expenses incurred in the performance of his duties.

Section 11. The Managing Editor of the organization's monthly magazine shall receive a travel expense allowance of $400.00 annually to compensate for personal expenses in the performance of his duties as long as the magazine is in existence.

Section 12. All officers shall have their books, records, and any other property belonging to the NHPA at the Convention; or, if unable to be present, they must forward these to the President by registered mail, before the first day of the Convention. All officers shall turn over to their successors in office all records and property of the NHPA that may or should be in their possession.

ARTICLE IV

Section 1. Any reputable person may become a member of the NHPA upon payment of annual dues as designated in the by-laws to the National Secretary-Treasurer or his officially approved agent or agents. This fee entitles one to membership in the NHPA from January 1 or from the date paid after January 1 through December 31 of the current year. Membership must be paid through the State Association where one is in existence. At National and World's Tournaments entrants must, if they have paid their dues locally, pay both State and National dues to be eligible to participate. A member must be accorded all courtesies and privileges extended by affiliated clubs and associations.

Section 2. All interstate sanctions shall be issued through the National Secretary-Treasurer, who shall notify the State Associations or state representatives in each state included in such territory assigned to an interstate tournament. All sanctions for intrastate tournaments shall be issued by State Associations or state representatives who shall require that National Rules be followed and each participant be a member of the NHPA. A copy of the sanction shall be forwarded to the National Secretary-Treasurer for recording. Championship certificates or insignias shall be issued through the National Secretary-Treasurer upon certification that National Rules were followed, legal shoes were used, and all participants were members of the NHPA.

Section 3. No sectional, national or world tournament game shall be played in the rain. The tournament committee shall decide whether it is raining sufficiently hard to stop play. When the game shall be stopped on account of rain it shall be resumed at exactly the same point as when stopped upon termination of the rain and satisfactory repair of the courts. The tournament committee shall also determine these two provisions.

ARTICLE V

Section 1. State Associations shall be organized under the NHPA and shall be known as (name of the state) Division of the NHPA. All National, State, Intersectional, and League Tournaments must have sanction of the NHPA before being held in order to be regarded as official.

Section 2. A state can at the discretion of the Executive Council be granted a second charter if a second organization is formed which shows the Executive Council it has fifty (50) members of the NHPA. If at any time after the second charter is granted either organization allows its membership to drop to less than twenty-five (25) members, that membership loss shall constitute grounds for the Executive Council to revoke the charter of the organization losing the members.

Section 3. In event a state has two charters and both apply for a sanction for the State Tournament the Executive Council may sanction the application it considers the most worthy, and the champion of that tournament will be officially recognized. NHPA members of both chapters shall be eligible to compete for the same entry fee.

Section 4. State Associations, and their affiliated members, must comply in all ways with this Constitution, By-Laws, Rules and the NHPA regulations.

Section 5. The officials of the organization affiliated with the NHPA shall be governed in their state by the provisions in their state constitution providing those shall not be contrary to the National Constitution, By-Laws, Rules and Regulations.

ARTICLE VI

Section 1. The winner of the authorized World's Tournament, shall be declared Champion Horseshoe Pitcher of the World, and shall hold the title until the next authorized World's Tournament, unless he is defeated in the interim by an officially recognized challenger in a title match authorized by the Executive Council with the title at stake. A challenge match can only be considered by the Executive Council in years when no World Tournament is held. At any nationally authorized tournament the champion shall again contest for the title, on the same basis, and under the same conditions, as all other contestants, except that the champion shall not be required to qualify for an authorized World Tournament. Qualifying shall be at least 200 consecutive shoes, 32 or more to qualify for the World's Championship, 16 or more for the "B" championship. Additional classes may be added at the discretion of the tournament committee.

Section 2. A Ladies Tournament may be held in conjunction with the Men's Tournament, and the winner will be declared the Champion Woman Horseshoe Pitcher of the World, and shall hold the title under the same conditions as the champion

OFFICIAL PLAYING RULES 51

man pitcher. Rules for qualifying and the finals shall be at the discretion of the tournament committee.

A Junior Tournament for boys and girls may be held in conjunction with the Men's Tournament, and the winner will be declared the Champion Junior Boys and Champion Junior Girls of the World, and shall hold the title under the same conditions as the champion man pitcher. Rules for qualifying and the finals shall be at the discretion of the tournament committee.

Playing rules for Juniors are the same as for men with the single exception that the pitching distance shall be a minimum of 30 feet between stakes (27) feet from foul line to the opposite stake).

A player will be considered a Junior for the entire season if his 17th birthday occurs on or after the start of the calendar year, January 1st.

Junior players may compete in the Men's division of sanctioned NHPA tournaments which have no Junior division without injury to their Junior standing in future tournaments as long as they do not accept any awards of cash or monetary value. If a Junior does compete in the men's division of a sanctioned tournament he must pitch the men's distance of 40 feet.

All Junior tournaments will be conducted strictly on an amateur basis with the only awards being trophies, ribbons and medals or other such awards having no monetary value.

It shall be the responsibility of each Junior player to make certain his participation in NHPA tournaments does not jeopardize his amateur standing in sports or activities in which he might be interested.

A Senior and an Intermediate tournament may be held in conjunction with the Men's Tournament, and the winner will be declared the Champion Senior and Intermediate Champion of the World, and shall hold the title under the same conditions as the Champion man pitcher. Rules for qualifying and the finals shall be at the discretion of the tournament committee.

A player is an Intermediate from his sixtieth birthday until his sixty-sixth birthday and is a Senior after his sixty-sixth birthday with the only exception being that if his birthday comes during an event he will be permitted to finish that event.

The Tournament Committee shall consist of all members of the Executive Council who are present at the World Tournament.

The Points System is to be optional in any and all pitching activities, except in World Championships. In World Championships, the Cancellation System must be used.

Section 3. The assembly of delegates in Convention shall award, by a majority vote, the privilege of conducting a world tournament two (2) years in advance. In case no bid from any city or locale is received at the Convention, the majority of the Executive Council has authority to award the tournament for the next year only. A city or organization desiring to sponsor and hold a World Tournament, shall place its bid in the hands of the NHPA Secretary at the first session of the delegates in Convention, if possible; and no later than ninety days prior to the date of the proposed tournament.

Section 4. No sealed bid will be considered by the assembly of delegates, unless the following rules are clearly observed:

1. The facilities available for conducting the tournament are stated.
2. The amount of cash money for prizes is stated.
3. The number and kind of trophy prizes are stated.
4. The miscellaneous advantages are stated.

Section 5. The NHPA may conduct any Sectional, National or International Tournament, under its own auspices in strict accord with the rules herein stated, and at a place agreeable to its members. Such action must, however, be approved by a majority of the delegates in Convention assembled.

Section 6. The bidder or bidders who are awarded a World Tournament, must place the total amount of the money offered in prizes, on deposit in a National Bank, at least thirty (30) days prior to the opening date of the tournament and certify same to the NHPA Secretary, or forward a signed contract that covers the above stipulation to the National Secretary.

ARTICLE VII

The NHPA may adopt such by-laws as it deems necessary. By-laws shall be adopted when approved by a majority vote of the members in good standing present at any regular meeting.

ARTICLE VIII—AMENDMENTS

The Constitution, and Article VI of the By-Laws, which are the official rules for horseshoe pitching may be amended at any Convention of delegates by a two-thirds vote of those present. All other by-laws may be amended at any convention of delegates by a simple majority of those present.

BY-LAWS

ARTICLE I

Section 1. The Executive Council shall be the judicial body and shall define and interpret the Constitution and By-Laws. Technical points shall be submitted to it, for decision, and the ruling declared official, unless delegates in Convention assembled, rule otherwise, by a two-thirds vote.

ARTICLE II

Section 1. A member may be suspended for: 1, Non-payment of dues or fees; 2, Willfully violating the Constitution, By-Laws, Rules, or Regulations; 3, By participating in a tournament under an assumed name, or being found guilty of fraud, fixing games, or other conduct unbecoming a member; 4, For directly or indirectly betting on a contestant, or self, when an entry in the competition; 5, using unsanctioned shoes in a tournament.

For all but the first of the above violations, a member may be suspended for a period of one year, and the Secretary of the NHPA shall notify all State Associations and state representatives, of said suspension.

Section 2. Members suspended for non-payment of dues or

fees, shall be reinstated upon payment of back dues or fees. Those members of the other violations listed in Article II, Section 1, shall be suspended for one year, and may be reinstated any time after that, on the discretion of the Executive Council, the majority vote of which is required.

Section 3. No member shall be suspended until given fair trial before the Executive Council.

ARTICLE III

Section 1. In any tournament involving a Sectional, National, or World title, the tournament committee shall estimate to the best of its ability, the number of players who will participate in the tournament, and confer with the NHPA President upon the method of conducting the tournament. In no case may the tournament rules be contrary to any of the provisions of the National Constitution, By-Laws, and Rules. Likewise, in no case shall a tournament committee retain any method of procedure that is objectionable to the President of the NHPA.

Section 2. In any intrastate tournament, the tournament committee shall confer with the President of the State Association, and follow his suggestions in regard to tournament procedure. In the event of no existing state association, the tournament committee shall outline its own plan of tournament procedure to the NHPA Secretary, at the time of application for sanction. Under these circumstances, the NHPA Secretary may act according to his own discretion, in-so-far as suggestions and awarding of sanctions are concerned.

Section 3. The title of Champion Horseshoe Pitcher of the World, can be contended for, only in World Tournaments that are authorized by the Executive Council, or in a series of games (not less than 6 wins in a scheduled 11-game match), the same to be authorized by a majority vote of the Executive Council, it being understood that the Executive Council, will give preference to those finishing among the first six in the last tournament. The Executive Council may, however, at its discretion, select some other opponent for the Champion. Not more than three such contests may be held annually. A representative selected by the Executive Council, shall be in attendance to conduct the match. No bid under $500, for sponsorship of the match, will be accepted, and twenty-five (25) percent of whatever amount is given, shall go to the NHPA.

Section 4. In a World Tournament, games won and lost, shall determine the order in which the winners are listed, as winning. For all other tournaments, method of play shall be decided by officials in charge. NHPA rules must be followed, however.

Section 5. In any tournament, ties between contestants for first place shall be settled by play-off. Other ties will be settled by percentage and/or total points.

Section 6. No player may indulge in actions, words, or phrases, disturbing to his opponent, nor will profane or abusive language by any member of the NHPA be permitted upon the tournament grounds. Violators of these rules shall be subject to suspension from the NHPA for one year.

Section 7. The Stokes Award, now given annually in memory of the late Arch Stokes, is awarded at the World Tournament to the person who has done the most during the preceding year to promote, foster and build the game of horseshoes in the world of horseshoes. Other territorial or special awards may be made in the discretion of the Executive Council.

It shall be the duty of the Executive Council to determine the kind, number and recipients of all awards.

ARTICLE IV

Section 1. The NHPA will not recognize nor sanction as an NHPA endorsed horseshoe, any brand of pitching horseshoe that is made by a manufacturer who has not made a written agreement with the NHPA, that the manufacturing firm will affix one of the NHPA's five-cent endorsement stamps to each pair of horseshoes, or the box containing same, the manufacturer puts on the market, for sale. The manufacturer shall have the option to pay the sum of $300.00 per year in lieu of the stamps.

At the end of each year, all endorsement stamps that have not been used by a manufacturing firm, may be returned to the NHPA and the NHPA will reimburse the manufacturer with cash, or an equal number of the new year's issue of the stamps, as the manufacturer chooses. Revenue from the NHPA's sale of the stamps, shall be used to promote and aid the game of horseshoes, in whatever way the NHPA believes is best.

In submitting a new model of horseshoe, or a change in an old model to the NHPA Secretary and Executive Council, a complete written description shall accompany the sample of shoes sent to the Secretary-Treasurer.

ARTICLE V

Section 1. A membership card is a combined State-National card. To be entitled to this card and enjoy its privileges a member must pay the national dues of $1.50 plus the amount set by his state charter.

Section 2. The annual cost for a twelve month subscription to the Horseshoe Pitchers' News Digest is $3.50.

Section 3. The entry fee for entry in the World Tournament shall be as follows:

	Men's Division	—	$10.00	
Women's Division — 5.00	Seniors		—	5.00
Intermediates — 5.00	Juniors		—	None

Entry fees in all tournaments other than the World Tournament shall be left to the discretion of the tournament committees running those tournaments.

OFFICIAL RULES FOR HORSESHOE PITCHING

(Revised 1972)

Rule 1. Section a: Layout of a Court: A court will occupy a level area of at least 50 feet in length (in a north-south direction if possible) by at least 10 feet in width and consists of two pitcher's boxes, each six feet square with a stake in its exact center. The pitcher's boxes shall be located in such a manner that their front edges are parallel and the stakes are 40 feet apart in the middle of the total area.

Section b: When a number of courts are constructed adjacent to each other as required for tournament play the stakes of one court shall be at least 10 feet, 12 feet is preferable, from

OFFICIAL PLAYING RULES 57

the stakes of adjacent courts. Foul lines in front of the pitcher's boxes shall be in a straight line across the entire layout.

Rule 2. Section a: Pitching Distance: The pitching distance for Men shall be 40 feet between the bottoms of the stakes where they emerge from the ground with a foul line three feet in front of each stake.

Section b: Pitching distance for Women and Juniors shall be 30 feet with a foul line three feet in front of each stake. When Women and Juniors play on a court constructed for Men foul lines shall be marked 10 feet in front of the Men's foul lines with an imaginary stake marked on the ground back of each of these foul lines. Women and Juniors may throw their shoes from any place back of these foul lines.

Note: The NHPA stipulates that Junior players must be under 17 years of age.

Rule 3. Indoor Pitching: When indoor courts are constructed, the height of pitching boxes shall not be over 6 inches above floor level. Ceiling height shall be at least 12 feet.

Rule 4. Section a: The Pitcher's Box: Each pitcher's box shall be six feet square with the stake in the exact center and consist of an area of clay, dirt or sand into which the players throw their shoes and flanked by two pitching platforms or areas from which the players throw their shoes.

Section b: The clay, dirt or sand area, clay is preferable, must be a minimum of 43 inches long in the direction in which the players throw their shoes and 31 inches wide. The maximum area is 72 inches long and 36 inches wide. This area must be located in the middle of the pitcher's box with the stake in its center. If clay is used the area must be filled to a depth of six to ten inches and kept in moist putty like condition.

Section c: The two pitching platforms or areas shall occupy the remaining portions of the pitcher's box flanking the clay, dirt or sand area. They must be six feet long, extending three feet in front of the stake and be at least 18 inches wide. They must be level with each other and with the platforms at the opposite stake. They should be as nearly flush as possible with the ground outside the pitcher's box.

Rule 5. Stakes shall be one inch in diameter—no larger. They may be of cold-rolled steel, milled iron, or soft steel. The top of each stake shall extend 14 inches nor more than 15 inches above the level of the pitcher's platform on each side of the stake, with a 3 inch incline toward each other.

Rule 6. Foul Lines: Foul lines shall be clearly defined three feet in front of each stake across the entire front edge of the pitcher's box. Raised foul lines should be used if possible and they are required in all National and World Championships. Raised foul lines of wood, concrete or metal should extend between one and two inches above the level of the pitching platforms and can be two inches wide.

PLAYING RULES

Rule 7. Section a—Conduct of Players and Members: No contestants, while opponent is in pitching position, shall make any remark, nor utter any sounds within the hearing of opponent, nor make any movement that does or might interfere with the opponent's playing.

Penalty—both shoes of the offender shall be declared foul in the inning about which complaint is made.

Section b—Any member of the NHPA of America, who indulges in heckling or unfair rooting against any opponent in a tournament, whether with malicious intent or otherwise, shall be expelled from the grounds, and from the National Association.

Section c—No contestant shall touch his own or opponent's shoe or shoes, until winner of point or points has been agreed upon by contestants, or decision rendered by the referee. Referee shall declare foul, shoes thrown by a contestant failing to comply with this rule, and awards points to the opponent, according to the position of his or her shoes.

Section d—No contestant shall walk to the opposite stake, or be informed of the position of shoes, prior to the completion of an inning.

Section e—A player, while not pitching, must remain on the opposite side of the stake to the player who is pitching, and on the rear one-fourth of the pitcher's platform, back of the stake. If standing back of the pitching platform the toe of one foot must remain on the rear one-fourth of the platform.

Section f—Any player repeatedly violating rules, or guilty of unsportsmanlike conduct, may be barred from further competition in the contest.

Rule 8. Section a—Foul lines: Any shoes pitched while the pitcher's foot extends on, or over, the raised foul line, shall be declared foul, and removed from counting distance.

section b—In pitching the shoe, the pitcher shall stand on the pitcher's platform, at one side or other of the stake.

Rule 9. In delivering a shoe, the pitcher must remain behind the foul line until the shoe has left his hand.

Rule 10. Choice of Pitch: Choice of first pitch, or follow, shall be determined by the toss of a coin or a flipped-up shoe. In successive games between the same players, the loser shall have choice.

Rule 11. Broken Shoes—When a shoe lands in fair territory and is broken into separate parts it shall be removed and the contestant allowed to pitch another shoe in its stead.

Rule 12. Section a: Foul Shoes: Any shoe pitched by a contestant in violation of Rule 9, or one which lands outside the clay area of the opposite pitching box is a foul shoe.

Section b—Foul shoes shall be removed from the opposite pitcher's box at the request of the opponent.

Section c—A foul shoe shall not be scored or credited except in the score sheet column headed "shoes pitched."

Rule 13. Measurements—Measurements to determine points shall be made with calipers and straight edge.

Official Shoe: A shoe shall not exceed 7¼ inches in width, 7⅝ inches in length, and shall not weigh more than two pounds ten ounces. On a parallel line ¾ of an inch from a straight edge touching the points of the open end of a shoe, the opening shall not exceed 3½ inches.

SCORING RULES

There are two official methods of scoring, the cancellation method and the count all method.

Cancellation Scoring

Rule 14. Section a—A regulation game shall consist of fifty (50) points in all contests where a National or Sectional title is involved. Any other contests may be decided in any manner acceptable to National Rules, Constitution and By-Laws are not violated.

Section b—Game points in other tournaments, leagues or contests may be determined by local authorities to fit their conditions.

Section c—A game is divided into innings and each inning constitutes the pitching of two shoes by each contestant.

Rule 15. *Section a*—A shoe must be within six (6) inches of the stake to score.

Section b—Closest shoe to stake scores .... 1 point
Section c—Two shoes closer than opponents .... 2 points
Section d—One (1) ringer scores .... 3 points
Section e—Two (2) ringers scores .... 6 points
Section f—One (1) ringer and closest shoe of same player scores .... 4 points
Section g—Party having two (2) ringers against one for opponent scores .... 3 points
Section h—All equals count as ties. If each contestant has a shoe touching the stake or each has a shoe equal distance from the stake, then the closer of the other two shoes will be scored as a point, if within six (6) inches of the stake.
Section i—In case each contestant has a ringer, the next closest shoe, if within six (6) inches shall score .... 1 point
Section j—In case of tie, such as four (4) ringers, or contestant's shoes are equal distance from the stake, causing no score for either, party pitching last in the inning will start the next inning.
Section k—A leaning shoe has no value over one touching the stake.

Rule 16. *Section a*—The points shall be scored according to the position of the shoes at the inning's end, that is, after the contestants have each thrown two shoes.

Section b—Ringer credits shall be given on the same basis.

Section c—The winner of points shall call the result. In case of a tie, the party pitching last shall call.

Rule 17—*Definition of a ringer:* A ringer is declared when a shoe encircles the stake far enough to allow the touching of both heel caulks simultaneously with a straight edge, and permit a clearance of the stake.

Rule 18. Section a—Count-All Scoring: A game shall consist of fifty (50) shoes pitched by each player (25 innings).

Section b—Each player shall receive credit for all points according to the position of the shoes at the end of each inning, regardless of what his opponent throws. Thus it is possible for each player to score six points in any one inning. Ringers count three points and shoes within six inches of the stake count one point each.

Section c—Players shall alternate first pitch, one player having first pitch in the even innings and the other player in the odd number innings.

Section d—Ties shall be broken by pitching an extra inning or as many extra innings as are necessary to break the tie.

Rule 19. Doubles Games: Two players are partners and pitch from opposite ends of the court against a similar combination of opponents. Partners points are added together, but the individual records of ringers and shoes pitched should be kept. Otherwise the game is the same as the conventional singles or walking game.

Rule 20. Three-handed Games: In three-handed games, when two of the players each have a ringer and a third player no ringer, the party without a ringer is out of the scoring and others score according to conditions pertaining if only two were in the game. Otherwise, the regulation rules apply.

Rule 21. Recording of Results: The recording of results shall be as follows:

W—Games Won; L—Games Lost; P—Points; R—Ringers; DR—Double Ringers; SP—Shoes Pitched; OP—Opponents Points; PR—Percentage of Ringers.

JURISDICTION

Rule 22. Section a—A tournament committee, satisfactory to the Executive Committee, shall supervise National contests.

Section b—A referee appointed by the committee shall decide points when contestants are in doubt. He shall also see that rules are complied with.

Section c—Appeal may be made to the committee if a ruling

of the referee is not considered proper. Decision of the committee shall be final.

Section d—All protests shall be made immediately when the occasion arises. Protests covering shoes or conditions of play can only be made before start of each game.

Section e—If rain or other elements interfere, players must stop play and not resume until officials authorize. On resuming play, score at time of interference will be in effect, also the same courts will be used by contestants unless they agree otherwise.

Section f—The interpretation of the tournament committee covering technical points and their rulings on matters uncovered by these rules shall be final.

Section g—An official scorer shall cover each game. When open scorers are also maintained, the official scorer shall watch closely the open score and correct immediately any error. The scoresheet kept by the official scorer shall be the official score. Not the scoring device.

Rule 23. An official contest between two players shall consist of best six (6) out of eleven (11) games.

6

How to Pitch Ringers

There was a day when a lucky ringer here and there along with a few close shoes would win a horseshoe game. This is still true at some family reunions or company picnics.

The tournament trail is a different story. A player who is interested in winning at any level of competition, and more particularly one who is interested in becoming a tournament champion, will have to learn how to throw ringers with regularity.

As I have studied and talked with pitchers from all across the United States and Canada I have been impressed by the many styles of pitching. One could come to the conclusion that there are as many pitching styles as there are pitchers. Up to a point this is true, because each pitcher adds his own personal touch to his delivery.

But just as true is the fact that certain fundamentals are common to all pitching styles. Looking back to earlier experiences in basketball, baseball, boxing and other sports it has been my observation that an athlete who masters the fundamentals of his sport will be able to work out the fine points and to fit his individual style to the framework of fundamentals.

To hold oneself out as a teacher is to invite disaster. At

times I am tempted to feel almost apologetic in view of the fact that I am not one of the outstanding pitchers myself. But I am bolstered by one of my idols, Coach Paul Brown of the Cincinnati Bengals of the National Football League. Paul was not a great football player, yet he is the greatest of all football coaches. Others who were great players have been wholly unsuccessful as coaches.

So it is with horseshoe pitching. Some of the greatest players in the game are either unable or unwilling to teach. Some of the best teachers are mediocre pitchers. My efforts to teach the game are made in the hope of filling a great void and causing the sport to grow.

My method is to divide the game into two phases and each phase into several steps.

Phase One: The Mechanics of Pitching a Ringer

1. *Select a brand of shoes.* Any one of the brands listed in Chapter 4 will go on the stake. If you have access to all brands you may choose one because some aspect of the shoe appeals to you more than another. The size of your hand might cause you to select a wide shank or a narrow one. Gripping a shoe near or on one of the calks might cause you to choose a shoe which has sloping calks. One part of the contour of a shoe might fit some finger so naturally that you will be able to get the same grip on the shoe each pitch without searching for your grip.

Once you decide to pitch a certain shoe, give it a good trial before going to another brand. The shoes are balanced differently and you cannot get a shoe to work for you unless you give it adequate time.

2. *Wear comfortable clothing.* It is important that you wear comfortable clothing whether you are practicing or playing in tournaments. The shoes on your feet should

be comfortable and should have soles that will grip the surface on which you are to stand. Without good footing you will be afraid to step freely. The shirt should have roomy shoulders so that there will be no binding or skin irritation in connection with your follow through. There should be no coattails or loose ends flapping in front of the arms or legs.

3. *Choose a grip and a turn.* Choosing a grip is one of the most important steps you will take on the road to ringer pitching. When you choose a grip you are also deciding which turn you will use.

The same grip can be used for more than one turn. For example, the most common grip is the 1¼ grip shown in Illustrated Grip No. 1. This grip can be used for the 2¼, reverse ¾ or reverse 1¾. The second most popular grip is the 1¾ shown in Illustrated Grip No. 2. This can also be used for the ¾ and for the reverse 1¼.

If you are just beginning I would recommend that you adopt either the 1¼ or the 1¾ turns. However, if you are already using some other turn and have confidence in it you must decide for yourself whether you will try to make it work or change to another turn. Any turn is permitted by the rules and most of them will work.

Ted Allen, Guy Zimmerman, Don Titcomb and John Monasmith pitched the 1¼ to perfection in winning World titles. Fernando Isais, Paul Focht and Elmer Hohl did the same with the 1¾. Harold Reno and Dan Kuchcinski won titles with a reverse 1¼ and Curt Day with a reverse ¾. With a flip shoe such as that shown in Illustrated Grip No. 3 Ruth Hangen has won the Women's World Championship four consecutive times beginning in 1970, Farron Eisemann the 1967 and 1968 Juniors, and in the men's division Jesse Gonzales is a perennial challenger in California and National tournaments with ringer percentages frequently above eighty.

PITCHING CHAMPIONSHIP HORSESHOES 66

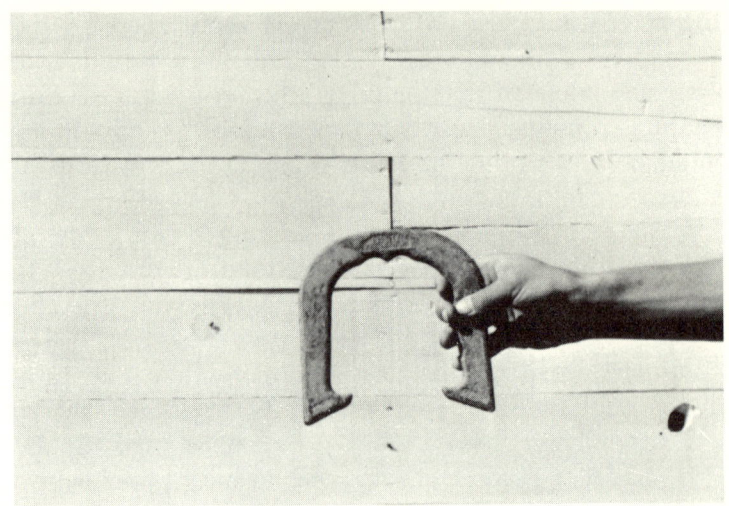

Illustrated Grip No. 1
1¼ viewed from top and bottom.

HOW TO PITCH RINGERS

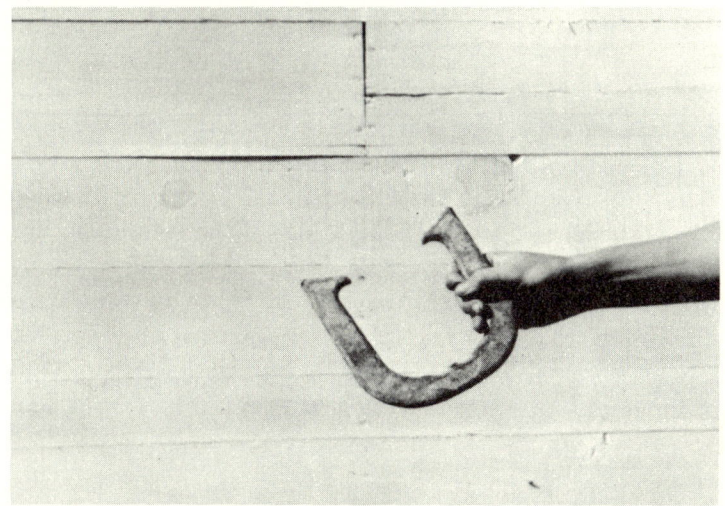

Illustrated Grip No. 2
1¾, viewed from top and bottom.

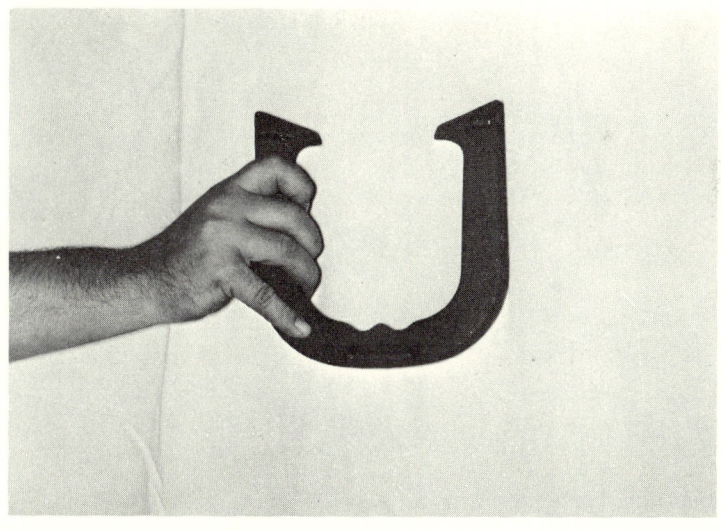

If you happen to be close to one of the outstanding pitchers there is some wisdom in adopting his turn. He has mastered it and will be able to teach you how to throw it. Don Titcomb who won the 1960 World Championship, had the rare privilege to be taught the ways of the 1¼ by the great Guy Zimmerman. All you have to do is to watch Gerald Schneider and Ron Simmons pitch to see the influence of Fernando Isais. The examples are endless.

4. *Adopt a stance.* The rules require that you stand even with or behind the stake. Just where you stand at the start of your step will depend upon the length of your stride. Stand so that your step will carry the front foot

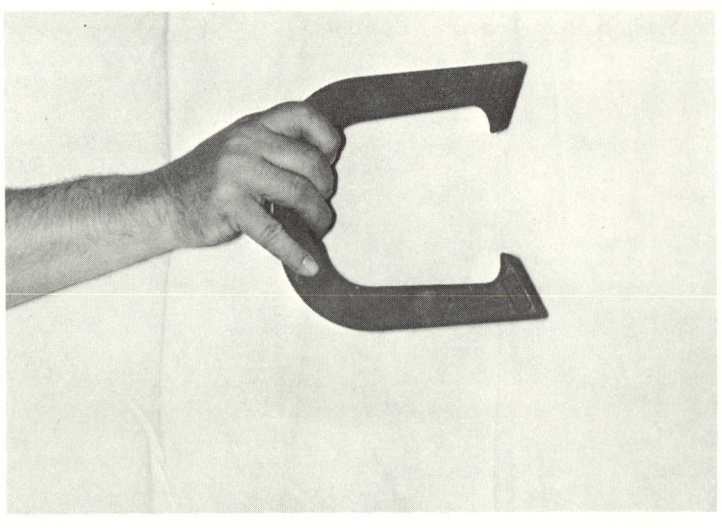

Illustrated Grip No. 3
The Flip

Jesse Gonzales
Californian beats 80% with flip shoe.

almost to the foul line. If you have a short stride stand even with the stake. If you have a long stride, back up as far as you must to keep from stepping on the foul line.

Right handed pitchers should stand on the left side of the stake. It is permissible to pitch from the other side if you have a good reason, but if you do pitch from the right side be sure to do so from both ends of the court.

The placement of the feet in relation to each other is a thing which varies widely. The most natural seems to be to stand with the feet even. However, good pitchers will

Lee Davis
1960 New Jersey Champion uses
overhead windup

trail with the right or the left foot. Placing the left foot forward ends to shorten the stride while placing the right foot forward will lengthen the stride. These different positions of the feet will change your entire delivery, so I recommend again that you adopt one which is comfortable and stay with it. At least I would not change until I became convinced that it would not work.

5. *Address the stake.* Whether you call it sighting, ad-

HOW TO PITCH RINGERS 71

Charles Stevens
1960 Florida Champion, used slow and elaborate delivery

dressing the stake, taking a bead on the target, or some other name, there is a precious moment just before you start your delivery which is very important. In that moment you get "ready" to pitch.

Some pitchers hold the shoe in front of their faces and look through it. Some hold it at various angles and look over it. Some hold it near the chest, over the head, beside the right ear or down at the side while staring at the

O. S. Plott
Louisiana Champion

opposite stake. Some swing their arms and others shuffle their feet.

All are trying to get the feel of the shoe and be at ease so that the delivery is natural and easy. Regardless of the method you choose I think it is fundamental to all that you square your shoulders with the target and avoid dropping the right side too low. My choice is to look over the center of the shoe at the stake.

6. *The step and the backswing.* At the beginning of the

HOW TO PITCH RINGERS 73

RALPH MADDOX
17 times West Virginia Champion
talks with the author about the fine points of the 1¾ grip. Maddox, a veteran of World Tournament play who averages in the eighties, uses a full hand grip and just "puts the shoe up where it will work by itself."

step the weight should be distributed equally between the two feet or in such a way that the pitcher feels perfectly balanced. The weight must shift to the right foot as the step begins toward the target stake just as though the pitcher were starting to walk. The knees bend and the pitcher leans forward as the backswing begins. The arm and the shoe should fall freely and close to the leg and should define an arc which is in line with the target stake. The forward step begins before the backswing is complete. A pitcher like Howard Shriver, West Virginia State Champion, has a short backswing of only a foot behind his leg. Dan Kuchcinski, present World Champion, has a long backswing which carries the shoe high above his head. If it is natural and allows you enough leverage to lift the shoe to the target any length of backswing will be satisfactory.

7. *The follow through and release.* The swing forward should retrace the path of the back swing with the release coming at eye level and the arm continuing upward after the release to the natural completion of the swing.

The follow through is all important because it is here that the finishing touch is put on the pitch. Once you have turned the shoe loose, its fate is decided. Many a pitcher has hurled epithets at shoes after they have been released but not one shoe has ever changed its course in flight as a result. The levelling of the shoe, the turn, the height and the alignment are all wrapped up in the point of release and the follow through. The lift of the shoe must come from the whole body as the knees straighten rather than from too much arm motion.

Generally speaking the height of the shoe should vary from seven to ten feet. The shoe should not be gripped too tightly. The whole routine should be as simple and

JIM SOLOMON
1964 Pennsylvania State Champion
He makes the unorthodox right foot lead work.

A right handed pitcher should lead with his left foot. But just as bowling has its Wrong Foot Louie, horseshoes has some very fine pitchers who lead with the right foot. A notable example is Jim Solomon, a Pennsylvania state champion who is shown in the accompanying picture. Solomon hits more than 80% ringers coming off the wrong foot (wrong can be right).

natural as possible. The simpler the delivery, the less the chance for error.

8. *Turning the shoe.* The turn is accomplished by shifting the weight of the shoe with a roll of the forearm. The shoe would not turn at all if you were able to hold it level from the beginning to the end of your delivery and release it without dragging your fingers or rolling your forearm. By letting the shoe hang down and levelling it before the release you cause it to turn. The amount of turn is increased by waiting longer to level the shoe and decreased by levelling it sooner. Each pitcher must learn to regulate the amount of turn so that it opens at the stake.

9. *Develop timing.* Timing or pitching rhythm is difficult to acquire and difficult to keep. Some never get it. Others who do get it lose it in some pressure-packed situation. A few seem to have it always. These men are the toughies.

Rhythm is nothing more than doing the right thing at the right time. The bending of the knees and the lean forward must blend with the back swing, the forward step must blend with the forward swing, and the lift of the body must end with the release of the shoe.

10. *Practice.* In the first phase of learning to pitch, practice is a must. It may be more beneficial to practice alone than to practice against an opponent. Your attention could more profitably be directed to the parts of your own game than to the thought of trying to win. Once you learn how to pitch you will develop confidence to compete against other pitchers.

The old saying that "Practice makes perfect" is still true. Practice every chance you get until you understand what makes a ringer go on the stake.

Phase Two—From Ringer Thrower to Complete Performer

The transition from the practice court to the tournament atmosphere is a big one. Fitting the mechanical aspect of pitching ringers into the game conditions requires many adjustments.

I am cautious to point out that since I am not one of the accomplished pitchers myself my analysis is based on games I have played against them, conversations with them and a close observation of them under game conditions. Fools rush in where angels fear to tread.

1. *Court manners.* A pitcher should follow the rules in every detail, particularly those rules which are designed to allow his opponent to pitch without interference. This includes standing at the back of the pitcher's box while he delivers his shoes and making no sound or motion that will hurt his concentration. Horseshoe pitching is seen at its beautiful best when both pitchers are "on" and battle each other on raw skill rather than on psychology and distraction.

You may insist on the enforcement of rules and on the measurement of shoes in doubt without being a poor sport. No pitcher will be offended by your insistence on the benefit of the rules but he will be offended by efforts to stretch or evade the rules in order to hurt his performance. In other words he wants to be outpitched rather than outfoxed.

2. *Dress.* Wearing apparel need not be expensive. Any type of sportswear will do. But it should be two things—comfortable and neat. A player's first and last name, his town and state should be lettered on his shirt in two inch letters which can be read 50 feet away. By wearing your pitching clothes every time you play you will never be conscious of your attire when you compete, thereby eliminating one more possible distraction.

3. *Hide your emotions.* You can never master the game

Ted Allen of Boulder, Colorado, won ten World Championships between 1933 and 1959. He was Colorado State Champion in 1922 and back as Colorado State Champion in 1968, 46 years apart! He is still firing and over half a century his record cannot be equalled. He has not missed a world tournament since 1933 and has held almost all the records at one time. Some have been broken, others still stand. Among these are 72 consecutive ringers in 1955 and 67 consecutive world tournament victories in 1955 and 1956.

of horseshoes unless you can first master your own temperament. Strive to be cool at all times and if you can't be cool, at least appear to be cool. Irritation can come from many sources: Opponents who try to "psyche" you, spectators who run behind the stake as you deliver the shoe, poor conditions of the playing courts, yesterday's

A great exhibitionist and promoter of the game Ted possesses that thing called color. He is one of the top attractions any where he hangs that ten gallon western hat.

The three shots of Ted show his grip (p. 78), his stance with the left foot trailing (p. 79), and above, his follow through.

quarrel with your wife, and perfect ringers bouncing off the stake are some good examples. A display of temper will only hurt your game and will take away something from the standpoint of spectator appeal.

4. *Develop your rhythm and mood.* Many of the best players seem to be in a state of self-hypnosis when they are at their best. They can almost rock themselves to sleep.

This requires a good general attitude toward the game

as a whole plus the ability to find one's timing. The physical and mental attitude of a pitcher will be different from time to time and he must learn how to make adjustments for it.

5. *Compete regularly.* Once you have mastered the art of throwing ringers you need to compete regularly to keep your competitive edge. Pitching on top of double ringers knowing that each miss will put three points on the scoreboard for your opponent makes a difference. Adjusting to the speed of your opponent is also different from practice where the tempo of the pitching is entirely up to you. The presence of the pencil has transformed 80 percent pitchers into 60 percent pitchers and regular competition will help in all these areas.

6. *Hunt for the bear.* There is a touch of grizzly bear in all of the champions. Sometimes the bear snarls where you can see and hear him. At other times he tracks you down quietly from behind. Either way his attack is inevitable and his attempt to kill you is certain.

If you study the facial expression in all of the action pictures you can see the bear. You can feel him in the handshakes and find his tracks on your scoresheet.

The logical reaction is to develop your own bear. This does not mean to use ugly behavior or to practice poor sportsmanship. Rather it means to develop a dogged determination to excel and to deliver your own best game regardless of the situation.

7. *Make plans and keep records.* While it is not necessary to make foolproof plans and to keep records in great detail, it is beneficial to do a reasonable amount of both. Making a long range plan to compete in certain events during the course of the year will help your overall attitude. With a little bit of planning you can have a tentative pitching schedule and some ready equipment nearby at

all times. Keeping track of your ringer percentage will tell you when you are up or down and what rate of improvement you have accomplished in any given period of time. It is helpful to keep a record of your practice because it causes you to bear down and creates a certain gamelike pressure.

8. *Correct mistakes immediately.* The great ones only make a mistake once. They correct it on the very next pitch. On your way through the first phase of pitching you have learned every detail about your pitch. You know how to increase or decrease the turn and the distance, adjust the alignment and level the shoe. Why keep repeating the same mistake? How often do you hear a pitcher say, "My pitch has been turning past the stake all day"? Why didn't that pitcher adjust his turn to slow it down?

9. *Confidence.* No pitcher is complete until he gets confidence in himself. This confidence comes only when he puts together all the parts of his game. There will always be differences in physical ability, experience and age of competitors which affect the peak performance each one can produce. Each man must determine how far his own abilities will take him and base his quest for confidence on his own capabilities.

10. *Pressure.* Every pitcher is plagued by pressure. There is no better way to combat pressure than to be ready ahead of time. If a man is in good physical condition, has a healthy mental attitude, and has confidence in his game, he has the battle half won before it gets under way. One must try to relax and this is doubly difficult in horseshoe pitching since it is a game of such intense and constant concentration. Pressure is a state of mind which can overcome a player to the point where his nerves and muscles do not respond normally and the result is a sub-

par performance. Some way must be found to free the mind from these shackles and different methods are employed by different players. Some think of their own game and are able to ignore all outside interference. Others will count to themselves, repeat short sentences or think of some object such as a snow-capped mountain. Anything that will work for you is the thing to use.

When you find the formula that will work every time write it down. You will be able to sell a copy of it to every pitcher in the world.

11. *Waste no practice.* Never pitch less than you can pitch, even in practice. Never practice without concentrating. Bad practice will develop bad habits that will be repeated in the games. If you are not mentally ready to concentrate don't practice. It will do more harm than good.

Less practice will be needed, of course, than when you were learning. But you will never reach the place where no practice is needed, and this is particularly true when you do not play in many tournaments.

12. *Goals.* The only goal worth setting is to do the best you can. It is a mistake to set a target which you will reach or else. There is no use to grieve over past performance. It is fine to profit by past mistakes, but look forward to tomorrow's performance. Tomorrow is a new day.

The rest of this chapter is devoted to a treatment of different phases of the game by men who are champions. They have made it work and their words of wisdom make good reading.

These two pictures of World Champion Dan Kuchinski reveal many things. The first one shows clearly his stance at the rear of the box to accommodate his long stride, the position of his feet and hands as he takes his stance

PITCHING CHAMPIONSHIP HORSESHOES 84

Two views of World Champion Dan Kuchcinski in action. (Courtesy Time, Inc.)

HOW TO PITCH RINGERS 85

and addresses the stake, his grips, and his intense concentration.

The second one shows the high backswing, straight arm and the start of his forward step.

A close look at the faces of the fans in both pictures shows an interest as keen as that of any baseball, football, basketball or hockey fans.

Carl F. Steinfeldt of Rochester, New York, is a master of the left-handed 1¼ turn. Carl constantly averages in the mid-eighties in ringer percentage and holds numerous state and world records. One outstanding world record is the 15 consecutive four-deads with Elmer Hohl, the Canadian champion, in the 1964 World Tournament.

Steinfeldt has won the New York state championship 15 times, the Eastern National six times and the World's left-handed championship six times.

Here are his comments on two aspects of the game:

Choice of Turn. I pitch the 1¼ turn because I think it is the easiest turn to control. The 1¾ turn is a better turn to throw if it is at all windy or the clay is hard.

Concentration. I have found it a great help to me, when I am up against a player of equal ability, to keep track of my own game as it progresses. My aim is to average between 8 and 9 ringers out of every 10 shoes. I know that if I obtain this goal my opponent is not scoring very often and it keeps my mind on my own game and not on his.

A Tip From Art Kamman, Arizona State Champ. To be successful in top flight competition a pitcher must have good distance, alignment, ability to concentrate on every pitch and finally to relax while his opponent makes his pitches. To me this is most important. I find that breathing deeply and looking up or around helps me to relax.

HOW TO PITCH RINGERS 87

CARL F. STEINFELDT
Rochester, New York

PITCHING CHAMPIONSHIP HORSESHOES 88

JIM KNISLEY
1968 Ohio State Champion—81.4%
1968 Runnerup to World Champion

How To Practice
By Jim Knisley

To get the most out of your practice session you should first have regulation equipment as well as good regulation courts. The stakes should be the right height and held securely in the ground. The clay should always be level and in a putty like condition at all times.

I feel that in the beginning you should practice alone. This is the best way to get the shoe working the way you want it to and to get your timing and rhythm right. Try to practice at least one hour a day. This is usually sufficient to put you in good form. Start bearing down when you first start warming up and then pitch your shoes in groups of 50 and count all points. Remember it is not how long you practice but how you train that is important.

But to do well in tournament play you must do more than practice by yourself. Many players learn to pitch very well by themselves in their own back yard. But when they go away from home in a different environment against strange pitchers they usually pitch poorly. There are two ways I have learned to overcome this.

1. When an opponent is not available at your home court simply use two or more pairs of horseshoes this way. Place a shoe around each stake and leave it there. I call these shoes my imaginary opponent. I usually use a scoreboard with players' names on it that I might meet in competition and keep score just like an actual game. Try to beat this opponent. With a shoe on each end you must pitch over 50 percent to defeat him. I usually use two shoes on one end and one on the other. This makes me throw over 75 percent to win. I feel that this is a great way of pitching against the iron of the opposing shoes and

is excellent practice in capping ringers.

2. But the best way I have found to improve at tournaments is to play in as many tourneys as possible. This will not only get you used to strange players but also strange courts.

Remember this, at home is the place to practice—not at the tournament site. You should do all of your experimenting before you come to play and when you get to the tournament you should have one thing on your mind—Ringers.

Ernolf "Red" Roland
1933 North Dakota Champion

When I was pitching horseshoes, I dedicated two hours daily to practice. I strung a wire for height and moved a marker along side the courts for consistency so that my turn could be studied more closely. I also had two spots, one about 6 feet out and one about 6 feet from the stake I was shooting at. This combination gave me proper elevation for my 1¼ turn, better direction, and forced me to follow through properly on my delivery. It also gave me a shoe that had completely exhausted all momentum upon reaching the stake. In fact, I at one time used brass shoes to throw a softer shoe to save ringers. I believe that a 1¼ turn with a flop in the final half-turn allows a greater margin for error. The shoe stays open longer and it is not as vulnerable to wind and air currents if you have drive behind the shoe and keep the elevation down. Of course, the secret is to keep your composure under control by shutting out the outside world, and above all free wheeling the shoe without guiding it. This can only come from practice and confidence.

HOW TO PITCH RINGERS 91

ERNOLF "RED" ROLAND
1933 North Dakota Champion

One of the best means of obtaining moderate exercise is the game of horseshoes. Your mind requires concentration, you walk at a moderate pace in good wholesome air, the arm activity is not strenuous, and it does not harm some of us to bend over now and then to pick up our shoes. How can you beat it?

Jim Solomon

Jim Solomon of Uniontown, Pennsylvania, is a state champion and winner of many open tournaments, averaging above 80 percent ringers.

One feature of Jim's pitching that is of particular interest to this book is the fact that he leads with the right foot. As a right handed pitcher he would normally lead with the left.

His reason for leading with the right foot is that he learned the habit at the age of ten. Pitching from 40 feet at that age made it a task to reach the stake. His foot work

JIM SOLOMON
Uniontown, Pennsylvania

consisted of one step and a push, starting out with the normal left foot lead but ending up on the right. When he became heavy enough to pitch 40 feet he abandoned the first step and retained the second with its follow through and release motion.

Solomon maintains that because of leading with the right foot he pitches only 39 feet instead of 40, which is less tiring for him than for pitchers who lead with the left. To see what he means one needs only to watch the point of release.

JIM SOLOMON ON CONCENTRATION:

The object of every pitch is a ringer. If you do not intend to concentrate on pitching a ringer, why pitch? I keep that object in mind at all times—every time a ringer!

To accomplish this object a pitcher must try to make himself into a robot or automaton, doing the same thing every time. My routine is to get into pitching position, take a bead on the top of the stake, and to put rhythm into my pitch as well as blot out everything except the stake. I do this by thinking to myself, "One, two, three and get them up."

I continue to watch the top of the stake and do not watch the shoe in flight. In this way I am aware only of the stake. It helps to keep out of my mind all interferences, the spectators, my opponent, the score or the situation.

Curt Day

Curt Day of Frankfort, Indiana, is regarded by many of the top ranked players as the "meanest man alive" when he is on the horseshoe courts. Regardless of the score or the situation Curt is always throwing ringers with the same deadly monotony. Points are hard to get against Curt Day.

Day won the World Championship in 1966 hitting 86.6 percent ringers at Murray City, Utah. On Labor Day of 1969 he hit an 88.8 percent clip for nine games to win his 14th Indiana State Championship and 11th in a row. There have been dozens of other tournament championships since he began organized play in 1947.

Induction into the Horseshoe Pitching Hall of Fame in 1969 at Erie, Pennsylvania, was the final recognition for this great pitcher.

Here are some tips from Curt Day:

Conditioning is important. Get plenty of rest and take care of your health generally.

What works for me might not work for everyone. For one thing I use the reverse three-quarters turn which is unusual. I also stand on the right side of the stake which is cross-fire for a right handed pitcher.

My step is a long one because it seems to give me a little extra distance. I start with my feet together, my shoulders square and my weight about equal on both feet. My weight seems to shift mostly to my right foot after I start my delivery.

My shoe is gripped on the tip of my fingers in a relaxed position. I bring it up and stop long enough to "feel" the shoe. I keep my eye on the stake and do not particularly watch the shoe in the air although I pick it up after the release and follow it to the stake. My aim is about three or four inches up on the stake.

Timing the step with the swing or getting the rhythm is important. My left foot is planted before the release and I try not to get too much arm in my pitch.

Patience is a big factor. A man has to be patient to work out the many different problems.

CURT DAY
World Champion in 1966 and 1971, Indiana State Champion 17 times, and a member of the Hall of Fame.

    To align the stake I sight over the center of the shoe, go straight down the stake, come straight back up the stake and push directly at the opposite stake. I stay relatively close to my leg. The lift and follow through affect the distance as well as the turn.
    More practice is needed while learning than later on.

I try to practice 45 minutes a day and play a tournament on each weekend through the summer months.

Distance is affected by tightening up, generally causing a pitcher to throw low. The secret is in the arm swing. Raise or lower the shoe to correct the distance.

To slow down my turn I cock the shoe slightly and always release it in the same position as I hold it to sight.

The simpler your routine the less chance there is to make mistakes.

To get up for a tournament I build up my endurance and make sure in practice that my shoe is working. I get one or two pairs of shoes in which I have confidence and which are working for me without extra attention.

To fight pressure I believe it is best to concentrate on your own game, stance, grip, release and so on, rather than the crowd, the score or your opponent. Find a way to get free and easy. You must come up with something to keep from tensing and gripping the shoe too tight.

Don Titcomb

Don Titcomb of Los Gatos, California, won the World Championship in 1960 at Muncie, Indiana. Although he was only 35 years old Don had been pitching for 23 years. During most of those 23 years he had aimed for the title.

Winning a world title takes more than the ability to throw ringers. It takes physical endurance, mental temperament, some luck in the form of breaks and an absolute refusal to yield to pressure.

It took Don six hours of pitching a day for six consecutive days to win the tournament, 2878 shoes and 2443 ringers. Getting ready for this performance was no accident.

Titcomb spends three months in training for a world championship tournament, gradually building up his strength. He throws 100 shoes a day for the first month. He increases the pace to 200 a day for the second month and the last month averages 300 to 400. Then there follows a week's rest before the big event.

The strain of competition is so great that each year Don told himself "never again." In 1958 and 1959 he was second. Each year he returned, however, until he won the dream title. Once that goal was achieved he relaxed. While he has remained active in the game, even winning the 1967 California state title, Don has not yet been able to build himself back to the fever pitch needed to go all the way.

TITCOMB TEACHES THE GAME

The game of horseshoes can be broken down into three basic steps: one, throwing an open shoe; two, acquiring alignment and distance; and three, developing a rhythm pitch.

I place opening the shoe first with a beginner to impress upon him the importance of controlling the action of a turning shoe. Once a beginner has confidence in opening his shoe, he can then concentrate on alignment and distance. The third step, that of developing a rhythm pitch, is a result of the first two and can be attained only by learning the first two.

Each pitcher will fall into a natural rhythm of his own and should not try to copy someone else in exact detail. The step, the swing and the release should blend into a natural movement.

A natural rhythm permits a pitcher to pitch with ease and comfort. A pitcher who forces his shoe is an erratic pitcher and can go only for a short period of time. He is a streak pitcher, blowing hot and cold. For the long game fought against a player of equal caliber, one cannot worry about anything except the job at hand.

OPENING THE SHOE

Whether your turn is as little as one quarter turn or as much as two and a half turns, it will be regulated by the position of the hand on the shoe and the angle at which the shoe leaves your hand. For example, my turn and a quarter can be held fairly flat during the release and will angle during the swing. Attempting to hold the shoe flat throughout the swing will destroy the alignment.

My advice is to use the shoe weight as much as possible in making the shoe turn. This will make your pitch easier and help in the development of a natural turn. Success in using shoe weight in your turn depends how much you use the weight in your swing. Just as in bowling, getting the shoe out away from the body and letting it drop will cause an increase in momentum, which in turn develops a natural release and turn.

ACQUIRING ALIGNMENT AND DISTANCE

Step One is part of alignment and distance, too. I have never been able to tell anyone exactly when the shoe leaves my hand. All I know is that it leaves when it is ready.

A pitcher should let his body help in the delivery of the shoe by bending it during the down swing, enough to help, but not enough to force the pitch.

I can control my alignment throughout the swing by keeping my aiming point down and up the stake with my eyes on a spot six inches from the bottom of the stake. I also try to control the direction of my step by making sure

DON TITCOMB
1960 World Champion

that my feet are turned in the direction of the stake. Right-handers stepping out with the left foot should control that step by having the right foot pointed toward the stake before taking the step.

DEVELOPING A RHYTHM PITCH

The third step is the most important step, and is at the same time the easiest one. A good athlete in any sport must be consistent. Horseshoes are no exception. One must develop and keep the same rhythm while he is pitching to maintain a steady game. When you find, keep and control this rhythm, you will be able to pitch your game through rainouts or other interruptions.

Search for the natural rhythm that will permit you to combine your step, your swing and your release into one continuous, easy movement.

Observations of Al Zadroga

Listed below are the two main items and following discussion which I feel are important in horseshoe pitching.
(1) Style or pitching routine
(2) Method of practice

Item No. 1: In order to bring out the best in every pitcher I believe it is essential that each individual develop his own personal style and routine and stick with it. The natural way is best and can be more readily developed and improved than one that is copied. Of course a person can and should observe other pitchers for ideas and methods. The turn of the shoe is irrelevant. They are all good. The natural turn is best, as it can more easily be mastered. In my own case I have never thrown anything but the 1¼ turn and expect that I will never change. I have experimented with other turns but found out quickly they were not for me.

Item No. 2: Practice and lots of it are a must for every pitcher. The first reason for practice is to get and keep in physical shape for tournament play. A 12- or 16-man round robin requires that a pitcher must be in good shape in order to do his best. Practice in the right way is very essential to improving your game. I have found in recent years that it has been important to me to keep a record of what I have been doing in practice. Get somebody to keep your score; preferably throw 100 shoes at a time. You then know exactly what you are pitching and if you are in need of more work. This item has been most important to me and I believe it will and should improve everybody's game. There is also a certain amount of pressure in this type of practice and helps out a lot in tournaments. Whenever the pencil appears a different atmosphere exits.

Miscellaneous Item: Courtesy on the court in my book is also a very important item in horseshoe pitching. Every pitcher should acquaint himself with the few rules, regulations and customs there are and live up to them. I make it a habit to show my opponent every courtesy he is entitle to and by the same token expect the same from him. I never hesitate to let my opponent know if he is doing something out of the ordinary that is contrary to the rules; sometimes these things are done unconsciously and a polite reminder is all that is necessary.

Paul Focht
1962 World Champion

Paul Focht of Dayton, Ohio, reached the pinnacle of his horseshoe pitching career in 1962 by winning the

AL ZADROGA
Pennsylvania State Champion 1965, 1969, and 1972.

PAUL FOCHT
1962 World Champion

World Championship. Over the gruelling week of play Focht posted 32 wins and three losses and an 81.8 ringer percentage.

Over the past 20 years Paul has been one of the most consistent, most active and toughest pitchers in the country. He won Ohio State titles in 1953, 1962 and 1963, an Eastern National and dozens of other tournament titles. Among his individual highs is a 95.4 percent game in the 1965 World Tournament in which he beat Marvin Craig 51-18, hitting 124 ringers out of 130 shoes. He hit 93 ringers out of 100 shoes and 286 points out of a possible 300 in a qualifying round at the Southwestern Ohio District tournament in 1968.

PITCHING TIPS FROM PAUL FOCHT

Some of the secrets of good horseshoe pitching are your position on the court, footwork, swing, release, rhythm, follow through and liking the game enough to practice about an hour a day. Make your pitch as easy and as natural as possible. I use the one and three-quarters and start with my up swing about eye level and my back swing as high as my head, then release it at eye level. This gives me good coordination and control of the shoe. Your left foot has to be on the concrete with your body leaning a little forward before your shoe passes your right leg. This gives you height and drive on your pitch. After you release your shoe your arm goes on up about two feet more for good follow through.

John Monasmith

John Monasmith, Yakima, Washington, won the World Title in 1963 at South Gate, California, with a 32-3 record,

JOHN MONASMITH
1963 World Champion

averaging 82.3 percent ringers. He owns 13 state championships in his native Washington.

Monasmith makes this interesting observation on competitive pressure:

PRESSURE

Horseshoe pitching has made a tremendous rise in ringer percentage in the past twenty years. Many players are averaging over 80 percent. Keeping relaxed under heavy pressure in a close game or when one is coming from behind is a must to survive today's tournaments. One

The great Elmer Hohl, thirteen times Canadian Champion and four times World Champion, wiped out all the records in 1968 at Keene, New Hampshire, on his way to the all-time record 88.5 percent tournament. These three pictures show his 1¾ grip, his stance, and his follow through. He possesses great natural ability and physical strength.

must not give signs of his problems or it will give his opponent an edge. No top horseshoe pitcher carries the same set of nerves in every tournament, so he must compensate by hiding his problems the best he can. Keeping cool and relaxed under heavy pressure won the 1963 World's Cham-

pionship Tournament for me. Most of the tournaments I have won in the Northwest in the past 20 years I attribute to my opponent's signs of trouble.

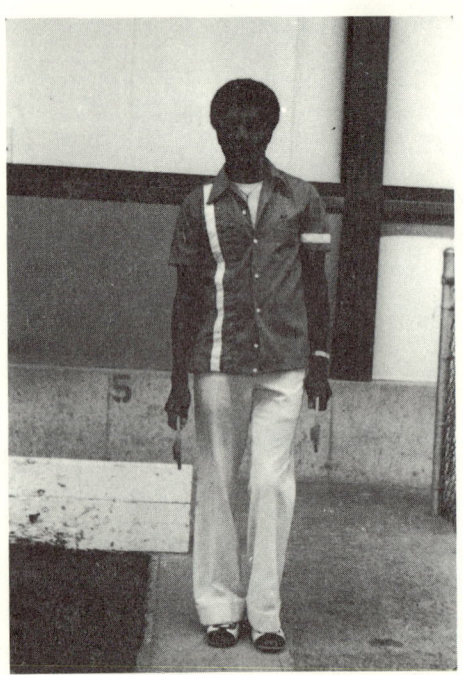

Art Tyson of Connecticut

Art Tyson is unquestionably the finest Negro horseshoe pitcher in America. In the 1973 World Tournament at Eureka he averaged 69.7% ringers, posting a 16-19 record and finishing 23rd. This is a remarkable achievement in view of the fact he started pitching in the New Haven league in 1969 and averaged 39% ringers. In 2 tournaments Art entered he has won 15 times in both A and B groups.

Art has a wife and three sons, enjoys the game, and looks forward to an improved showing.

HOW TO PITCH RINGERS 109

From left to right are: Norman Rioux, Connecticut state champion; Ed Domey, who built Heritage Recreation at Sutton, Massachusetts; Art Tyson, unquestionably the greatest Negro pitcher in America; and Peter Shepard, Director of the Northeastern States and manufacturer of the American horseshoe. These men are examples of what can be done with a fine indoor facility such as Heritage.

Practice

Elmer Hohl, Wellesley, Ontario, Canada, earned a place for himself in Horseshoe Pitching's Hall of Fame in one year, 1968. In winning his second World Championship Elmer set the all-time world record ringer percentage, hitting 88.5 percent for 35 games. Included in his 35 straight wins was one perfect game in which he hit 30 ringers out of 30 shoes.

To achieve this kind of accuracy one would assume that

endless hours of practice must be involved. Elmer destroys that notion, however, with this statement:

"From November through April is a five-month period during which I never touch a horseshoe. Between June and Ocotber I play in about three tournaments in the United States and four in Canada, ten at the most. I never practice over two hours a week or play over once a week.

"I have hit over 80 percent for all my pitching since I started in organized play in 1950 but I am not too me-

CLYDE MARTZ
Pennsylvania State Champion 1970 and 1973 and designer of the Imperial shoe.

chanical about it. I would just call it a natural coordination."

Clyde Martz, Pittsburgh, Pennsylvania, averages in the high seventies and is a threat to win any tournament he enters. He reached a peak individual performance of 89.7 percent against Al Zadroda in the 1968 Pennsylvania State Tournament.

On the subject of practice Clyde says that practice is an absolute must for him.

"I am not a natural pitcher. My improvement came hard. I work at it, pitching three hours or 500 shoes a day and trying little different things in my practice. My movements are all mechanical, all committed to memory and repeated time after time. My efficiency at throwing ringers is directly related to the amount of practice I get."

Sam Sutton on Alignment

"Once I learned how to throw an open shoe, alignment became 95 percent of my problem. Alignment is still the hardest thing for me to control, but the progress I have made has been from following this simple pattern: I aim at the top of the stake, step straight at the opposite stake and keep my eye on the stake throughout the complete delivery."

Dan and Sue Kuchcinski are doing much to promote the growth of horseshoe pitching. Dan owns the 1967 and 1969 World Championships. Sue owns Women's World Titles for 1962, 1964 and 1965.

They are presently travelling all over the country putting on exhibitions at sports shows, fairs and clubs. They have appeared on national TV. Their performance consists of trick pitching and acrobatics.

SAM SUTTON
Averages in seventies

In the accompanying pictures the husband and wife team are attired for exhibition pitching. In the first one Dan is about to turn loose a ringer. Beside him is his portable court and behind him the stage curtain. In the other two Sue is shown placing her head on the block giving hubby a beautiful target.

Dan Kuchcinski offers some tips:

A person should learn the fundamentals of the game before anything else. Then he should concentrate on

HOW TO PITCH RINGERS 113

Rod Hatton, 1973 Texas Champion and Class B World Champion. With Rod on the backyard court in San Antonio is son Stevie, who is just three but enthusiastically tries to imitate Dad.

Rod Hatton learned to pitch horseshoes in his native Indiana and was hitting at a 70% clip in 1961 when he made it into the Championship Division of the World Tournament at Muncie. He can pitch the 1¼ turn or the 1¾ turn equally well and has spent as much time experimenting and testing the different theories of horseshoes as any pitcher his age. This constant experiment has undoubtedly kept Rod from rising higher in his percentage but has given him a background that could produce anything.

At present Rod Hatton is promoting the game in Texas and the Southwest and exhibiting his unusual style in many tournaments. He builds musical instruments as his occupation.

Dan Kuchcinski turns loose a ringer during an exhibition.

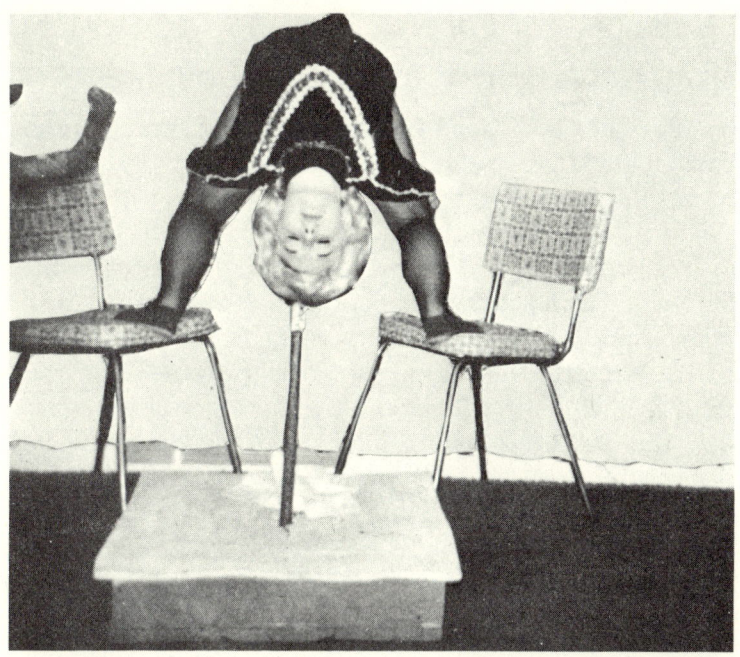

Sue stands on two chairs with her head near the stake as Dan pitches. (Notice the shoe coming in toward the stake at the middle left)

Now Sue does a straddle split in front of the stake as Dan pitches over her head and onto the stake.

opening the shoe. Good concentration and timing are important in improving one's game. He must always keep trying to put everything together.

The pitcher should be "mentally up" to pitch well even in just simple practice. He should practice at least three or four times a week, two hours a day if possible. Being relaxed and letting the shoe turn by itself is important. Never force the shoe. One should learn something every time he goes out to pitch, and the more practice a person has, the less he is apt to forget and the better he will become.

Correcting Mistakes

Generally speaking, a shoe that turns too much may be slowed down either by pitching it lower or leveling it up sooner. A shoe that turns too little may be speeded up either by pitching it higher or waiting longer to level it up. A shoe that is bouncing is either too low and hard or landing on its edge. When the shoe lands on its edge, you have simply not leveled it at the point of release. Roll your arm a little more to the right.

If you find yourself pitching high or low, don't change your stance. A short shoe has been released too soon. Holding on too long can carry it over the stake or pull it out of line.

Harold Reno

Harold Reno, a Clinton County, Ohio, farmer won the World Championship in 1961 and repeated in 1964. He owns 11 Ohio state titles and averages constantly in the

HOW TO PITCH RINGERS 117

HAROLD RENO, GARY ROBERTS, OTTIE RENO
1964 was a good year in the Reno family. Harold won his second World Championship, Gary (a nephew) his fourth consecutive Junior World Championship and Ottie the Stokes Memorial Award.

eighties. In the 1964 Ohio tournament Reno averaged 88.6 percent for 11 games.

Over the past 15 years Reno has been one of the real toughies, winning titles in the Eastern National, Midwest Ringer Roundup, Lakeside Open and dozens of other major events.

One of the quiet gentlemen who play the game, he offers these hints on how to pitch.

1. Try to stay in good health, get plenty of sleep, good food, plenty of exercise, and avoid bad habits that hurt your health.

2. Pick out a spot to stand and stand in the same place every time. This will help you get your distance.
3. Set no goals, except to do your best. Goals put unnecessary pressure on you.
4. Find a way to relax before you pitch each shoe. I do this by an extra swing of my arms, but other pitchers do it other ways.
5. Don't change anything without a good reason or without giving it a fair chance. If you are improving with your turn, with your brand of shoe, with your stance, don't go to another.
6. Try to practice some every day, if time will permit. I cannot find time to do this myself, but I would recommend that you pitch 100 shoes or more each day.
7. Blot out interferences. Don't talk to people, listen to noises, or watch something going on outside the courts while you play.
8. Pitch one shoe at a time and play one game at a time. Worrying about percentages or about upcoming opponents can lessen your concentration.
9. Try to get an early lead. This will put the pressure on your opponent and give you confidence.
10. Be a good sport.

How To Become a Top Player
Roy Smith, Michigan

The first thing you have to have is confidence in yourself and you can obtain this by your stance, which should be comfortable and from the same spot for each throw. The second thing is your swing and follow through which should be worked on so your shoe is always released at the same point. This in turn will give you the right height so your shoe will drop at 40 feet.

After the shoe is released you should watch the action

of your shoe all the way to the stake. In this way you will be able to correct your height and turn. I have found that for me it is better to change the height and let the shoe work itself instead of trying to change the turn myself.

After these ingredients have been put together the most important one is good competition. Join a local club or state organization and try to play someone who is better than you and when you get beat mark their names down in a book with the idea sooner or later you'll scratch their names out.

The most important thing to me is the people I have met. I think the nicest people in the world play horseshoes.

Danny Kuchcinski Makes TV Appearance on Johnny Carson's Tonight Show

Horseshoe pitching received its greatest single shot exposure during a 12-minute appearance by Danny Kuchcinski on Johnny Carson's *Tonight* show, April 16, 1968.

An estimated 30 million viewers watched the 1967 World Champion during the interview and pitching session over the NBC network.

Carson, in his usual rare form, placed his chin on the stake while the poised 19 year old from Erie, Pennsylvania, fired a ringer on his second attempt.

"He didn't move a muscle while I was pitching," Kuchcinski related after the show. "I was nervous before the show started, but once I got out there it was okay."

Carson gave Kuchcinski the 12 minutes immediately following his opening monologue. Dan fielded Carson's questions like a pro while giving the game of horseshoe pitching a boost at every opportunity.

Portions of the question and answer session went like this:

CARSON: How did you get started pitching horseshoes?

KUCHCINSKI: My father taught me the game and some tricks and later I showed him a few.

CARSON: What about the popularity of the game?

KUCHCINSKI: It has grown 100 percent in the last year and is going to rival some of the sports like tennis, hockey and others before long.

CARSON: By winning the title are you a professional?

KUCHCINSKI: Yes, although both professionals and amateurs are permitted to pitch in the world tournament.

CARSON: Where will you defend your championship?

KUCHCINSKI: At Keene, New Hampshire, and in 1969 the tournaments will be in Erie, Pennsylvania.

Carson straddled the stake during one of the series of three trick shots performed by Kuchcinski. A master at getting laughs, Johnny had to be shown how to straddle the stake by the champ. Earlier, Carson had mentioned having a sore eye. When positioning himself with one foot on each side of the horseshoe box, Carson set himself up for the barb from fellow showman Ed McMahon, who said, "and you thought your eye hurt."

Kuchcinski's first shoe slipped past the stake, giving Carson reason to ham it up again. Then came the second pitch and it was a perfect ringer, bringing loud applause from the responsive audience.

Another of Danny's acts was pitching ringers while the stake was hidden by a blind rigged up by the Carson staff. Both shoes hit the box, but did not ring the stake although the effort drew a compliment from Carson. The blind was unlike that used by Dan during his tour.

Carson introduced the climactic chin on the stake act

by mentioning "Danny says this is the easiest one." The amiable Carson sent chills through the audience as he knelt in his position to set himself up as Danny's "target."

A serious-looking Carson watched Dan's first pitch hit the rubber mat, just missing the stake. It caused Johnny to pop a couple of his comments as Dan poised for the second pitch.

This time it was a perfect ringer, leaving a smile on Carson's face, a satisfied look on Kuchcinski's face and a thrilled audience.

Johnny and Danny shook hands over a job well done before Carson went on with the rest of the show.

Kuchcinski's gold uniform with bright red and blue letters was striking on color TV. Will Gullickson, NHPA publicity head; John Gilroy, head talent man for Carson, and writer Walter Kempley were responsible for making the arrangements.

7

Your Local Club and Its Pitching Program

A club is worth organizing any time you get half a dozen pitchers interested in playing horseshoes.

There are many advantages to organization; in fact, it is necessary if there is to be anything worthwhile accomplished.

Prior to the organization meeting, several interested persons should do some advance planning. A few of the things they should do are:

1. Select a temporary chairman and secretary for the first or Organizational Meeting.
2. Decide on a place and a time for the meeting.
3. Decide on what agencies or groups should be asked to help foster the club.
4. Prepare a short constitution to be acted on at the first meeting.
5. Prepare a prospective list of individuals who should be interested in the club and present at the meeting.
6. Discuss who would be best fitted for officers of the club and find at least one person who would be willing to hold each office if elected.
7. Decide on what publicity should be given the first meeting.

8. Organize an order of business for the first meeting.
9. Discuss a tentative program for the club during the season.
10. Have someone obtain the N.H.P.A.'s World Tournament film or some suitable substitute to show at the first meeting in order to provide both entertainment and to stimulate attendance at the first meeting.
11. Between the preliminary meeting and the organizational meeting keep arousing interest in the new horseshoe club at every opportunity.
12. Notify every interested person who might attend, preferably in person or by phone.

The Organization Meeting

The Organization Meeting should be held at a convenient place, called to order promptly at time scheduled, should be as enthusiastic as possible and above all, not too long. While it is well to give as many persons as possible an opportunity to express their desires for the new club it must not be forgotten that the meeting must not drag and that certain things are to be accomplished as quickly as possible. Details should be worked out beforehand and be ready for action at the meeting. Few persons care about business meetings of clubs. It is always well to have some entertainment or social feature in connection with the meeting.

A "Live-wire" peppy talker should act as Temporary Chairman and someone with experience should be previously appointed Temporary Secretary. The chairman should call the gathering to order and explain the purpose of the meeting and make the following recommendations:

1. That the Club affiliate with the National Horseshoe Pitchers' Association.
2. That the Club hold an informal tournament at an early date.

3. That the Club meet regularly—once a week, bi-weekly, or monthly.
4. That the Club have a drive for members.
5. That the Club hold one big Annual Championship Meet for Club titles and records.

The remaining Order of Business should be as follows:

1. Short, snappy talks by boosters on such subjects:
   a. Why should we have a Horseshoe Club, and what it can mean to the Community.
   b. Advantages to be secured by affiliating with the National Horseshoe Pitchers' Association.
2. Set date of the Annual Meeting at the beginning of the Horseshoe season, either April or May.
3. Decide on monthly or bi-monthly meetings.
4. Membership dues—$1.00 a year or more.
5. Decide on what agencies will be asked to help foster the Club.
6. Decide on a Club Program for the year, including maintenance and improvement of horseshoe courts.
7. Reading and accepting of Constitution.
8. Election of officers.
9. Election of following Committee Chairmen for: Horseshoe Courts, Horseshoe Contests, Club Program, Membership, Prizes, Pitching Records and Publicity.

The very life of your club will depend on the success of your program. The only reason interested persons join a club is to participate. If they have no chance to participate, they will drift away.

Most important is to provide all the pitching that the members want. Tournaments and leagues can keep them busy every night of the week. Special events once in a while, like exhibitions or matches between top players, keep the interest high.

Award a sufficient number of trophies, but do not

overdo it. Post figures on all pitchers, so that they will be able to study and discuss their performance.

Hold meetings at least once a month and include social events that will include wives, at least occasionally.

If possible, get a man who does not pitch to serve as president or program committee chairman. It will benefit your club, because he can devote his whole interest to organization and promotion. It will benefit him by giving him a role to play. This end of the club activities is often underrated; it takes so much attention that it can adversely affect the game of a good pitcher.

The more members who can be persuaded to work the stronger your club will be and the better its program.

Suggested Program of Activities

The following is merely a suggestion for a Club Program. It may be revised and added to, to suit local conditions.

1. All meetings to be short and snappy followed by a smoker or mixer making use of members with musical or entertainment talent.
2. Have wives serve refreshments and have at least one big picnic or outing during the year.
3. Organize dancing or card parties for entertainment and to raise funds.
4. Organize team league play on a weekly basis, making sure the strength of the teams are fairly equal.
5. Conduct a club tournament with the players divided into classes of six or eight each according to ability.
6. Sponsor a city or county tournament at the end of the season.
7. Hold at least one N.H.P.A. sanctioned open tournament for players from your club and neighboring clubs and cities.

8. Arrange team matches between your club and clubs from neighboring cities and areas.
9. Sponsor some type of Junior or boys' horseshoe pitching program as well as a program for women.

A Model Constitution
(For Horseshoe Clubs)

PREAMBLE

We, the horseshoe pitchers of Pike County, Ohio, in order to promote and foster the game of horseshoe pitching as a sport, to provide the opportunity and facilities for all persons interested in horseshoes in our area to participate in the game, and to insure its continued existence and growth, do hereby establish this constitution for the Pike County Horseshoe Pitchers' Association.

Article I—Name

The name of this association shall be "The Pike County Horseshoe Pitchers' Association."

Article II—Purpose

The purpose of this association shall be to further the cause of horseshoe pitching by all proper means in Pike County and throughout the area of our influence.

Article III—Membership

The requirements for membership shall be set out in the by-laws.

Article IV—Officers

The officers of this club shall consist of a president, a first vice-president, a second vice-president, and a secretary-treasurer. These officers are to be elected annually by a majority vote of all regular members present and entitled to vote at the annual meeting of the club, and they shall hold office until the next annual meeting, or until their successors are elected and qualified.

Article V—Duties of Officers

1. President: The duties of the president shall be to preside at all meetings and to administer the business of this association, to pass on any obligations the association may wish to incur, and to handle whatever other duties may come to his attention in promoting the best interest of the association.

2. First Vice-President: The first vice-president shall have the same duties as the president, but will assume them only in the absence of the president.

3. Second Vice-President: The second vice-president shall have the same duties as the first vice-president, but will assume them only in the absence of the president and the first vice-president.

4. Secretary-Treasurer: The duties of the secretary-treasurer shall be to keep accurate minutes of all meetings, act as custodian of all funds of the association, sign all warrants for club expenditures, keep accurate financial records of club funds, and attend to correspondence and any other duties which may come to his attention as necessary to promote the best interests of the association.

Article VI—Executive Board

The elected officers shall constitute the executive board and may act on behalf of the association in all matters.

Meetings of the executive board shall be held at such times and places as the executive board may decide, and at least three of the four members must be present to constitute a quorum.

Article VII—Committees

The president shall appoint such committees as he feels are necessary.

Article VIII—By-Laws

The association may adopt such by-laws as it shall deem necessary. By-laws shall be adopted when approved by a majority vote of the members in good standing present at any regular meeting.

Article IX—Meetings

The regular annual meeting for the election of officers shall be held on the first Wednesday night of November in each year. A second regular meeting shall be held on the first Wednesday night in May of each year. Such other meetings as are necessary may be called either by the president or by any two other officers notifying all members in good standing of the time, place and purpose of such meeting at least three days before such meeting.

Article X—Amendment

This constitution may be amended by two-thirds affirmative vote of all voting members present at any regular meeting; provided however, that no proposed constitutional amendment may be considered or voted upon unless the notice of the regular or special meeting at which the amendment is proposed shall have contained a brief statement that amendments are to be proposed.

(End of Constitution)

By-Laws

1. NHPA Rules to Govern

The rules of the National Horseshoe Pitchers' Association shall govern in all cases except those specifically stated as otherwise in these by-laws.

2.

3. and so forth.

NOTE: It is better to cover most of the rules and other items covering the operation of your association in the by-laws than in the constitution since the by-laws can be changed so much more easily.

There can be as many by-laws as are needed. Examples

are: membership, voting requirements, dues, affiliation with the NHPA, league or tournament directors, posting of rules, make-up of classes for league or tournament play, type of game (whether count-all or cancellation), drinking, profane language, trophies and awards, records and statistics, method of conducting meetings, removal of officers and deposit of funds. We have given the president and secretary-treasurer a great deal of liberty. If you wish, you may require two signatures on checks and more approval on actions to be taken.

How To Conduct Tournaments, Leagues and Team Matches

The only way a local club can be really successful is to keep all its members pitching regularly. No matter what other activities the club may try to carry on in connection with its pitching program, the heart of it all will remain the pitching. If the officers of the club will bear in mind that 98 percent of the ordinary member's interest lies in his own pitching, they will not make many wrong decisions.

Many of the players will be satisfied to practice when the courts are open, either alone or with other members. Most of them will want to take part in some organized competition.

There are many different ways to conduct organized play. There are team matches between your club and other local clubs; there are leagues that can be played on either a team or an individual basis; and there are tournaments on a local level, as well as the bigger tournaments conducted by the National Horseshoe Pitchers' Association, in which your most interested players might take part.

In this chapter are set out some of the schedules and charts needed for these types of play.

LEAGUES

For the pitchers who want to bind themselves to a steady diet of pitching, your club can set up a league for a convenient number of weeks. Ten to fifteen weeks should be long enough, and one night a week should be often enough.

Depending on the size of your area and the number of members in your club, you may want to choose a team league or an individual league, or even both.

If an individual league is your choice, it is important to group the pitchers as nearly as you can with other pitchers of the same ability. You may accomplish this by putting them together in small classes. Each pitcher on whom you have no record should pitch at least 200 shoes in a qualifying round to determine his ability.

Once you have grouped the pitchers, you must decide on a schedule of play, type of games to be played, and a method of deciding a winner. For a schedule, round robin can be used in which one pitcher plays only one other pitcher on a single league night. They should play at least three games. The type of game can be cancellation or count-all, and the winner can be decided on the won and lost record, on total points, or possibly by other methods.

When the count-all scoring method is used, the champion is usually the man who has the most points for all games. When cancellation games are played, the champion is usually the man with the best won-and-lost record. Another way to schedule games is to have the first player in the standings oppose the second player, the third player oppose the fourth, and so on. There are other methods, and you will have to choose the method that best suits your club.

If you choose to have a team league, it is again important to try to balance the teams. If teams representing different areas or different sponsors are already formed, it may take handicap play to balance the teams. If teams are made up out of your player pool, it is very easy to group players who have nearly the same average. For example, you may group these men into two five-man teams of equal ringer percentage:

Team One	%	Team Two	%
Player 1	75	Player 1	50
2	60	2	50
3	30	3	45
4	25	4	40
5	20	5	25
Average %	42	Average %	42

You may also group two teams on their average number of total points per 50 shoes:

Team One	Pts.	Team Two	Pts.
Player 1	127	Player 1	98
2	103	2	95
3	90	3	90
4	60	4	86
5	35	5	46
Average Pts.	83	Average Pts.	83

Team matches between your club and other clubs will be the same as matches between teams within your own club. To schedule the games, assign one team consecutive numbers beginning with one, and the other team with consecutive numbers immediately following the last player on the first team. Then turn to the right schedule.

TOURNAMENTS

There are a number of ways to run a tournament. Tournaments may be elimination events (either single or double) if this fits the occasion. Or they may be round robin. Elimination type of play is not too popular, for the reason that one poor game can put a pitcher out of the tournament. Horseshoe pitchers who enter a tournament come to play. They like more games, whether they are winning or losing. And often a pitcher who loses an early game can come back in round robin play to win the tournament.

Tournaments have been run on a count-all basis, with the title being decided on total points for the entire event, and with the won-and-lost column being disregarded. The argument in favor of this type of scoring is that the steadiest and best pitcher will always win out instead of being beaten by one or two hot games by an opponent. For example, Casey Jones in cancellation play averaged 87.5 percent ringers for the entire national tournament in 1948, but he lost the tournament. The argument against this type of play is that it lessens the man-to-man competition and takes away the chance a lower percentage man may hit a big game at the right time and win the event.

The most successful way to run a tournament seems to be to permit each man to play each other man in his class, the man winning the most games being declared the winner.

With this thought in mind, I have set out round-robin master schedules in Chapter 8, beginning with four men and going all the way to the full 36 men played in the World Tournament. For those occasions where single or double elimination tournaments may be needed because of time or number of partcipants, I have set out an eight-man chart for each type. A large field can be run off in groups of eight.

Before any tournament can be a success, a great deal of planning has to be done. Here are some of the essentials:

1. Inform all contestants in plenty of time for them to make preparations.
2. Appoint a tournament committee to handle any disputes.
3. Assign persons to care for courts and make sure they have equipment.
4. Assign judges, and equip them with a ruler, straight edge and calipers.
5. Assign scoring personnel and equip them with shore sheets, pencils, scoreboards, summary sheets, rules and playing schedules.

Round-robin tournaments are most interesting, if the best player is given number one, the second best player number two, and so on. This places the most even and best games last.

Placement can be made on existing averages. However, the most common practice is to have a qualifying round of 50, 100 or 200 shoes prior to the tournament. This permits a player to find his level for that day. If he has made a recent improvement, he can get in a higher class. If he has dropped in his percentage or is ill, he will play in a lower class.

Groups of six or eight players are best for most tournaments. Five to seven games, plus possible play-off of ties, will give the average pitcher all the action he needs for one day. However, any number of players can be used to fit the occasion.

These tournaments will attract not only your regulars, but the occasional player who wants to pitch only when the mood hits him, or whose schedule will not permit him to pitch in a league.

It is important to have some award or recognition for your class winners. Trophies are best, since they can be kept as reminders for a long time. It is good practice to award a runner-up trophy also. Some clubs have gone trophy-happy and awarded trophies down to fourth or fifth place, but this seems to me to rob a trophy of any significance, unless the tournament is a major one. Prize money is frequently given, as well as merchandise, but it is generally not large enough to be of any real help and is soon forgotten.

If you end up with an uneven number of players, just add an imaginary man named George Bye to the list and draw a schedule for the even number of players, including Bye. As each player comes to Bye in regular play, he is awarded a 50-0 victory over Bye, which is included as a victory in the final standings for each player.

The qualifying is important, because it groups the pitchers closely and makes competition keen. The round-robin play is the most important part of the tournament, because it is here that all the players get in their little bit, be it good or bad. And if play-offs occur, they can be the high point from the standpoint of fan interest. All ties for first place should be played off.

BREAKING TOURNAMENT TIES

The breaking of ties, especially multiple ties, in the final tournament standings should follow a definite formula adopted prior to the start of play. The N.H.P.A. recommends the following formula.

Only first place ties are decided by a playoff. All other ties are decided by total ringer precentage or by total

DONNIE ROBERTS

1959 Junior World Champion—1972 Ohio's State Champion Listed among the highlights of his pitching are a perfect NHPA Sanctioned game of 38 consecutive ringers against Ernie Danielson in a 1972 Day-Bel Tournament, Dayton, Kentucky; a tournament high of 86.9 for 15 games at Statesville, North Carolina; and many tournament titles. Donnie has just completed a four-court indoor facility near his home, which will be the scene of many leagues and tournaments in the future.

points scored. Total ringer percentage is generally used. If total points are used points over 50 in a game should be used. This occurs when a player scores more points than needed to reach the winning total of 50 in the final frame.

Some clubs use a playoff for other than first place when trophies are involved, but this can sometimes become quite complicated and the N.H.P.A. recommends it be avoided.

MARINES TAMBOER
Ten times Kansas Champion, Alternates between a 1¼ and 1¾ turn

YOUR LOCAL CLUB 137

If two players tie for first the playoff can either be best two out of three or a sudden death one game decision. The larger events use the best two out of three formula, but in most weekend tourneys time is always important and the sudden death one game is generally used.

If three players are involved in a tie the formula is to figure the overall ringer percentage of the players with the

ROGER VOGEL
Winner of State Championship in both Arizona and Colorado and a consistent Class A performer in World Tournament play.

GLEN HENTON
Seven times Iowa State Champion
He and Ray Martin pitched the longest
game in history, 194 shoes.

two having the lower percentages playing one game. The loser automatically takes 3rd place while the winner plays the high percentage player for 1st and 2nd places. An alternative formula is to have each player pitch 50 shoes as in qualifying with the low man taking 3rd and the two high playing for 1st and 2nd. To have the three play a round robin is undesirable for it means one man is always

YOUR LOCAL CLUB 139

JIM WEEKS
1959 California Champion

sitting out a game and the round robin is very apt to end in another tie.

If four men tie they should play a round robin if time permits, and if a two way tie still exists at the end of the round robin a sudden death can decide the issue. An alternate formula is to pair the four men off as opponents with the two winners playing each other for 1st and 2nd place and the two losers playing for 3rd and 4th. This elimination formula is not as desirable as the round robin method.

John Rademacher, of Plant City, Florida, has won many tournaments including eight Florida state titles. He has averaged 80% in World Tournament play, his best finish being a fifth in 1973. John is a great promoter of the game and is Second Vice-President of the NHPA.

Once in a great while a five man tie will occur, usually in a six man round robin. It would not be practical for the five to play a round robin playoff. The best formula for deciding this type of tie is to have each man throw 50 or 100 shoes as in a qualifying round with the top two playing off for 1st and 2nd and the others being ranked on the basis of their score in 50 or 100 shoe round.

If ties occur in the qualifying round for the last position in a class the players involved should throw an additional 50 shoes to break the tie. An alternate formula is to give

YOUR LOCAL CLUB 141

preference to the player throwing the most ringers. If a tie still exists double ringers are used and if a tie still exists consecutive ringers would be used.

All rules and formulas for breaking ties should be decided prior to the tournament and the formula to be used posted.

TOURNAMENT FORFEITS

When a player withdraws or fails to show up at the

CLIVE WAHLIN
14 times Utah State Champion. He is an 80 percenter with one of the smoothest 1¼ deliveries in the business.

scheduled time for round robin play he forfeits all games, each of the other players receiving a forfeit win.

When a player withdraws after playing part of his schedule he forfeits all games, even those he has completed and won, and the records are revised accordingly.

There may be unusual circumstances beyond control of the player such as illness, injury or late arrival. In these cases the tournament committee must render a decision. The common and recommended practice in NHPA events is to allow a player to forfeit one game of his schedule under such conditions, but the forfeit of a second game means forfeiture of all games including those already played.

James Burns is a left hander who uses a 1¾ turn. He has hit 75% or better consistently and in addition to his three Tennessee titles has won many other tournaments. He is one of the real "toughies" of the South.

A more serious problem sometimes arises when an individual makes a practice of withdrawing after playing part of his schedule, usually because he has lost some games. This disrupts the schedule and is very irritating to both officials and the other players. This practice actually is one of unsportsmanlike conduct and should be treated as such by the tournament committee. Chronic offenders should be warned and if they continue the practice should be barred from the next or future competition.

8

Useful Charts and Tables

Master Schedules

For matches between two teams of four, five, six and eight men each. The court number appears at the top of the sheet, and the round number appears at the left.

FOUR MEN

	1	2	3	4
1	1-5	3-8	2-6	4-7
2	4-8	2-5	3-7	1-6
3	2-7	4-6	1-8	3-5
4	3-6	1-7	4-5	2-8

FIVE MEN

	1	2	3	4	5
1	4-6	3-7	5-9	2-8	1-10
2	3-8	2-10	4-7	1-9	5-6
3	2-9	1-6	3-10	5-7	4-8
4	1-7	5-8	2-6	4-10	3-9
5	5-10	4-9	1-8	3-6	2-7

PITCHING CHAMPIONSHIP HORSESHOES 145

SIX MEN

	1	2	3	4	5	6
1	5-10	6-9	3-8	4-7	1-12	2-11
2	2-9	1-10	6-7	5-8	4-11	3-12
3	3-11	4-12	2-10	1-9	5-7	6-8
4	4-8	3-7	1-11	2-12	6-10	5-9
5	1-7	2-8	5-12	6-11	3-9	4-10
6	6-12	5-11	4-9	3-10	1-8	2-7

EIGHT MEN

	1	2	3	4	5	6	7	8
1	2-12	3-9	4-10	1-11	6-16	7-13	8-14	5-15
2	1-9	2-10	3-11	4-12	5-13	6-14	7-15	8-16
3	7-11	8-12	5-9	6-10	3-15	4-16	1-13	2-14
4	8-10	5-11	6-12	7-9	4-14	1-15	2-16	3-13
5	6-13	7-14	8-15	5-16	2-9	3-10	4-11	1-12
6	3-16	4-13	1-14	2-15	7-12	8-9	5-10	6-11
7	4-15	1-16	2-13	3-14	8-11	5-12	6-9	7-10
8	5-14	6-15	7-16	8-13	1-10	2-11	3-12	4-9

Round Robin Schedules for Uneven Numbers of Pitchers

FIVE MEN ON TWO STAKES

	1	2
1	2-5	1-4
2	1-5	2-3
3	1-3	4-5
4	2-4	3-5
5	1-2	3-4

SEVEN MEN ON THREE STAKES

	1	2	3
1	3-7	1-5	2-6
2	1-3	4-6	5-7
3	1-7	2-4	3-5
4	3-6	2-7	1-4
5	4-5	6-7	2-3
6	2-5	4-7	1-6
7	1-2	3-4	5-6

NINE MEN ON FOUR STAKES

	1	2	3	4
1	4-6	3-7	5-9	2-8
2	3-8	4-7	1-5	6-9
3	2-5	1-6	7-9	4-8
4	1-7	8-9	2-6	3-5
5	2-9	4-5	1-3	6-8
6	5-7	1-9	2-4	3-6
7	5-8	1-4	3-9	2-7
8	4-9	6-7	2-3	1-8
9	1-2	3-4	5-6	7-8

Round Robin Master Schedules

Court numbers appear at the top of each schedule and round numbers appear at the left side.

FOUR-MAN ROUND ROBIN

	1	2
1	1-4	2-3
2	2-4	1-3
3	1-2	3-4

USEFUL CHARTS AND TABLES

SIX-MAN ROUND ROBIN

	1	2	3
1	2-5	3-6	1-4
2	4-6	1-5	2-3
3	1-3	2-6	4-5
4	2-4	3-5	1-6
5	5-6	1-2	3-4

EIGHT-MAN ROUND ROBIN

	1	2	3	4
1	3-7	4-8	1-5	2-6
2	2-8	1-3	4-6	5-7
3	1-7	2-4	3-5	6-8
4	3-6	5-8	2-7	1-4
5	4-5	6-7	1-8	2-3
6	3-8	2-5	4-7	1-6
7	1-2	3-4	5-6	7-8

TEN-MAN ROUND ROBIN

	1	2	3	4	5
1	4-6	3-7	5-9	2-8	1-10
2	3-8	2-10	4-7	1-5	6-9
3	2-5	1-6	3-10	7-9	4-8
4	1-7	8-9	2-6	4-10	3-5
5	2-9	4-5	1-3	6-8	7-10
6	5-7	1-9	8-10	2-4	3-6
7	6-10	5-8	1-4	3-9	2-7
8	4-9	6-7	2-3	5-10	1-8
9	1-2	3-4	5-6	7-8	9-10

PITCHING CHAMPIONSHIP HORSESHOES 148

TWELVE-MAN ROUND ROBIN

	1	2	3	4	5	6
1	4-7	1-12	2-11	3-8	6-9	5-10
2	6-11	3-9	4-10	5-12	2-8	1-7
3	5-8	4-11	3-12	6-7	1-10	2-9
4	1-9	5-7	6-8	2-10	4-12	3-11
5	2-12	6-10	5-9	1-11	3-7	4-8
6	3-10	1-8	2-7	4-9	5-11	6-12
7	8-11	9-12	1-4	7-10	3-6	2-5
8	3-5	8-10	7-12	1-6	2-4	9-11
9	7-9	2-6	10-11	4-5	8-12	1-3
10	10-12	7-11	2-3	8-9	1-5	4-6
11	1-2	3-4	5-6	11-12	9-10	7-8

14-MAN ROUND ROBIN

	1	2	3	4	5	6	7
1	2-9	6-12	1-13	8-10	3-11	4-7	5-14
2	3-10	2-14	4-5	7-11	6-9	1-12	8-13
3	4-12	1-9	8-14	6-13	5-7	2-3	10-11
4	2-13	4-11	6-10	9-12	1-8	7-14	3-5
5	6-11	5-10	7-9	1-14	4-13	3-12	2-8
6	9-14	7-13	5-11	2-12	3-8	1-10	4-6
7	3-13	4-14	6-8	1-11	2-10	5-9	7-12
8	5-12	2-7	3-14	4-9	1-6	8-11	10-13
9	7-10	11-13	9-8	3-6	12-14	2-5	1-4
10	6-14	8-12	2-11	5-13	1-7	4-10	3-9
11	4-8	1-5	3-7	10-12	11-14	9-13	2-6
12	9-11	10-14	12-13	2-4	5-8	6-7	1-3
13	1-2	3-4	5-6	7-8	9-10	11-12	13-14

USEFUL CHARTS AND TABLES 149

16-MAN ROUND ROBIN

	1	2	3	4	5	6	7	8
1	1-9	2-10	3-11	4-12	5-13	6-14	7-15	8-16
2	2-12	3-9	4-10	1-11	6-16	7-13	8-14	5-15
3	7-11	8-12	5-9	6-10	3-15	4-16	1-13	2-14
4	8-10	5-11	6-12	7-9	4-14	1-15	2-16	3-13
5	6-13	7-14	8-15	5-16	2-9	3-10	4-11	1-12
6	3-16	4-13	1-14	2-15	7-12	8-9	5-10	6-11
7	4-15	1-16	2-13	3-14	8-11	5-12	6-9	7-10
8	5-14	6-15	7-16	8-13	1-10	2-11	3-12	4-9
9	3-6	9-16	10-13	4-7	11-14	1-8	2-5	12-15
10	12-14	2-8	9-15	3-5	4-6	10-16	1-7	11-13
11	1-5	11-15	2-6	12-16	9-13	3-7	10-14	4-8
12	9-11	10-12	14-16	13-15	1-3	2-4	6-8	5-7
13	13-16	6-7	1-4	10-11	5-8	14-15	9-12	2-3
14	10-15	4-5	3-8	9-14	2-7	12-13	11-16	1-6
15	7-8	13-14	11-12	1-2	15-16	5-6	3-4	9-10

18-MAN ROUND ROBIN

	1	2	3	4	5	6	7	8	9
1	2-9	1-17	10-12	4-8	3-18	6-14	5-7	13-15	11-16
2	8-13	9-12	3-15	7-10	2-6	11-17	14-16	1-18	4-5
3	6-18	2-16	8-17	1-15	9-11	5-13	4-10	12-14	3-7
4	4-16	15-17	2-12	3-5	10-13	7-18	6-9	8-11	1-14
5	7-15	6-11	5-9	4-17	8-16	3-12	1-13	2-14	10-18
6	5-17	8-10	14-18	2-7	1-12	4-15	3-11	6-13	9-16
7	3-14	4-18	1-11	6-8	5-15	2-10	16-17	7-9	12-13
8	1-10	3-13	6-7	11-18	4-14	5-16	2-15	12-17	8-9
9	16-18	4-11	10-17	14-15	2-13	1-9	7-12	5-8	3-6
10	7-17	8-15	9-14	2-5	1-16	12-18	3-10	4-6	11-13
11	3-9	2-18	1-8	13-16	10-15	6-17	5-12	11-14	4-7
12	6-15	3-16	5-18	14-17	4-12	10-11	9-13	1-7	2-8
13	4-13	7-14	12-16	8-18	3-17	9-15	2-11	5-10	1-6
14	10-14	1-5	2-17	4-9	7-11	3-8	6-16	13-18	12-15
15	8-12	13-17	11-15	6-10	9-18	7-16	1-4	2-3	5-14
16	5-11	6-12	7-13	1-3	8-14	2-4	15-18	9-17	10-16
17	1-2	9-10	3-4	11-12	5-6	13-14	7-8	15-16	17-18

PITCHING CHAMPIONSHIP HORSESHOES 150

20-MAN ROUND ROBIN

	1	2	3	4	5	6	7	8	9	10
1	1-20	2-19	3-18	4-17	5-16	6-15	7-14	8-13	9-12	10-11
2	4-15	5-14	6-13	7-12	9-10	18-20	8-11	3-16	2-17	1-19
3	8-9	4-13	5-12	2-15	16-20	7-10	17-19	6-11	1-18	3-14
4	14-20	16-18	4-11	5-10	7-8	3-12	2-13	1-17	15-19	6-9
5	13-19	12-20	15-17	14-18	3-10	2-11	1-16	6-7	4-9	5-8
6	5-6	1-15	10-20	3-8	2-9	14-16	13-17	12-18	11-19	4-7
7	11-17	10-18	1-14	2-7	4-5	8-20	9-19	13-15	3-6	12-16
8	10-16	7-19	2-5	1-13	8-18	9-17	12-14	3-4	11-15	6-20
9	11-13	2-3	8-16	9-15	1-12	5-19	4-20	6-18	10-14	7-17
10	2-20	9-13	7-15	10-12	6-16	1-11	3-19	5-17	4-18	8-14
11	8-12	6-14	9-11	20-19	7-13	3-17	1-10	4-16	5-15	2-18
12	18-19	7-11	6-12	8-10	3-15	5-13	4-14	1-9	2-16	17-20
13	7-9	20-15	3-13	16-19	17-18	4-12	6-10	2-14	1-8	5-11
14	3-11	6-8	14-19	5-9	4-10	15-18	2-12	20-13	16-17	1-7
15	1-6	3-9	5-7	4-8	14-17	2-10	11-20	15-16	12-19	13-18
16	14-15	12-17	2-8	9-20	11-18	4-6	3-7	10-19	13-16	1-5
17	10-17	8-19	1-4	2-6	13-14	3-5	12-15	9-18	7-20	11-16
18	2-4	12-13	7-18	1-3	6-19	8-17	9-16	5-20	11-14	10-15
19	8-15	7-16	10-13	11-12	1-2	9-14	5-18	4-19	6-17	3-20

USEFUL CHARTS AND TABLES 151

24-MAN ROUND ROBIN

	1	2	3	4	5	6	7	8	9	10	11	12
1	1-24	2-23	3-22	10-15	4-21	12-13	6-9	8-17	9-16	7-18	11-14	5-20
2	12-11	13-10	14-9	8-15	7-16	23-1	22-24	2-21	4-19	3-20	5-18	6-17
3	4-17	3-18	8-13	20-24	1-22	5-16	21-23	6-15	7-14	2-19	9-12	10-11
4	20-22	1-21	18-24	9-10	2-17	4-15	8-11	5-14	6-13	7-12	3-16	19-23
5	6-11	16-24	1-20	18-22	4-13	3-14	2-15	7-10	5-12	19-21	17-23	8-9
6	7-8	6-9	4-11	3-12	14-24	18-20	5-10	1-19	17-21	15-23	2-13	16-22
7	3-10	14-22	2-11	1-18	17-19	6-7	13-23	12-24	4-9	16-20	15-21	5-8
8	5-6	15-19	13-21	11-23	3-8	12-22	1-17	16-18	10-24	2-9	4-7	14-20
9	8-24	20-12	14-18	4-5	11-21	1-16	9-23	15-17	3-6	13-19	10-22	2-7
10	1-15	2-5	10-20	13-17	12-18	9-21	14-16	8-22	7-23	3-4	11-19	6-24
11	10-18	11-17	12-16	9-19	4-24	2-3	8-20	7-21	1-14	6-22	5-23	13-15
12	12-14	18-8	7-19	4-22	6-20	11-15	3-23	1-13	9-17	2-24	10-16	5-21
13	8-16	9-15	10-14	11-13	1-12	23-24	2-22	3-21	4-20	5-19	6-18	7-17
14	21-24	22-23	9-13	10-12	8-14	7-15	6-16	5-17	4-18	3-19	2-20	1-11
15	1-10	2-18	4-16	3-17	5-15	9-11	19-24	20-23	21-22	8-12	7-13	6-14
16	5-13	7-11	18-23	4-14	2-16	17-24	8-10	1-9	6-12	3-15	19-22	20-21
17	7-9	6-10	17-22	16-23	5-11	18-21	19-20	4-12	15-24	2-14	1-8	3-13
18	3-11	13-24	2-12	1-7	4-10	6-8	14-23	15-22	5-9	17-20	21-16	18-19
19	16-19	14-21	11-24	15-20	3-9	17-18	1-6	4-8	2-10	13-22	5-7	12-23
20	6-4	1-5	3-7	8-2	12-21	13-20	11-22	14-19	17-16	15-18	10-23	24-9
21	12-19	14-17	15-16	13-18	9-22	3-5	7-24	2-6	8-23	10-21	4-1	11-20
22	6-23	9-20	2-4	5-24	11-18	8-21	12-17	13-16	3-1	7-22	10-19	14-15
23	7-20	8-19	5-22	6-21	12-15	4-23	2-1	9-18	13-14	3-24	11-16	10-17

PITCHING CHAMPIONSHIP HORSESHOES 152

32-MAN ROUND ROBIN

	1	2	3	4	5	6	7	8	9	10	11	12	13	14	15	16
1	1-17	2-18	3-19	4-20	5-21	6-22	7-23	8-24	9-25	10-26	11-27	12-28	13-29	14-30	15-31	16-32
2	5-13	6-14	7-15	8-16	1-9	2-10	3-11	4-12	21-29	22-30	23-31	24-32	17-25	18-26	19-27	20-28
3	18-16	1-19	2-20	3-21	4-22	5-23	6-24	7-25	8-26	9-27	10-28	11-29	12-30	13-31	14-32	15-17
4	7-9	5-15	6-16	4-14	8-10	1-11	2-12	3-13	23-25	21-31	22-32	20-30	24-26	17-27	18-28	19-29
5	15-19	16-20	10-30	2-22	3-23	4-24	5-25	6-26	7-27	8-28	9-29	1-21	11-31	12-32	13-17	14-18
6	18-30	24-28	20-32	21-25	19-31	22-26	23-27	17-29	2-14	5-9	4-16	8-12	3-15	1-13	6-10	7-11
7	14-20	15-21	16-22	1-23	2-24	3-25	4-26	5-27	6-28	7-29	15-25	9-31	10-32	11-17	12-18	13-19
8	17-31	18-32	19-25	20-26	21-27	22-28	23-29	24-30	1-15	2-16	3-9	4-10	5-11	6-12	7-13	8-14
9	13-21	14-22	15-23	16-24	1-25	2-26	3-27	4-28	5-29	6-30	7-31	8-32	9-17	10-18	11-19	12-20
10	1-10	2-11	3-12	4-13	5-14	6-15	7-16	8-9	17-26	18-27	19-28	20-29	21-30	22-31	23-32	24-25
11	12-22	13-23	14-24	15-25	16-26	1-27	2-28	3-29	4-30	5-31	6-32	7-17	8-18	9-19	10-20	11-21
12	19-30	17-28	18-29	20-31	21-32	22-25	24-27	23-26	7-10	1-12	2-13	3-14	4-15	5-16	8-11	6-9
13	11-23	12-24	13-25	14-26	15-27	16-28	1-29	2-30	3-31	4-32	5-17	6-18	7-19	8-20	9-21	10-22
14	8-13	1-14	2-15	3-16	4-9	5-10	6-11	7-12	24-29	18-31	19-32	20-25	17-30	22-27	23-28	21-26
15	10-24	11-25	12-26	13-27	14-28	15-29	16-30	1-31	2-32	3-17	4-18	5-19	6-20	7-21	8-22	9-23
16	22-29	23-30	24-31	21-28	20-27	17-32	18-25	19-26	7-14	6-13	5-12	8-15	4-11	3-10	2-9	1-16
17	9-26	10-27	11-28	12-29	13-30	14-31	15-32	16-17	1-18	2-19	3-20	4-21	5-22	6-23	7-24	8-25
18	11-15	12-16	1-5	2-6	10-14	4-8	9-13	3-7	27-31	28-32	26-30	25-29	17-21	18-22	19-23	20-24
19	8-27	9-28	10-29	11-30	12-31	13-32	14-17	15-18	16-19	1-20	2-21	3-22	4-23	5-24	6-25	7-26
20	19-22	27-32	26-31	17-23	25-30	18-24	28-29	20-21	3-6	11-16	10-15	9-14	1-7	2-8	12-13	4-5
21	7-28	8-29	9-30	10-31	11-32	12-17	13-18	14-19	15-20	16-21	1-22	2-23	3-24	4-25	5-26	6-27
22	11-13	10-16	12-14	4-7	3-8	2-5	1-6	9-15	27-29	26-32	28-30	25-31	17-22	20-23	19-24	18-21
23	6-29	7-30	8-31	9-32	10-17	11-18	12-19	13-20	14-21	15-22	16-23	1-24	2-25	3-26	4-27	5-28
24	19-21	26-29	20-22	27-30	28-31	25-32	18-23	17-24	3-5	10-13	4-6	11-14	12-15	9-16	2-7	1-8
25	5-30	6-31	7-32	8-17	9-18	10-19	11-20	12-21	13-22	14-23	15-24	1-26	16-25	2-27	3-28	4-29
26	10-12	13-15	1-3	9-11	2-4	14-16	5-7	6-8	26-28	29-31	17-19	18-20	30-32	21-23	22-24	25-27
27	4-31	5-32	6-17	7-18	8-19	9-20	10-21	11-22	12-23	13-24	14-25	15-26	16-27	1-28	2-29	3-30
28	22-23	21-24	25-28	26-27	29-32	18-19	30-31	17-20	6-7	5-8	1-4	9-12	2-3	10-11	13-16	14-15
29	3-32	4-17	5-18	6-19	7-20	8-21	9-22	10-23	11-24	12-25	13-26	14-27	15-28	16-29	1-30	2-31
30	7-8	1-2	13-14	3-4	15-16	9-10	11-12	5-6	17-18	23-24	29-30	19-20	31-32	25-26	27-28	22-21

USEFUL CHARTS AND TABLES 153

36-MAN ROUND ROBIN

	1	2	3	4	5	6	7	8	9	10	11	12	13	14	15	16	17	18
1	1-36	2-35	3-34	4-33	5-32	6-31	7-30	8-29	9-28	10-27	11-26	12-25	13-24	14-23	15-22	16-21	17-20	18-19
2	17-18	34-36	16-19	15-20	14-21	13-22	12-23	11-24	10-25	9-26	8-27	7-28	6-29	5-30	4-31	3-32	2-33	1-35
3	8-25	9-24	10-23	11-22	13-20	14-19	15-18	16-17	32-36	33-35	12-21	6-27	5-28	4-29	3-30	2-31	1-34	7-26
4	32-34	15-16	14-17	13-18	12-19	11-20	10-21	9-22	8-23	7-24	6-25	5-26	4-27	3-28	2-29	1-33	31-35	30-36
5	9-20	11-18	29-35	12-17	6-23	30-34	31-33	10-19	7-22	13-16	5-24	8-21	3-26	2-27	1-32	14-15	28-36	4-25
6	29-33	30-32	26-36	27-35	10-17	9-18	8-19	7-20	6-21	5-22	4-23	3-24	2-25	1-31	13-14	28-34	12-15	11-16
7	6-19	8-17	27-33	9-16	29-31	28-32	11-14	12-13	5-20	4-21	3-22	2-23	1-30	26-34	25-35	24-36	7-18	10-15
8	10-13	25-33	28-30	24-34	22-36	23-35	26-32	27-31	11-12	3-20	7-16	2-34	9-14	8-15	6-17	5-18	4-19	2-21
9	5-16	1-28	6-15	7-14	3-18	4-17	20-36	21-35	2-19	25-31	27-29	22-34	23-33	24-32	26-30	9-12	10-11	8-13
10	26-28	5-14	7-12	23-31	24-30	25-29	1-27	4-15	3-16	9-10	20-34	6-13	8-11	21-33	18-36	19-35	2-17	22-32
11	22-30	23-29	21-31	1-26	25-27	7-10	24-28	18-34	17-35	2-15	19-33	20-32	16-36	6-11	8-9	4-13	3-14	5-12
12	4-11	19-31	24-26	21-29	16-34	3-12	2-13	1-25	14-36	7-8	15-35	17-33	18-32	5-10	22-28	20-30	23-27	6-9
13	21-27	6-7	2-11	3-10	15-33	5-8	23-25	20-28	1-24	12-36	18-30	4-9	17-31	13-35	19-29	22-26	16-32	14-34
14	15-31	20-26	3-8	11-35	2-9	19-27	5-6	14-32	13-33	1-23	10-36	16-30	12-34	4-7	21-25	17-29	22-24	18-28
15	2-7	8-36	4-5	16-28	11-33	1-22	15-29	3-6	18-26	14-30	12-32	9-35	20-24	19-25	10-34	21-23	13-31	17-27
16	18-24	1-21	17-25	15-27	14-28	9-33	3-4	2-5	8-34	13-29	20-22	11-31	7-35	12-30	16-26	10-32	6-36	19-23
17	12-28	18-22	1-20	2-3	5-35	14-26	16-24	4-36	10-30	6-34	9-31	15-25	19-21	17-23	7-33	13-27	8-32	11-29
18	15-23	10-28	16-22	6-32	4-34	2-36	17-21	8-30	7-31	11-27	13-25	1-19	12-26	9-29	14-24	18-20	5-33	3-35
19	14-22	3-33	9-27	12-24	10-26	15-21	6-30	17-19	4-32	1-18	2-34	8-28	13-23	16-20	35-36	11-25	7-29	5-31
20	3-31	7-27	2-32	4-30	13-21	6-28	12-22	11-23	5-29	8-26	1-17	14-20	16-18	10-24	15-19	34-35	9-25	33-36
21	32-35	2-30	13-19	7-25	3-29	8-24	31-36	1-16	9-23	4-28	6-26	33-34	10-22	14-18	5-27	15-17	11-21	12-20
22	10-20	9-21	30-35	31-34	8-22	5-25	32-33	29-36	3-27	11-19	14-16	13-17	1-15	2-28	4-26	7-23	12-18	6-24
23	29-34	4-24	7-21	5-23	12-16	11-17	28-35	2-26	13-15	31-32	30-33	10-18	3-25	27-36	8-20	6-22	9-19	1-14
24	1-13	10-16	8-18	9-17	7-19	30-31	27-34	28-33	25-36	12-14	5-21	29-32	6-20	11-15	3-23	2-24	26-35	4-22
25	26-33	25-34	10-14	2-22	9-15	23-36	5-19	27-32	4-20	6-18	7-17	24-35	29-30	8-16	11-13	1-12	3-21	28-31

PITCHING CHAMPIONSHIP HORSESHOES 154

26	6-16	3-19	1-11	25-32	4-18	2-20	9-13	10-12	26-31	23-34	28-29	21-36	5-17	22-35	24-33	8-14	27-30	7-15
27	9-11	8-12	24-31	26-29	27-28	4-16	20-35	7-13	22-33	3-17	2-18	5-15	19-36	21-34	1-10	25-30	6-14	23-32
28	4-14	17-36	25-28	20-33	23-30	21-32	7-11	18-35	19-34	24-29	3-15	6-12	22-31	1-9	2-16	26-27	5-13	8-10
29	24-27	5-11	22-29	1-8	20-31	18-33	25-26	21-30	16-35	15-36	19-32	2-14	7-9	3-13	4-12	6-10	23-28	17-34
30	19-30	14-35	13-36	21-28	6-8	1-7	4-10	23-26	2-12	16-33	22-27	18-31	15-34	17-32	5-9	3-11	20-29	24-25
31	5-7	15-32	3-9	18-29	11-36	12-35	13-34	14-33	1-6	2-10	23-24	17-30	4-8	22-25	20-27	19-28	16-31	21-26
32	20-25	18-27	12-33	14-31	1-5	13-32	16-29	3-7	15-30	17-28	9-36	19-26	10-35	4-6	11-34	22-23	21-24	2-8
33	8-35	12-31	2-6	13-30	17-26	9-34	20-23	19-24	14-29	21-22	1-4	7-36	11-32	10-33	15-28	16-27	18-25	3-5
34	18-23	16-25	15-26	5-36	7-34	14-27	19-22	9-32	17-24	11-30	10-31	8-33	13-28	20-21	6-35	2-4	1-3	12-29
35	3-36	6-33	5-34	12-27	4-35	19-20	1-2	17-22	8-31	13-26	11-28	15-24	14-25	7-32	16-23	18-21	10-29	9-30

USEFUL CHARTS AND TABLES 155

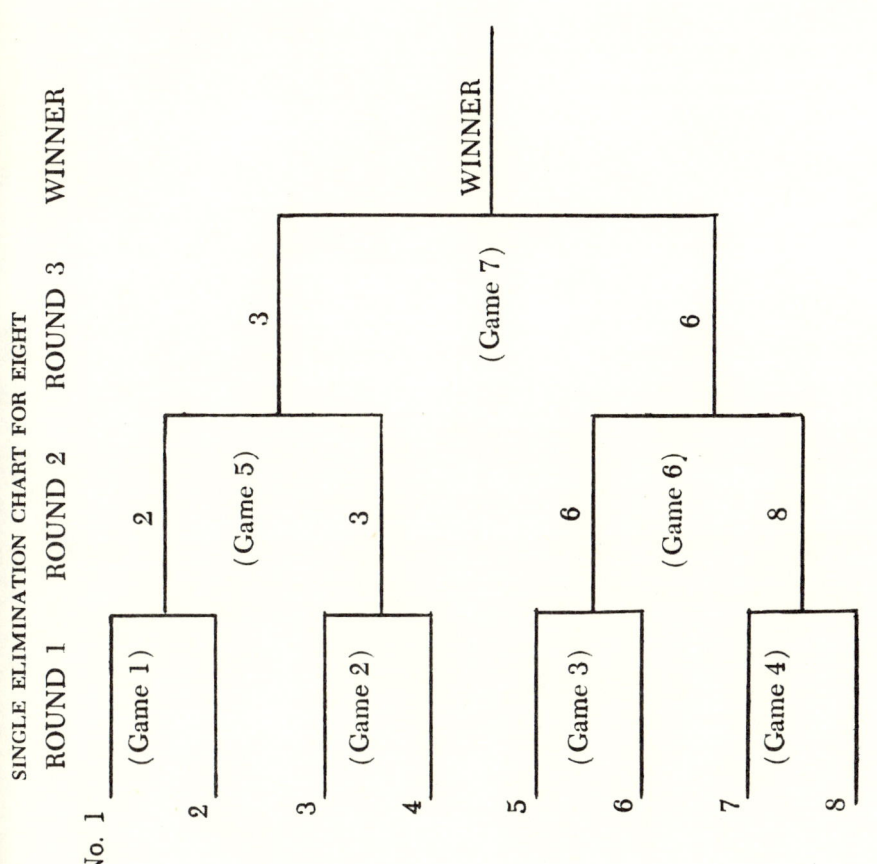

THE WINNERS' BRACKET — DOUBLE ELIMINATION CHART FOR EIGHT

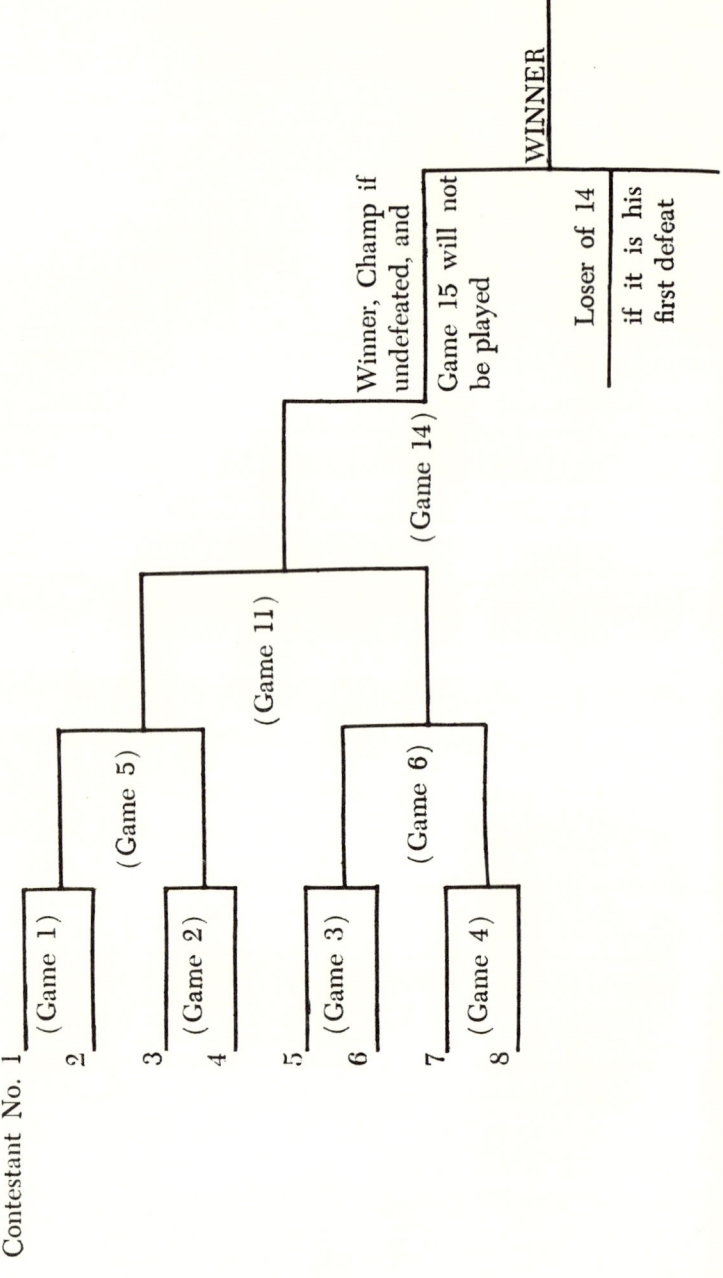

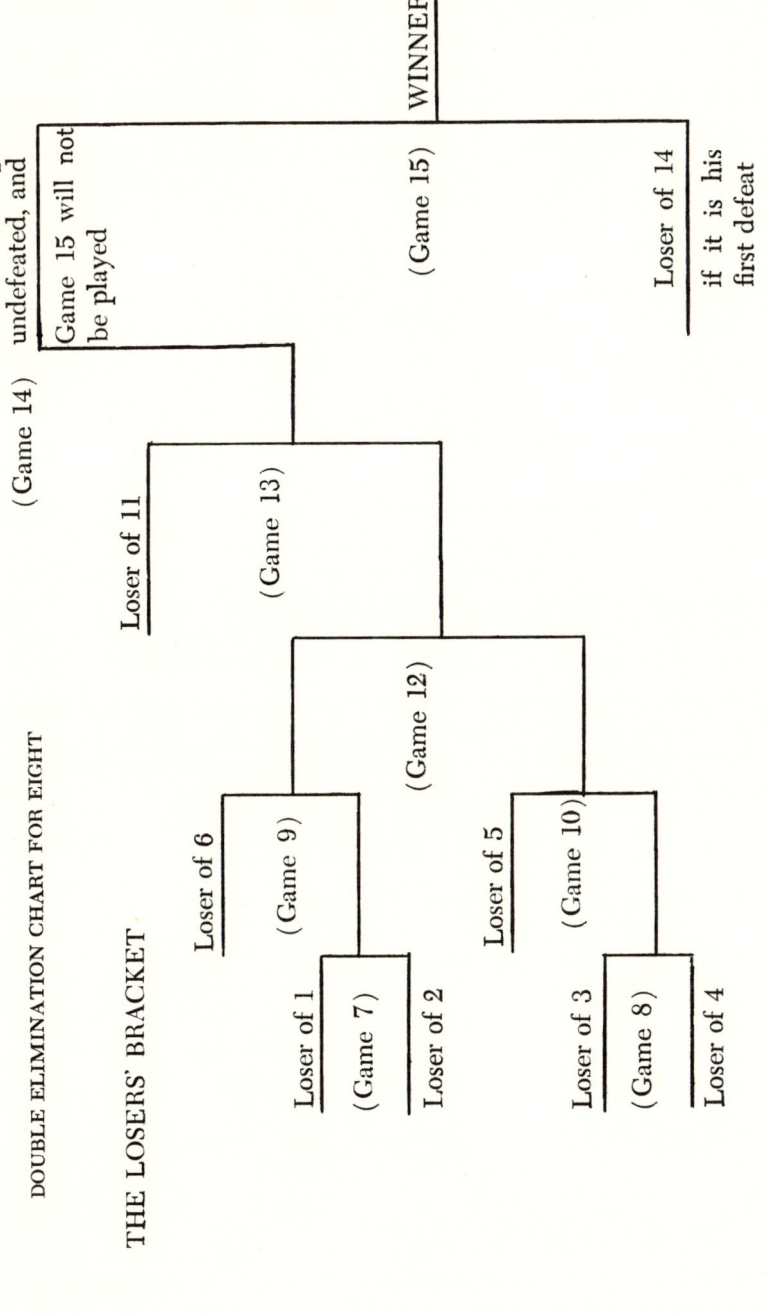

PITCHING CHAMPIONSHIP HORSESHOES 158
MASTER SUMMARY CHART

MASTER SUMMARY CHART - for 6 or 8 man round robin

Tournament: 1969 National   Class: B Finals   at: Erie, PA   Date:

#1 Ancil Copeland, Akron, Ohio

Opponent	W/L	Score	Ring	Shoes	%
Wright	W	50/40	80	104	76.9
W. Kuchcinski	W	51/39	64	82	78.0
Winston	W	51/22	65	78	83.3
Baker	L	41/51	48	70	68.6
Rogers	L	23/52	48	70	68.6
Semans	W	52/30	40	58	69.0
Craig	W	51/25	71	86	75.9
Totals	W 5 L 2		416	548	75.9

A master summary chart like the one pictured (above) should be kept by the tournament director. It provides a complete but concise record of each player's performance, all on one sheet that is easy to handle and easy to keep even after the individual game scoresheets have been destroyed.

USEFUL CHARTS AND TABLES 159

ROUND ROBIN CARD FOR INDIVIDUAL PLAYERS

NATIONAL HORSESHOE PITCHERS ASSOCIATION

OFFICIAL ROUND ROBIN TOURNAMENT SCHEDULES

Tournament: *1968 Columbus Open*
Name: *Jim Knisley*
Class: *Champ*   Number: *2*
Use the *8* Man Schedule

6 MAN ROUND ROBIN

ROUND	COURT 1	COURT 2	COURT 3
1	1-6	2-3	4-5
2	2-4	1-5	3-6
3	3-5	2-6	1-4
4	4-6	1-3	2-5
5	1-2	5-6	3-4

RESULTS

OPPONENT	Opp Pts.	Self Pts.	Shoes	Ringers	%
Young	16	53	60	45	75.0
Von Dach	17	57	50	42	84.0
Harris	6	50	42	36	85.7
Montgomery	13	51	56	44	78.6
Daniels	10	55	48	39	81.2
Bennett	0	54	30	28	93.3
Manker	20	50	68	56	82.3
TOTALS	(7-0)		354	290	81.9

This round robin schedule contains the round robins for 6, 8, 10 and 12 men as well as space for the name of the tournament, the name of the player, his class and number and all his game by game results. By giving each man one of these at the start of the tournament and letting him find his opponent and record his results, the tournament director frees himself from these extra duties. The players are happier, too, and take the results home with them.

Ringer Percentage Chart—Its Use

In cancellation play, it is impossible to tell how well you pitch by checking your score. If you pitch against a man who throws very few ringers, you may be inclined to think you are pitching well simply because you defeat him. But you may pitch the same game against a better opponent and be defeated.

For an average pitcher, a game of 26 ringers out of 44 shoes pitched, good for a 59.1 ringer percentage, is an excellent game. With that game he could defeat a 25 percent pitcher by a very lopsided score, possibly even shut him out. On the other hand, he can be shut out himself with the same game. It happened in the 1960 National Tournament at Muncie, Indiana.

Marines Tamboer, a former champion of the state of Kansas, hit 26 out of 44 against the eventual winner of the tournament, Don Titcomb. Titcomb countered with the highest percentage game of the tournament, for 97.7 percent, defeating Tamboer 51-0.

The point in this illustration is that a 59.1 game is a game you can be equally proud of, regardless of whether you win with it 51-0 or lose with it 51-0. If you check the score only, you may be inclined to think you are doing very well in the first instance and very poorly in the second. The best way to measure your game is by using the ringer percentage. If you are a 33 percent pitcher, you need not be alarmed at the score, as long as you pitch your usual one out of three. In other words, you can measure the game you are playing by comparing it to your own average rather than to the game your opponent is throwing. This is the value of the ringer percentage chart in measuring the consistency of your game.

Using the chart is very simple. Just go across the

USEFUL CHARTS AND TABLES 161

top until you find the column showing the number of shoes, and run the two lines to where they intersect. The figure in that square is your ringer percentage for that game.

In games which go beyond 100 shoes, you can divide both the shoes and ringers by two and find the ringer percentage. Eighty ringers out of 200 shoes is 40 percent just the same as 40 out of 100.

THE RINGER PERCENTAGE CHART

Shoes Pitched Ringers	4	5	6	7	8	9	10	11	12	13	14	15	16
20	20.0	25.0	30.0	35.0	40.0	45.0	50.0	55.0	60.0	65.0	70.0	75.0	80.0
22	18.1	22.7	27.2	31.8	36.3	40.9	45.5	50.0	54.5	59.1	63.6	68.2	72.7
24	16.6	20.8	25.0	29.1	33.3	37.5	41.6	45.8	50.0	54.2	58.3	62.5	66.6
26	15.3	19.2	23.0	26.9	30.7	34.6	38.5	42.3	46.1	50.0	53.8	57.7	61.5
28	14.3	17.8	21.4	25.0	28.5	32.1	35.7	39.3	42.8	46.4	50.0	53.6	57.1
30			20.0	23.3	26.6	30.0	33.3	36.7	40.0	43.3	46.7	50.0	53.3
32			18.7	21.8	25.0	28.1	31.2	34.4	37.5	40.6	43.7	46.9	50.0
34			17.6	20.6	23.5	26.4	29.4	32.3	35.3	38.2	41.2	44.1	47.0
36			16.6	19.4	22.2	25.0	27.8	30.5	33.3	36.1	38.9	41.7	44.4
38			15.8	18.4	21.0	23.6	26.3	28.9	31.6	34.2	36.8	39.5	42.1
40					20.0	22.5	25.0	27.5	30.0	32.5	35.0	37.5	40.0
42					19.0	21.4	23.8	26.2	28.5	30.9	33.3	35.7	38.1
44					18.1	20.4	22.7	25.0	27.3	29.5	31.8	34.1	36.4
46					17.4	19.5	21.7	23.9	26.1	28.2	30.4	32.6	34.7
48					16.6	18.7	20.8	22.9	25.0	27.1	29.1	31.2	33.3
50							20.0	22.0	24.0	26.0	28.0	30.0	32.0
52							19.2	21.1	23.0	25.0	26.9	28.8	30.8
54							18.5	20.4	22.2	24.1	25.9	27.8	29.6
56							17.8	19.6	21.4	23.2	25.0	26.8	28.6
58							17.2	19.0	20.7	22.4	24.1	25.9	27.5
60									20.0	21.6	23.3	25.0	26.6
62									19.3	20.9	22.5	24.2	25.8
64									18.7	20.3	21.9	23.4	25.0
66									18.2	19.7	21.2	22.7	24.2
68									17.6	19.1	20.6	22.0	23.5

(Continued)

THE RINGER PERCENTAGE CHART

Shoes Pitched													
Ringers	4	5	6	7	8	9	10	11	12	13	14	15	16
70									17.6	19.1	20.6	22.0	23.5
72											20.0	21.4	22.8
74											19.4	20.8	22.2
76											18.9	20.3	21.6
78											18.4	19.7	21.0
80											17.9	19.2	20.5
82													20.0
84													19.5
86													19.0
88													18.6
90													18.2
92													
94													
96													
98													

Shoes Pitched Ringers	17	18	19	20	21	22	23	24	25	26	27	28	29
20	85.0	90.0	95.0	90.9	95.4								
22	77.3	81.8	86.4	83.3	87.5	91.7	95.8						
24	70.8	75.0	79.2	76.9	80.8	84.6	88.5	92.3					
26	65.4	69.2	73.1	71.4	75.0	78.6	82.1	85.7	96.1				
28	60.7	64.3	67.8	66.6	70.0	73.3	76.7	80.0	89.3	92.8			
30	56.7	60.0	63.3	62.5	65.6	68.7	71.9	75.0	83.3	86.7	90.0	93.3	96.7
32	53.1	56.2	59.4	58.8	61.8	64.7	67.6	70.6	78.1	81.2	84.4	87.5	90.6
34	50.0	52.9	55.9	55.5	58.3	61.1	63.9	66.7	73.5	76.5	79.4	82.4	85.3
36	47.2	50.0	52.8	52.6	55.3	57.9	60.5	63.1	69.4	72.2	75.0	77.8	80.6
38	44.7	47.4	50.0	50.0	52.5	55.0	57.5	65.0	65.8	68.4	71.0	73.7	76.3
40	42.5	45.0	47.5	47.6	50.0	52.4	54.8	57.1	62.5	65.0	67.5	70.0	72.5
42	40.5	42.8	45.2	45.4	47.7	50.0	52.2	54.5	59.5	61.9	64.3	66.7	69.0
44	38.6	40.9	43.2	43.5	45.6	47.8	50.0	52.2	56.8	59.1	61.4	63.6	65.9
46	36.9	39.1	41.3	41.7	43.7	45.8	47.9	50.0	54.3	56.5	58.7	60.9	63.0
48	35.4	37.5	39.6	40.0	42.0	44.0	46.0	48.0	52.1	54.2	56.2	58.3	60.4
50	34.0	36.0	38.0	38.5	40.4	42.3	44.2	46.1	50.0	52.0	54.0	56.0	58.0
52	32.7	34.6	36.5	37.0	38.8	40.7	42.6	44.4	48.0	50.0	51.9	53.8	55.8
54	31.5	33.3	35.2	35.7	37.5	39.2	41.0	42.8	46.3	48.1	60.0	51.8	53.7
56	30.3	32.1	33.9	34.5	36.2	37.9	39.5	41.4	44.6	46.4	48.2	50.0	51.8
58	29.3	31.0	32.7	33.3	35.0	36.6	38.3	40.0	43.0	44.8	46.5	48.3	50.0
60	28.3	30.0	31.6	32.2	33.8	35.4	37.1	38.7	41.6	43.3	45.0	46.6	48.3
62	27.4	29.0	30.6	31.2	32.8	34.3	35.9	37.5	40.3	41.9	43.5	45.1	46.7
64	26.5	28.1	29.7	30.3	31.8	33.3	34.8	36.3	39.0	40.6	42.2	43.8	45.3
66	25.7	27.3	28.8	30.3	31.8	33.3	34.8	36.3	37.9	39.4	40.9	42.4	43.9
68	25.0	26.4	27.9	29.4	30.9	32.3	33.8	35.3	36.7	38.2	39.7	38.2	39.7
70	24.3	25.7	27.1	28.6	30.0	31.4	32.8	34.3	35.7	37.1	38.6	40.0	41.4

(Continued)

Ringers	Shoes Pitched 17	18	19	20	21	22	23	24	25	26	27	28	29
72	23.6	25.0	26.4	27.8	29.2	30.5	31.9	33.3	34.7	36.1	37.5	38.9	40.3
74	23.0	24.3	25.7	27.0	28.4	29.7	31.1	32.4	33.8	35.1	36.5	37.8	39.2
76	22.4	23.7	25.0	26.3	27.6	28.9	30.3	31.6	32.9	34.2	35.5	36.8	38.1
78	21.8	23.1	24.3	25.6	26.9	28.2	29.5	30.8	32.0	33.3	34.6	35.9	37.2
80	21.2	22.5	23.7	25.0	26.2	27.5	28.7	30.0	31.2	32.5	33.7	35.0	36.2
82	20.7	21.9	23.2	24.4	25.6	26.8	28.0	29.3	30.5	31.7	32.9	34.1	35.4
84	20.2	21.4	22.6	23.8	25.0	26.2	27.4	28.6	29.8	30.9	32.1	33.3	34.5
86	19.8	20.9	22.1	23.2	24.4	25.6	26.7	27.9	29.1	30.2	31.4	32.5	33.7
88	19.3	20.4	21.6	22.7	23.9	25.0	26.1	27.3	28.4	29.5	30.7	31.8	32.9
90		20.0	21.1	22.2	23.3	24.4	25.5	26.7	27.8	28.9	30.0	31.1	32.2
92		19.6	20.6	21.7	22.8	23.9	25.0	26.1	27.2	28.3	29.3	30.4	31.5
94		19.1	20.2	21.3	22.3	23.4	24.5	25.5	26.6	27.6	28.7	29.8	30.8
96		18.7	19.8	20.8	21.9	22.9	23.9	25.0	26.0	27.1	28.1	29.2	30.2
98		18.4	19.4	20.4	21.4	22.4	23.5	24.5	25.5	26.5	27.5	28.6	29.6

Shoes Pitched Ringers	30	31	32	33	34	35	36	37	38	39	40	41	42
32	93.7	96.9											
34	88.2	91.2	94.1										
36	83.3	86.1	88.9	91.6	94.4		94.7						
38	78.9	81.5	84.2	86.8	89.4	92.1	90.0	92.5	95.0	92.8	95.2		
40	75.0	77.5	80.0	82.5	85.0	87.5	85.7	88.1	90.5	88.6	90.9	93.2	95.4
42	71.4	73.8	76.2	78.5	80.9	83.3	81.8	84.1	86.4	84.8	86.9	89.1	91.3
44	68.2	70.4	72.7	75.0	77.3	79.5	78.3	80.4	82.6	81.2	83.3	85.4	87.5
46	65.2	67.4	69.6	71.7	73.9	76.0	75.0	77.1	79.2	78.0	80.0	82.0	84.0
48	62.5	64.6	66.7	68.7	70.8	72.9	72.0	74.0	76.0	75.0	76.9	78.8	80.8
50	60.0	62.0	64.0	66.0	68.0	70.0	69.2	71.1	73.1	72.2	74.1	75.9	77.8
52	57.7	59.6	61.5	63.5	65.4	67.3	66.6	68.5	70.4	69.6	71.4	73.2	75.0
54	55.5	57.4	59.2	61.1	62.9	64.8	64.3	66.1	67.8	67.2	69.0	70.7	72.4
56	53.6	55.3	57.1	58.9	60.7	62.5	62.1	63.8	65.5	65.0	66.6	68.3	70.0
58	51.7	53.4	55.1	56.9	58.6	60.3	60.0	61.6	63.3	62.9	64.5	66.1	67.7
60	50.0	51.6	53.3	55.0	56.6	58.3	58.0	59.7	61.3	60.9	62.5	64.0	65.6
62	48.3	50.0	51.6	53.2	54.8	56.4	56.2	57.8	59.3	59.0	60.6	62.1	63.6
64	46.8	48.4	50.0	51.6	53.1	54.6	54.5	56.0	57.6	57.3	58.8	60.3	61.8
66	45.4	47.0	48.4	50.0	51.5	53.0	52.9	54.4	55.9	55.7	57.1	58.6	60.0
68	44.1	45.6	47.0	48.5	50.0	51.4	51.4	52.9	54.3	54.2	55.5	56.9	58.3
70	42.8	44.3	45.7	47.1	48.6	50.0	50.0	51.4	52.8	52.7	54.0	55.4	56.7
72	41.7	43.0	44.4	45.8	47.2	48.6	48.6	50.0	51.3	51.3	52.6	53.9	55.3
74	40.5	41.9	43.2	44.6	45.9	47.3	47.4	48.7	50.0	50.0	51.3	52.6	53.8
76	39.5	40.8	42.1	43.3	44.7	46.0	46.1	47.4	48.7	48.7	50.0	51.2	52.5
78	38.5	39.7	41.0	42.3	43.6	45.0	45.0	46.2	47.5				
80	37.5	38.7	40.0	41.2	42.5	43.7							

(Continued)

USEFUL CHARTS AND TABLES 167

Ringers	Shoes Pitched 30	31	32	33	34	35	36	37	38	39	40	41	42
82	36.6	37.8	39.0	40.2	41.4	42.7	43.9	45.1	46.3	47.6	48.8	50.0	51.2
84	35.7	36.9	38.1	39.3	40.5	41.7	42.8	44.0	45.2	46.4	47.6	48.8	50.0
86	34.9	36.0	37.2	38.4	39.5	40.7	41.9	43.0	44.2	45.3	46.5	47.7	48.8
88	34.1	35.2	36.4	37.5	38.6	39.8	41.0	42.0	43.2	44.3	45.4	46.6	47.7
90	33.3	34.4	35.5	36.7	37.8	38.9	40.0	41.1	42.2	43.3	44.4	45.5	46.7
92	32.6	33.7	34.8	35.9	36.9	38.0	39.1	40.2	41.3	42.4	43.5	44.6	45.6
94	31.9	33.0	34.0	35.1	36.2	37.2	38.3	39.4	40.4	41.5	42.5	43.6	44.7
96	31.2	32.3	33.3	34.4	35.4	36.4	37.5	38.5	39.6	40.6	41.7	42.7	43.7
98	30.6	31.6	32.6	33.7	34.7	35.7	36.7	37.7	38.8	39.8	40.8	41.8	42.8

PITCHING CHAMPIONSHIP HORSESHOES

Shoes Pitched Ringers	43	44	45	46	47	48	49	50	51	52	53	54
46	93.4	95.5	93.7									
48	89.6	91.7	90.0	92.0								
50	86.0	88.0	86.5	88.5	94.0	96.0						
52	82.7	84.6	83.3	85.2	90.4	92.3	94.2					
54	79.6	81.4	80.3	82.1	87.0	88.9	90.7	92.6				
56	76.8	78.6	77.6	79.3	83.9	85.7	87.5	89.3	91.0	92.8	94.6	93.1
58	74.1	75.9	75.0	76.6	81.0	82.7	84.5	86.2	87.9	89.6	91.4	90.0
60	71.6	73.3	72.7	74.2	78.3	80.0	81.6	83.3	85.0	86.6	88.3	87.1
62	69.3	70.7	70.3	71.8	75.8	77.4	79.0	80.6	82.2	83.8	85.4	84.4
64	67.2	68.7	68.2	69.7	73.4	75.0	76.5	78.1	79.6	81.2	82.8	81.8
66	65.1	66.6	66.2	67.6	71.2	72.7	74.2	75.7	77.2	78.8	80.3	79.4
68	63.2	64.7	64.3	65.7	69.1	70.6	72.0	73.5	75.0	76.5	77.9	77.1
70	61.4	62.8	62.5	63.9	67.1	68.6	70.0	71.4	72.8	74.3	75.7	75.0
72	59.7	61.1	60.8	62.2	65.3	66.7	68.0	69.4	70.8	72.3	73.6	73.0
74	58.1	59.4	59.2	60.5	63.5	64.9	66.2	67.6	68.9	70.3	71.6	71.0
76	56.6	57.9	57.7	59.0	61.8	63.2	64.5	65.8	67.1	68.4	69.7	69.2
78	55.1	56.4	56.2	57.5	60.2	61.5	62.8	64.1	65.4	66.7	67.9	67.5
80	53.7	55.0	54.9	56.1	58.7	60.0	61.2	62.5	63.7	65.0	66.2	65.9
82	52.4	53.6	53.6	54.8	57.3	58.5	59.9	61.0	62.2	63.4	64.6	64.3
84	51.2	52.4	52.3	53.5	55.9	57.1	58.3	59.5	60.7	61.9	63.1	62.8
86	50.0	51.2	51.1	52.3	54.7	55.8	57.0	58.1	59.3	60.5	61.6	61.4
88	48.9	50.0	50.0	51.1	53.4	54.5	55.7	56.8	57.9	59.1	60.2	60.0
90	47.8	48.9	48.9	50.0	52.2	53.3	54.4	55.5	56.7	57.8	58.9	58.7
92	46.7	47.8	47.9	48.9	51.1	52.2	53.3	54.3	55.4	56.5	57.6	57.4
94	45.7	46.8	46.9	47.9	50.0	51.1	52.1	53.2	54.2	55.3	56.4	56.2
96	44.8	45.8	46.9	47.9	48.9	50.0	51.0	52.0	53.1	54.2	55.2	55.1
98	43.9	44.9	45.9	46.9	47.9	49.0	50.0	51.0	52.0	53.1	54.1	55.1

USEFUL CHARTS AND TABLES

Shoes Pitched Ringers	55	56	57	58	59	60	61	62	63	64	65	66	67
58	94.8												
60	91.6	93.3	95.0										
62	88.7	90.3	91.9	93.5	95.1								
64	85.9	87.5	89.0	90.6	92.2	93.7	95.3						
66	83.3	84.8	86.3	87.8	89.4	90.9	92.4	93.9	95.4				
68	80.9	82.3	83.8	85.3	86.8	88.2	89.7	91.2	92.6	94.1			
70	78.6	80.0	81.4	82.8	84.3	85.7	87.1	88.6	90.0	91.4	92.8	94.3	95.7
72	76.4	77.8	79.2	80.5	81.9	83.3	84.7	86.1	87.5	88.9	90.3	91.7	93.0
74	74.3	75.7	77.0	78.4	79.7	81.1	82.4	83.8	85.1	86.5	87.8	89.2	90.5
76	72.4	73.7	75.0	76.3	77.6	78.9	80.3	81.6	82.9	84.2	85.5	86.8	88.1
78	70.5	71.8	73.1	74.3	75.6	76.9	78.2	79.5	80.8	82.0	83.3	84.6	85.9
80	68.7	70.0	71.2	72.5	73.7	75.0	76.2	77.5	78.7	80.0	81.2	82.5	83.7
82	67.1	68.3	69.5	70.7	71.9	73.2	74.4	75.6	76.8	78.0	79.3	80.5	81.8
84	65.5	66.7	67.8	69.0	70.2	71.4	72.6	73.8	75.0	76.2	77.4	78.6	79.8
86	63.9	65.1	66.3	67.4	68.6	69.8	70.9	72.1	73.2	74.4	75.6	76.7	77.9
88	62.5	63.6	64.8	65.9	67.0	68.2	69.3	70.4	71.6	72.7	73.9	75.0	76.1
90	61.1	62.2	63.3	64.4	65.5	66.7	67.8	68.9	70.0	71.1	72.2	73.3	74.4
92	59.8	60.9	61.9	63.0	64.1	65.2	66.3	67.4	68.5	69.6	70.6	71.7	72.8
94	58.5	59.6	60.6	61.7	62.8	63.8	64.9	65.9	67.0	68.1	69.1	70.2	71.3
96	57.3	58.3	59.4	60.4	61.4	62.5	63.5	64.6	65.6	66.7	67.7	68.7	69.8
98	56.1	57.1	58.2	59.2	60.2	61.2	62.2	63.3	64.3	65.3	66.3	67.3	68.4

PITCHING CHAMPIONSHIP HORSESHOES 170

Shoes Pitched Ringers	68	69	70	71	72	73	74	75	76	77	78	79	80
72	94.4												
74	91.9	93.2	94.6										
76	89.5	90.8	92.1	93.4	94.7								
78	87.1	88.5	89.7	91.0	92.3	93.6	94.9						
80	85.0	86.2	87.5	88.7	90.0	91.2	92.5	93.7	95.0				
82	82.9	84.1	85.4	86.7	87.8	89.0	90.2	91.4	92.7	93.9	95.2		
84	80.9	82.1	83.3	84.5	85.7	86.9	88.1	89.3	90.5	91.7	92.8	94.0	95.2
86	79.1	80.2	81.4	82.5	83.7	84.9	86.0	87.2	88.4	89.5	90.7	91.9	93.0
88	77.3	78.4	79.5	80.7	81.8	82.9	84.1	85.2	86.4	87.5	88.6	89.8	90.9
90	75.5	76.7	77.8	78.9	80.0	81.1	82.2	83.3	84.4	85.5	86.7	87.8	88.9
92	73.9	75.0	76.1	77.2	78.3	79.3	80.4	81.5	82.6	83.7	84.8	85.9	86.9
94	72.3	73.4	74.4	75.5	76.6	77.6	78.7	79.8	80.8	81.9	83.0	84.0	85.1
96	70.8	71.9	72.9	73.9	75.0	76.0	77.1	78.1	79.2	80.2	81.2	82.3	83.3
98	69.4	70.4	71.4	72.4	73.5	74.5	75.5	76.5	77.5	78.5	79.6	80.6	81.6

USEFUL CHARTS AND TABLES 171

Ringers	\multicolumn{13}{c	}{Shoes Pitched}

Ringers	81	82	83	84	85	86	87	88	89	90	91	92	93
86	94.2	95.3											
88	92.0	93.2	94.3	95.4									
90	90.0	91.1	92.2	93.3	94.4	95.5							
92	88.0	89.1	90.2	91.3	92.4	93.5	94.6	95.6					
94	86.2	87.2	88.3	89.4	90.4	91.5	92.6	93.6	94.7	95.7			
96	84.4	85.4	86.4	87.5	88.5	89.6	90.6	91.7	92.7	93.7	94.8	95.8	
98	82.6	83.7	84.7	85.7	86.7	87.7	88.8	89.8	90.8	91.8	92.8	93.9	94.9

PITCHING CHAMPIONSHIP HORSESHOES

Odd Man Round Robins for two & three courts

It has come to the NHPA's attention that throughout the country there are probably more clubs that have two or three courts than any other number. How to get the maximum use out of the courts, and how to accommodate as many pitchers as possible are problems that must surely plague the tournament and program managers. As far as the author knows, there has been little or no use made of the odd man round robins. These types of round robins have definite advantages over the even, or conventional, round robins for a small number of courts. Two of the obvious are: they allow one more man to compete in comparison with the even round robin, and they free players to keep score (a much needed function in small groups). It is hoped that the following round robin schedules will be of assistance in setting up small tournaments and program activities.

FIVE MAN ROUND ROBIN FOR TWO COURTS

Round	Court #1	Court #2	Sit Out
1	1 - 5	2 - 4	3
2	2 - 3	1 - 4	5
3	3 - 4	2 - 5	1
4	4 - 5	1 - 3	2
5	1 - 2	3 - 5	4

SEVEN MAN ROUND ROBIN FOR THREE COURTS

Round	Court #1	Court #2	Court #3	Sit Out
1	2 - 7	3 - 6	4 - 5	1
2	3 - 5	1 - 7	2 - 6	4
3	1 - 6	2 - 5	4 - 7	3
4	4 - 6	3 - 7	1 - 5	2
5	2 - 3	1 - 4	5 - 7	6
6	1 - 3	6 - 7	2 - 4	5
7	1 - 2	5 - 6	3 - 4	7

9

Methods of Scoring

Cancellation and Count-All Scoring

There are two official methods of scoring provided for in the rules, Cancellation and Count-All.

Cancellation is the traditional method familiar to most players and used in practically all tournaments, where almost all players prefer it—especially in competition involving contestants from different clubs, cities and areas.

Ringers or shoes of equal value thrown by opposing players in a given frame cancel each other and points by the best remaining shoe are tallied in the scoring column. The first player to reach 50 points wins the game. This makes for head-on competition between opposing pitchers on every pitch. Cancelled ringers can prolong the game, making them vary greatly in length. An average player can have ringer after ringer cancelled by a superior opponent and consequently score very few points. This is why tournament players are placed in classes on the basis of past records, thus making all opponents of the same approximate ability.

Count-all scoring gives each player full credit for each

shoe pitched regardless of what his opponent does. Games last a specified number of shoes, usually 50, and total points scored over the entire competition count instead of games won and lost.

Thus count-all provides for games of uniform length, gives the beginner a chance to score against the expert and removes some of the tension resulting from head-on competition.

Count-all lends itself readily to a handicap system, which properly used can stimulate interest in beginning players. For these reasons it is used chiefly in local club programs with weekly league competition, either team or individual, where count-all has been very successful. A number of clubs use count-all for its weekly league program and cancellation for their championship tournaments during the season.

Handicap Systems

When the relative ability of the players participating in a horseshoe pitching program varies widely, a good handicap system is essential to success. This problem is taken care of in tournaments by the system of placing the players in classes on the basis of ability determined by a qualifying round or past records. It is the league play of local clubs that has need of a good handicap system.

Applying a handicap system calls for an accurate rating of the players kept up to date by a league secretary or recorder. A player's average will decrease or increase during the course of the season and his handicap must fluctuate accordingly.

The initial rating of the players can be obtained by having each player pitch 100 shoes by himself in a qualifying round using this score to determine his handicap.

METHODS OF SCORING

After that each individual handicap will change as the season progresses.

The handicap system must give the beginning player the chance to compete on even terms with the expert. This will stimulate interest and constantly bring in fresh blood in the form of beginning and new players.

Since there are two official methods of scoring we present a handicap system for both the cancellation and the count-all method of scoring. Handicap systems are much harder to apply to cancellation.

CANCELLATION HANDICAP SYSTEM

The handicap system employed by the New Jersey State Horseshoe Pitcher's Association has been found the most satisfactory for the cancellation method.

The system is based on the difference in ringer percentage of the two players over a total of 100 shoes. All that is needed is to know the ringer percentage of the players involved and then apply the difference to the two charts listed at the end of this article. This difference in ringer percentage is converted into points, three points for each percentage of difference.

Since in cancellation games one never knows the length of the game in advance it is impractical to apply the full handicap at one time. Therefore the handicap is applied gradually—one-tenth of it every ten shoes or five frames.

For example, if the difference in ringer percentage between two players is 10 percent that figures to a difference of 30 points in 100 shoes. Since it is impractical to give the lower percentage player 30 points at one time, because one does not know the eventual length of the game, one-tenth, or three points, of the handicap is applied every ten shoes or five frames. These three points are distributed one each in the first, third and fifth frames.

This process continues each ten shoes as long as the game lasts.

Here is a chart on how to figure the number of handicap points for each ten shoes followed by a chart showing how to distribute those points in each ten shoes of each game.

CHART FOR FIGURING HANDICAP
Chart to Apply Handicap Each 5 Frames (10 shoes)

1 point handicap in each third frame.
2 point handicap—1 point in 2nd and 4th frames.
3 point handicap—1 point in 1st, 3rd and 5th frames.
4 point handicap—1 point in the 1st, 2nd, 4th and 5th frames.
5 point handicap—1 point in each frame.
6 point handicap—2 points in the 1st, 3rd and 5th frames.
7 point handicap—2 points in 1st and 5th frames, 1 point in the 2nd, 3rd and 4th frames.
8 point handicap—2 points in the 1st, 3rd and 5th frames, 1 point in the 2nd and 4th frames.
9 point handicap—2 points in the 1st, 2nd, 4th and 5th frames, 1 point in the 3rd frame.
10 point handicap—2 points in each frame.

In order for a player to receive his handicap in any given frame he must have one shoe within counting distance.

With this system a tie game is possible and in that case the game is extended to five additional points until the tie is broken.

Prior to tournament or league play scoresheets are made up in advance for each possible handicap situation with the handicap points being marked in the designated frames in red pencil. Then only the name of the players need be added to the proper scoresheet at the start of each game.

METHODS OF SCORING

CHART FOR FIGURING HANDICAP

Ringer % 100 shoes	Difference in points 100 shoes	Handicap for each 10 shoes	Ringer % 100 shoes	Difference in points 100 shoes	Handicap for each 10 shoes
1%	3	none	18%	54	5
2%	6	none	19%	57	6
3%	9	1	20%	60	6
4%	12	1	21%	63	6
5%	15	1	22%	66	7
6%	18	2	23%	69	7
7%	21	2	24%	72	7
8%	24	2	25%	75	8
9%	27	3	26%	78	8
10%	30	3	27%	81	8
11%	33	3	28%	84	8
12%	36	4	29%	87	9
13%	39	4	30%	90	9
14%	42	4	31%	93	9
15%	45	5	32%	96	10
16%	48	5	33%	99	10
17%	51	5	34%	102	10

"COUNT ALL" HANDICAP SYSTEM

The handicap system for "Count All" scoring is based on points pitched in a 50 shoe game with 100 points considered the "scratch" score.

Each player's individual handicap is figured on the difference between his average points for 50 shoes and the "scratch" score of 100 points.

The "scratch" score can and should be set higher than 100 if there are players in the group who consistently score more than 100 points in 50 shoes.

There are many mathematical variations of this system in use, but basically they are the same.

Some clubs use the full difference between the player's average and the "scratch" score of 100 as the handicap. Others use ¾ or 75 percent of the difference.

The most common variation in usage is ⅘ or 80 percent of the difference and this is the one illustrated by the chart below.

Thus under this variation a player who has an average of 80 points for 50 shoes will receive a handicap of 16 points which is ⅘ or 80 percent of the difference between his average of 80 points and the "scratch" score of 100. Therefore if he pitches an actual score of 85 in a 50 shoe "Count All" game he will receive 101 points (85 plus his handicap of 16 points).

Player's Ave. Pts. 50 shoes	Player's Handicap 50 shoes	Player's Ave. Pts. 50 shoes	Player's Handicap 50 shoes	Player's Ave. Pts. 50 shoes	Player's Handicap 50 shoes
99 pts.	1 pt.	79 pts.	17 pts.	59 pts.	33 pts.
98 pts.	2 pts.	78 pts.	18 pts.	58 pts.	34 pts.
97 pts.	2 pts.	77 pts.	18 pts.	57 pts.	34 pts.
96 pts.	3 pts.	76 pts.	19 pts.	56 pts.	35 pts.
95 pts.	4 pts.	75 pts.	20 pts.	55 pts.	36 pts.
94 pts.	5 pts.	74 pts.	21 pts.	54 pts.	37 pts.
93 pts.	6 pts.	73 pts.	22 pts.	53 pts.	38 pts.
92 pts.	6 pts.	72 pts.	22 pts.	52 pts.	38 pts.
91 pts.	7 pts.	71 pts.	23 pts.	51 pts.	39 pts.
90 pts.	8 pts.	70 pts.	24 pts.	50 pts.	40 pts.
89 pts.	9 pts.	69 pts.	25 pts.	49 pts.	41 pts.
88 pts.	10 pts.	68 pts.	26 pts.	48 pts.	42 pts.
87 pts.	10 pts.	67 pts.	26 pts.	47 pts.	42 pts.
86 pts.	11 pts.	66 pts.	27 pts.	46 pts.	43 pts.
85 pts.	12 pts.	65 pts.	28 pts.	45 pts.	44 pts.
84 pts.	13 pts.	64 pts.	29 pts.	44 pts.	45 pts.
83 pts.	14 pts.	63 pts.	30 pts.	43 pts.	46 pts.
82 pts.	14 pts.	62 pts.	30 pts.	42 pts.	46 pts.
81 pts.	15 pts.	61 pts.	31 pts.	41 pts.	47 pts.
80 pts.	16 pts.	60 pts.	32 pts.	40 pts.	48 pts.

Proper Scoring Methods Illustrated

The purpose of a scoresheet is to make a written record

METHODS OF SCORING

of every pitch in game in such a manner that the result can be tabulated and checked for accuracy.

Different symbols are used in various sections of the country and some scoresheets are of a vertical type and others a horizontal type. The system illustrated here is the one the NHPA has found to be the most satisfactory.

Ringers which score points—that is "live ringers"—are indicated by a 0 in the ringer column of the player who threw the ringer.

Cancelled ringers are indicated by an X in the ringer column. For each X registered in the ringer column of one player there must be an X in the ringer column of his opponent.

No count is indicated by a dash (-).

Points scored in a frame are listed in the point column of the player scoring the points, and a running total is kept in the score column. Horizontal type scoresheets usually do not have a point column, having only the column for the running score.

It is possible to score 0, 1, 2, 3, 4, or 6 points in any given frame.

Scoring under the "Count All" system follows the same pattern except that there are no cancelled ringers and all points scored by both players are tallied.

Following are reproduced copies of the greatest game ever played in World Tournament competition using the cancellation system and a sample cancellation score sheet.

Of the four scoresheets that follow, three are genuine, one imaginary.

The first one is Don Titcomb's qualifying round at Murray, Utah in 1958. Titcomb hit 105 ringers out of 108 shoes and 97 of a consecutive 100 at one interval.

The second is the game between Ted Allen and Cletus

Scorekeeper — Harold Wolfe
O—Ringer OO—Double Ringer X—Dead —No Count

Second Sheet —
O—Ringer OO—Double Ringer X—Dead —No Count

National Horeshoe Pitchers Association
OFFICIAL SCORE SHEET

Date 8-7-1965 Court No. 10 Game No. 18
Ray Martin vs Glen Henton

Shoes	Ringers	Points	Score	Ringers	Points	Score
2	XX	—	—	XX	—	—
4	XX	—	—	XX	—	—
6	XO	3	3	X	—	—
8	X	—	—	XO	3	3
10	XX	—	—	XX	—	—
12	XX	—	—	XX	—	—
14	XX	—	—	XX	—	—
16	XX	—	—	XX	—	—
18	XX	—	—	XX	—	—
20	XX	—	—	XX	—	—
22	X	—	—	XO	3	6
24	XX	—	—	XX	—	—
26	X	—	—	XO	3	9
28	XX	—	—	XX	—	—
30	X	—	—	XO	3	12
32	XX	—	—	XX	—	—
34	XX	—	—	X	1	13
36	XX	—	—	XX	—	—
38	XX	—	—	XX	—	—
40	XX	—	—	XX	—	—
42	XO	3	6	X	—	—
44	XX	—	—	XX	—	—
46	XX	—	—	XX	—	—
48	XX	—	—	XX	—	—
50	XX	—	—	XX	—	—
52	XO	3	9	X	—	—
54	XX	—	—	XX	—	—
56	XX	—	—	XX	—	—
58	XX	—	—	XX	—	—
60	XX	—	—	XX	—	—
62	XX	—	—	XX	—	—
64	XX	—	—	XX	—	—
66	XX	—	—	XX	—	—
68	XX	—	—	XX	—	—
70	O	3	12	—	—	—
72	XX	—	—	XX	—	—
74	XX	—	—	XX	—	—
76	XX	—	—	XX	—	—
78	XX	—	—	XX	—	—
80	X	—	—	XO	3	16
82	XX	—	—	XX	—	—
84	XX	—	—	XX	—	—
86	XX	—	—	X	—	—
88	XO	3	15	X	—	—
90	XX	—	—	XX	—	—
92	XO	3	18	X	—	—
94	XX	—	—	XX	—	—
96	XO	3	21	X	—	—
98	XX	—	—	XX	—	—
100	XX	—	—	XX	—	—

National Horeshoe Pitchers Association
OFFICIAL SCORE SHEET

Date 8-7-1965 Court No. 10 Game No. 18
Ray Martin vs Glen Henton

Shoes	Ringers	Points	Score	Ringers	Points	Score
2	XX	—	—	XX	—	—
4	XX	—	—	XX	—	—
6	XX	—	—	XX	—	—
8	XX	—	—	XX	—	—
10	XX	—	—	XX	—	—
12	XX	—	—	XX	—	—
14	XX	—	—	XX	—	—
16	XO	3	24	X	—	—
18	XO	3	27	X	—	—
20	XO	3	30	X	—	—
22	X	—	—	XO	3	19
24	XX	—	—	XX	—	—
26	XX	—	—	XX	—	—
28	X	—	—	XO	3	22
30	XX	—	—	XX	—	—
32	X	—	—	XO	3	25
34	X	—	—	XO	3	28
36	X	—	—	XO	3	31
38	XX	—	—	XX	—	—
40	XX	—	—	XX	—	—
42	X	1	31	X	—	—
44	X	—	—	XO	3	34
46	X	—	—	XO	3	37
48	XX	—	—	XX	—	—
50	XX	—	—	XX	—	—
52	XX	—	—	XX	—	—
54	XX	—	—	XX	—	—
56	X	—	—	XO	3	40
58	X	—	—	XO	3	43
60	XO	3	34	X	—	—
62	XX	—	—	XX	—	—
64	XX	—	—	XX	—	—
66	XX	—	—	XX	—	—
68	XX	—	—	XX	—	—
70	XX	—	—	XX	—	—
72	XX	—	—	XX	—	—
74	XX	—	—	XX	—	—
76	XO	3	37	X	—	—
78	XX	—	—	XX	—	—
80	X	—	—	XO	3	46
82	XO	3	40	X	—	—
84	XX	—	—	XX	—	—
86	OO	6	46	—	—	—
88	X	—	—	XO	3	49
90	XO	3	49	X	—	—
92	XX	—	—	XX	—	—
94	X	—	—	XO	3	52
96						
98						
100						

SUMMARY

Points	49		Points	52
Ringers	174		Ringers	175
Doubles	77		Doubles	80
Shoes Pitched	194		Shoes Pitched	194
Percent Ringers	89.7		Percent Ringers	90.2

This 194 shoe marathon was played at Keene, New Hampshire in the 1965 World Tournament and set many records. There were 312 ringers cancelled and 63 four-deads.

METHODS OF SCORING 181

O—Ringer OO—Double Ringer X—Dead — — —No Count

National Horeshoe Pitchers Association

OFFICIAL SCORE SHEET

Date 9-1-1969 Court No. 2 Game No. 3

Bob Wilson vs. Jim Watkins

Shoes	Ringers	Points	Score	Ringers	Points	Score
2	XX	—	—	XX	—	—
4	X	—	—	X	—	—
6	— —	—	—	— —	—	—
8	— —	1	1	— —	—	—
10	— —	—	—	— —	1	1
12	X	1	2	X	—	—
14	X	—	—	X	1	2
16	— —	2	4	— —	—	—
18	— —	—	—	— —	2	4
20	O	3	7	— —	—	—
22	— —	—	—	O	3	7
24	XO	3	10	X	—	—
26	X	—	—	XO	3	10
28	O	4	14	— —	—	—
30	— —	—	—	O	4	14
32	OO	6	20	— —	—	—
34	— —	—	—	OO	6	20
36	OO	6	26	— —	—	—
38	O	4	30	— —	—	—
40	— —	—	—	O	3	23
42	— —	2	32	— —	—	—
44	— —	—	—	— —	1	24
46	XO	3	35	X	—	—
48	X	—	—	X	—	—
50	X	1	36	X	—	—
52	X	—	—	X	1	25
54	X	—	—	X	—	—
56	— —	1	37	— —	—	—
58	OO	6	43	— —	—	—
60	— —	—	—	OO	6	31
62	XO	3	46	—	—	—
64	O	3	49	—	—	—
66	X	1	50	X	—	—
68						
70						
72						
74						
76						
78						
80						
82						
84						
86						
88						
90						
92						
94						
96						
98						
100						

SUMMARY

Points - - - - - 50		Points - - - - - 31	
Ringers - - - - 27		Ringers - - - - 21	
Doubles - - - - 7		Doubles - - - - 4	
Shoes Pitched - - 66		Shoes Pitched - - 66	
Percent Ringers - - 40.9		Percent Ringers - - 31.8	

This sample scoresheet illustrates all possible combinations of scoring in a 50 point cancellation game.

PITCHING CHAMPIONSHIP HORSESHOES 182

National Horseshoe Pitchers Association
OFFICIAL SCORE SHEET
Qualifying Round

Date 7-22-58 Court No. Murray, Utah Game No. ___

Don Titcomb vs. ___

Shoes	Ringers	Points	Score	Ringers	Points	Score
2	OO	6	6	OO	6	6
4	OO	6	12	OO	6	12
6	O	3	15	OO	6	18
8	OO	6	21	OO	6	24
10	O	4	25	OO	6	30
12	O	3	28	OO	6	36
14	OO	6	34	OO	6	42
16	OO	6	40	OO	6	48
18	OO	6	46	OO	6	54
20	O	3	49	OO	6	60
22	OO	6	55	OO	6	66
24	OO	6	61	OO	6	72
26	OO	6	67	OO	6	78
28	OO	6	73	OO	6	84
30	OO	6	79	O	4	88
32	OO	6	85	OO	6	94
34	OO	6	91	O	4	98
36	OO	6	97	OO	6	104
38	OO	6	103	OO	6	110
40	OO	6	109	OO	6	116
42	O	3	112	OO	6	122
44	OO	6	118	OO	6	128
46	OO	6	124	OO	6	134
48	OO	6	130	OO	6	140
50	OO	6	136	O	4	144
52	OO	6	142	OO	6	150
54	OO	6	148	OO	6	156
56	OO	6	154	OO	6	162
58	OO	6	160	OO	6	168
60	OO	6	166	OO	6	174
62	O	3	169	OO	6	180
64	OO	6	175	OO	6	186
66	OO	6	181	OO	6	192
68	OO	6	187	OO	6	198
70	O	3	190	OO	6	204
72	OO	6	196	—	2	206
74	OO	6	202	O	4	210
76	OO	6	208	OO	6	216
78	OO	6	214	OO	6	222
80	OO	6	220	OO	6	228
82	OO	6	226	OO	6	234
84	OO	6	232	OO	6	240
86	OO	6	238	OO	6	246
88	OO	6	244	OO	6	252
90	OO	6	250	O	4	256
92	OO	6	256	OO	6	262
94	OO	6	262	OO	6	268
96	OO	6	268	OO	6	274
	OO	6	274	OO	6	280
	OO	6	280	OO	6	286

SUMMARY

Points		Points	566
Ringers		Ringers	186
Doubles		Doubles	87
Shoes Pitched		Shoes Pitched	200
Percent Ringers		Percent Ringers	93%

National Horseshoe Pitchers Association
OFFICIAL SCORE SHEET

Date 7-26-55 Court No. ___ Game No. 30

Ted Allen vs. Clayton Chappelle

Shoes	Ringers	Points	Score	Ringers	Points	Score
2	XX			XX		
4	XO	3	3	X		
6	XO	3	6	X		
8	X			OX	3	3
10				OX	3	6
12	XX			XX		
14	XX			XX		
16	XX			XX		
18	XO	3	9	X		
20	X			OX	3	9
22	XX			XX		
24	OX	3	12	X		
26	XX			XX		
28	OX	3	15	X		
30	OX	3	18	X		
32	XX			XX		
34	XX			XX		
36	XX			XX		
38	XX			XX		
40	XX			XX		
42	XX			XX		
44	OX	3	21	X		
46	OX	3	24	X		
48	XX			XX		
50	XX			XX		
52	XX			XX		
54	XX			XX		
56	XX			XX		
58	OO	6	30	—		
60	XX			XX		
62	XX			XX		
64	XX			XX		
66	OX	3	33	XX		
68	XX			XX		
70	OX	3	36	X		
72	XX			XX		
74	OX	3	39	X		
76	OX	3	42	X		
78	OX	3	45	X		
80	OX	3	48	X		
82	XX			XX		
84	XX			XX		
86	XX			XX		
88	XX			XX		
90	XX			XX		
92	OX	3	51	X		

SUMMARY

Points	51	Points	9
Ringers	89	Ringers	75
Doubles	43	Doubles	30
Shoes Pitched	92	Shoes Pitched	92
Percent Ringers	96.7	Percent Ringers	81.6

METHODS OF SCORING 183

O—Ringer OO—Double Ringer X—Dead —No Count

National Horseshoe Pitchers Association
OFFICIAL SCORE SHEET

Date 8-5-68 Court No. 7 Game No. 30

CRAIG vs. KNISLEY

Shoes	Ringers	Points	Score	Ringers	Points	Score
2	XX	—	—	XX	—	—
4	XO	-3	3	X	—	—
6	XO	3	6	X	—	—
8	XX	—	—	XX	—	—
10	X	—	—	XO	3	3
12	XO	3	9	X	—	—
14	XO	3	12	X	—	—
16	XX	—	—	XX	—	—
18	X	—	—	XO	3	6
20	X	—	—	XO	3	9
22	X	—	—	XO	3	12
24	XX	—	—	XX	—	—
26	X	—	—	XO	3	15
28	XX	—	—	XX	—	—
30	XO	3	15	X	—	—
32	XX	—	—	XX	—	—
34	XX	—	—	XX	—	—
36	X	—	—	XO	3	18
38	X	—	—	XO	3	21
40	—	—	—	OO	6	27
42	X	—	—	XO	3	30
44	X	—	—	XO	3	33
46	XX	—	—	XX	—	—
48	XX	—	—	XX	—	—
50	XX	—	—	XX	—	—
52	X	—	—	XO	3	36
54	XX	—	—	XX	—	—
56	XO	3	18	X	—	—
58	XX	—	—	XX	—	—
60	XX	—	—	XX	—	—
62	XX	—	—	XX	—	—
64	XX	—	—	XX	—	—
66	XX	—	—	XX	—	—
68	XX	—	—	XX	—	—
70	XX	—	—	XX	—	—
72	X	—	—	XO	3	39
74	XO	3	21	X	—	—
76	X	—	—	XO	3	42
78	X	—	—	XO	3	45
80	XX	—	—	XX	—	—
82	XX	—	—	XX	—	—
84	XX	—	—	XX	—	—
86	XX	—	—	XX	—	—
88	X	—	—	XO	3	48
90	X	—	—	XO	3	51
92						
94						
96						
98						

SUMMARY

Points - - - -	21	Points - - - -	51
Ringers - - -	73	Ringers - - -	83
Doubles - - -	29	Doubles - - -	38
Shoes Pitched -	90	Shoes Pitched -	90
Percent Ringers -	81.1	Percent Ringers -	92.2

O—Ringer OO—Double Ringer X—Dead —No Count

50 SHOE COUNT ALL SCORING

National Horseshoe Pitchers Association
OFFICIAL SCORE SHEET

Date July 4, 1970 Court No. 1 Game No. 1

LEO McGRATH vs. HAL PORTER

Shoes	Ringers	Points	Score	Ringers	Points	Score
2	—	—	—	—	—	—
4	—	1	1	—	1	1
6	—	—	—	—	1	1
8	—	2	3	—	—	—
10	—	—	—	—	2	3
12	O	3	6	—	—	—
14	—	—	—	O	3	6
16	O1	4	10	—	—	—
18	—	—	—	O1	4	10
20	OO	6	16	—	—	—
22	—	—	—	OO	6	16
24	—	1	17	—	1	17
26	—	2	19	—	2	19
28	O	3	22	O	3	22
30	O1	4	26	O1	4	26
32	OO	6	32	OO	6	32
34	—	1	33	—	2	34
36	—	1	34	O	3	37
38	—	1	35	O1	4	41
40	—	1	36	OO	6	47
42	OO	6	42	—	2	49
44	OO	6	48	O1	4	53
46	OO	6	54	—	1	54
48	—	2	56	O1	4	58
50	O1	4	60	—	2	60

SUMMARY

Points - - - -	60	Points - - - -	60
Ringers - - -	15	Ringers - - -	14
Doubles - - -	5	Doubles - - -	3
Shoes Pitched -	50	Shoes Pitched -	50
Percent Ringers -	30	Percent Ringers -	28

-154-A-

NHPA scoring device.

METHODS OF SCORING

RALPH DYKES
NHPA President
Posting the scoreboard during the qualifying round at a world tournament.

Chapelle in which Allen set the all-time record for consecutive doubles. After being tied with Chapelle at 9-all, Allen closed out the game with 72 ringers in a row. Chapelle hit 82.6 percent and scored only nine points.

The third sheet is a game between Marvin Craig and Jim Knisley in which Knisley hit one streak of 77 out of 80.

The fourth sheet is an imaginary sheet made up for the purpose of showing how to score a game of 50 shoe count-all. In it all possible scores have been included.

Pictured here is the scoring device used by the NHPA in the last three World Tournaments.

The device was designed and made by Vern Fuller and Jim Davis of Battle Creek, Michigan, long time

NHPA members and players in the Wolverine State. The name plate holders and mounting were made by NHPA President Ralph Dykes and his buddy Jack Stout.

The two-inch numbers are on two inner disks numbered from 1 to 5 and two outer rings numbered from 0 to 9. The diameter of the inner disks is eight inches.

There is a viewing window on the other side of the device as well as name plate slots so the score can be seen from both sides.

The overall size of the device is 24 by 12 inches and one inch thick. It weighs only six pounds.

The bottom of the device has a fitting into which a piece of thin wall pipe can be inserted for mounting in the ground. The entire device will swivel freely so that the score can be seen from all angles.

The NHPA now has blueprints for scoring devices and mounting equipment that can be obtained by writing the national secretary. Any local club can build them on a "do it yourself" basis. Experience has been that a good set of scoreboards does a great deal to increase spectator interest.

10

The National Horseshoe Pitchers' Association

Chapter 2 gave some of the background behind the National Horseshoe Pitchers' Association. Here, the association is discussed in greater detail.

The National Horsheshoe Pitchers' Association of America (N.H.P.A.) is an incorporated non-profit organization, which is actually a federation of 54 State Associations in the U. S. and Canada, each with numerous club affiliates and individual members. Each State Association is self-governing and formulates its own program.

The purpose of the N.H.P.A. is to promote and foster the game, standardize the rules, equipment and playing procedures and above all to serve as a unifying agent between State Associations, local clubs, unorganized groups and individual players. Many improvements and good ideas have not only been developed in the N.H.P.A. but have originated in local club affiliates and passed on to the general membership, thereby benefiting every horseshoe player in the country.

Competitive championships are N.H.P.A. sponsored and sanctioned on all levels from purely local leagues and tournaments up to the annual World Tournament including State, Regional and many open events. These events greatly stimulate interest in the game and the N.H.P.A. gives championship insignias to the winners of all classes in every sanctioned tournament.

There is a place in the N.H.P.A. for everybody regardless of their experience or degree of playing skill. All tournaments are conducted in "classes" with the entrants grouped on the basis of their skill as determined by past performance or a qualifying round at the start of each event. Thus everybody, even novices and beginners, competes only with opponents of their same approximate skill, and can move up to a higher class when their ability and skill increases.

An important function of the N.H.P.A. is to provide information which enables local clubs to organize, formulate a good program of events or improve an existing program. Many local clubs have gotten under way or improved their program through contact with the N.H.P.A.

The N.H.P.A. makes game related items available to its members. These include all makes of official shoes, horseshoe trophies, films of the World Tourament, scoresheets, ringer % charts, sport shirts and T shirts, round robin schedules and many other items.

The NHPA's monthly magazine, *The Horseshoe Pitchers News Digest* is an excellent means of communication and enables subscribers to keep up with the news of games, tournament dates and results, and to observe how other clubs operate. Its pages are always open for news items of local clubs and groups. A 12-month subscription is $3.50.

For a very small amount of money you can become an N.H.P.A. member. The membership card is a combined State-National card good everywhere. The cost is only

$1.50 for the National portion of the dues. The state portion of the dues vary slightly from state to state.

National Officers

Ralph E. Dykes, 433 West North Avenue, Lombard, Illinois 60148	President
Leo McGrath, 1937 Lawn Avenue, Cincinnati, Ohio 45237	1st Vice-President
John Rademacher, 408 N. Pevetty Drive, Plant City, Florida 33566	2nd Vice-President
Earl Winston, Rte. 1, La Monte, Missouri 65337	3rd Vice-President
Dorothy Pinch, 592 Hull Street, Sharon, Pennsylvania 16146	4th Vice-President
W. Ray Williams, P.O. Box 3150, 819 Eye Street, Eureka, California 95501	Secretary-Treasurer

Editor of *The Horseshoe Pitchers' News Digest*,
F. Ellis Cobb, P.O. Box 1606, Aurora, Illinois 60507

State Secretaries and NHPA Representatives

Alabama — Johnnie P. Glass, P.O. Box 33, Calera, Al. 35040
Alaska — Harold Samuelson, 300 Glacier Ave., Fairbanks, Alaska 99701*
Arkansas — Floyd Toole, 7215 Shetland Drive, Little Rock, Arkansas 72204*
Arizona — Walter Stearns, 332 West 9th Street, Mesa, Arizona 85201
California, North — Verdan Zelmar, 2183 Abbey Lane, Campbell, California 95008
California, South — Jim Weeks, 12133 Graystone Avenue, Norwalk, California 90650
Colorado — Robert W. Cheline, 4585 Garland, Wheat Ridge, Co. 80033
Connecticut — Ervin Van Dine, 11 Harbison Avenue, Hartford, Connecticut 06106
Delaware — Dave Bowen, 125 Roosevelt Avenue, Dover, Delaware 19901*
District of Columbia — Allen Bertschey, 8016 Carey Branch Dr., Oxon Hill, Md. 20022
Florida — John Rademacher, 408 N. Pevetty Dr. Plant City, Fl. 33566
Georgia — Carl Gammon, Rt. 2, Duluth, Georgia 30577*
Hawaii — Herschel Jones, Chief Petty Officer, Q and A Dept., U.S. Naval Submarine Base, Pearl Harbor, Hawaii 96610*

PITCHING CHAMPIONSHIP HORSESHOES 190

Idaho — Walter McGarvey, 709 Prospect Avenue, Lewiston, Idaho 83501 — $ .50
Illinois — Ellis Cobb, Box 1606, Aurora, Illinois 60507 — $1.50
Indiana — Betty Whilhoite, 120 North Allen Drive, Lebanon, Indiana 46052 — $1.50
Iowa — Lucille Hopkins, 124 South Cherry Street, Ottumwa, Iowa 52501 — $2.50
Kansas — K.W. Hunter, 952 Amidon, Wichita, Kansas 97203
Kentucky — Daniel Webb, 1321 Licking Pike, Cold Springs, Kentucky 41076
Louisiana — Al Lucas, 621 - 27th St., Kenner, Louisiana 70062
Maine — Emily Woods, R.F.D., Greene, Maine 04236
Maryland — Parker Sturgis, R.F.D. 303A., Salisbury, Maryland 21801
Massachusetts — Russ Sweeney, 114 Montclair Ave., Quincy, Mass. 02171 — $2.00
Michigan Upper Peninsula — Bernice Houtari, Rt. 1 Box 66, Mass, Michigan 49948*
Michigan Wolverene — Duane Gillen, 12505 Crocket, Metamora, Ohio 43540*
Minnesota — Arthur L. Moran, Box 98, Webster, Minnesota 55088 — $1.00
Mississippi — Bruce Lloyd, 265 Venetian Gardens, Mississippi City, Miss. 39562*
Missouri — James Acock, 16315 East Pacific, Independence, Missouri 64050 — $1.00
Montana, East — William Driver, 415 - 6th Avenue, NE, Sidney, Montana 59270
Montana, West — Nat B. Clark, McLeod, Montana 59052
Nebraska — Janice Heist, Box 157, DeWitt, Nebraska 68341
Nevada — Marge Bower, 2880 Kietzke Lane No. 31, Reno, Nevada 89502
New Hampshire — Virginia Traquari, Surry, New Hampshire 03431
New Jersey — Bill Herrmann, 3 Orchard Street, Clark, New Jersey 07066
'bw
New Mexico — Don Hanes, 10608 Constitution N.E. Albuquerque, N.M. 87112
New York — Beryle Greenfield, R.D. No. 1, Richland, New York, 13144
North Carolina — Leslie Brendle, 260 Stewart Road, Winston-Salem, N.C. 27107
North Dakota — Ruben H. Zeller, Carson, North Dakota 58529
Ohio Buckeye — Francis Asher, 1425 Mulberry St. Pigua, Ohio, 45356
Oklahoma — John W. Brewer, Drawer 'U', Davenport, Oklahoma 74026
Oregon — Ken Lukens, 1130 N.W. 91st Avenue, Portland, Oregon 97229
Pennsylvania — Joe Abbott, 5840 Peck Road, Erie, Pennsylvania 16510
Pennsylvania East — Ray Greenlaw, 28 Balsam Road, Levittown, Pennsylvania 17657
Rhode Island — Tom Robertson, Stump Hill, Lincoln, Rhode Island 02865
South Carolina — Charles Brakefield, Rt. 4 Box 824, York, South Carolina 29745
South Dakota — Leigh Dunker, Warner, South Dakota 57478
Tennessee — Dexter Stallings, Rt. 3, Powell, Tennessee 37849
Texas — Lake Parlett, 1815 Lee Hall, San Antonio, Texas 78201
Utah — Clarence Giles, 1348 S. 1700 W. Riverton, Utah, 84065
Vermont — Ralph E. Watson, East Road, Bennington Vermont 05201
Virginia — Floyd Hix, 107 MacMurdo Street, Ashland, Virginia 23005*
Washington — Herb Okeson, 6910 N.E. 107th St., Bothell, Wash. 98011 — $3.00
West Virginia — Howard Barnett, 126 Valley Drive, Nitro, West Virginia 25143
Wisconsin — Robert Phelan, 215 South Walnut St., Kimberly, Wisconsin 54136 — $ .50
Wyoming — Harold Bindschadler, 520 S. 12th St., Laramie, Wyo. 82070 — $1.50
Alberta, Canada — Robert Moodie, 1314 - 3rd Ave., North Lethbridge, Alberta, Canada
British Columbia — Stan Hoffard, 3651 Van Ness Ave., Vancouver 16, B.C., Canada
Manitoba — Bert Snart, 231 - 3rd Avenue NE, Dauphin, Manitoba, Canada
MA
Maritime Prov. — Charles Dupius, 206 MacLaren Blvd., St. John, New Brunswick, Can.
Ontario — Norman Prange, 11 Nelson Street, Bridgeport, Ontario, Canada
Saskatchewan — Alvin Ross, 708 Grey Street, Regina, Saskatchewan, Canada
Quebec — Fernand Thibeault, 18 Rue Reine, Sorel, Quebec, Canada
Canadian National — Russ Martin, 212 Boniface Ave., Kitchener, Ontario, Canada

11
Horseshoe Pitching's Hall of Fame

In 1964 Harold Craig, President of the National Horseshoe Pitchers' Association, appointed a committee to set up a Hall of Fame. That committee consisted of Carl Steinfeldt, Rochester, New York, Chairman; Elmer Beller, Bellflower, California; Bob Pence, Gary, Indiana; Leland Mortenson, Des Moines, Iowa; and Marvin Chrisman, Connersville, Indiana.

This committee reported to the 1965 National Convention at Keene, New Hampshire.

Upon the motion of Amos Whitaker of Massachusetts and the second of Glen Henton of Iowa the committee report was adopted, calling for "establishment of a permanent Hall of Fame with three players and three non-players to be installed at the 1966 World Tournament and two players and one non-player to be selected each year thereafter. The original Hall of Fame Committee will serve during the coming year with replacements being appointed by the NHPA President in each succeeding year. The committee will make the final Hall of Fame selections based on recommendations by the NHPA membership."

Through 1973 a total of 26 pitchers and promotors have been enshrined in the Hall of Fame. The pictures of each of these persons and a brief statement about each appear in this chapter.

Listed below is the present Hall of Fame committee:

Chairman: Bernard Herfurth, 17 Fort Street, Northampton, Massachusetts, 01060.

Members: Cletus Chapelle, 7018 North Greenwich, Portland, Oregon, 97217.

Lt. Col. Jack Adams, 45335 Westview Avenue, Chilliwack, B. C., Canada

Ted Allen, 1045 Linden Avenue, Boulder, Colorado, 80302.

Elmer Beller, 9725 Beach Street, Bellflower, California, 90706.

Alvin Dahlene, 947½ Illinois Street, Lawrence, Kansas, 66044.

Dale Dixon, 2616 49th Street, Des Moines, Iowa, 50310 and 2701 Allred, Mesa, Arizona, 85204

Ruth Hangen, 630 Heim Road, Getzville, New York, 14068

Arthur Holter, 4417 Brunswick Avenue, Crystal, Minnesota, 55422

Lee Davis, 13595 - 86th Avenue North, Seminole, Florida, 33542

Ed McFarland, 211 Wroxton Drive, Conroe, Texas, 77301

Paul Puglise, 200 Luddington Avenue, Clifton, New Jersey, 07011

Donnie Roberts, Route 5, Lucasville, Ohio, 45648

Earl Winston, Route 1, La Monte, Missouri, 65337

At the present time there is no permanent home for the Hall of Fame. The plaques holding the pictures of

HORSESHOE PITCHING'S HALL OF FAME 193

the members are kept at the home of the National Secretary and brought each year to the site of the World Tournament for display.

Ed Domey is making an attempt to locate the Hall of Fame at the Heritage Recreation Center at Sutton, Massachusetts. There may be others who will suggest a home for the hall. Regardless of the location it seems that the Hall of Fame is destined to have a permanent home in the near future. Rome, New York, and Greenville, Ohio, have expressed an interest.

Here are the twenty-six members through 1973:

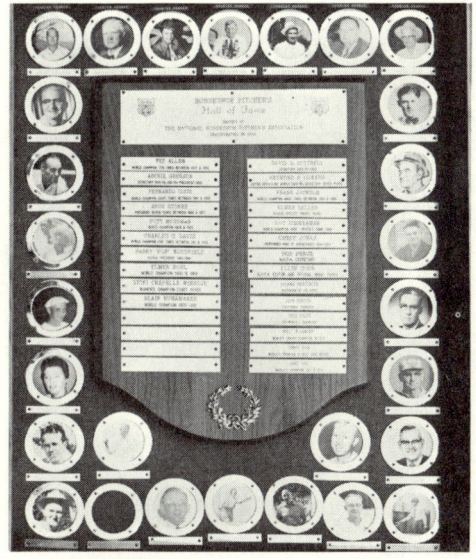

HALL OF FAME PLAQUE
The Horseshoe Pitching Hall of Fame was established in 1965 but as of now has no permanent home. The members of the select group are pictured on the above plaque and it is brought to the World Tournament each year by the NHPA Secretary and kept in his custody throughout the following year.

TED ALLEN
Original Charter Member 1966
Ted Allen of Boulder, Colorado holds ten World Championships. He has pitched exhibitions in many parts of the world, holds the record for 72 consecutive ringers in World Tournament competition. Possessing a unique color Allen has established himself over 50 years of play as the Babe Ruth of horseshoe pitching.

FRANK JACKSON
Original Charter Member 1966
Frank Jackson, an Iowa farmer, is part legend and part man. He won the first recognized World Tournament in 1909 as well as the first one to be sanctioned by the NHPA in 1915. He toured the nation and with his three sons, Hanford, Carroll and Vyril, to spark interest in the game everywhere. He won World Championships in 1920, 1921, and 1926, finished 5th in 1935 at age 65 and pitched until his death at age 85 in 1955. He could be called the pioneer champion or the man who was born too soon.

FERNANDO ISAIS
Original Charter Member 1966
Fernando Isais was born in Mexico and came to California in 1927. He won eight World Championships and his six consecutive titles beginning in 1947 may never be equalled. His one and three-quarters pitch must rank as one of the classic deliveries of all time for style, ease and consistency.

HORSESHOE PITCHING'S HALL OF FAME

ARCH STOKES
Original Charter Member 1966

Arch Stokes of Salt Lake City, Utah, made himself one of the most loved men in the game. Chiefly because of his work the 18-court layout at Murray City became the home of the World Tournament from 1947 through 1959. As the guiding father of the NHPA he served four terms as President. Although he died in 1957, he still influences the game in the form of the Arch Stokes Memorial Award given each year to the person who makes the biggest contribution to the game.

DAVID D. COTTRELL
Original Charter Member 1966

David D. Cottrell was owner and founder of a magazine distribution agency. A brilliant organizer and promoter he published the first comprehensive book on the history of the game and how to play it in 1927. Serving as NHPA Secretary from 1925 through 1933 he set up an orderly method of keeping tournament results and designed the first horseshoe scoresheets.

ARCHIE GREGSON
Original Charter Member 1966

Archie Gregson and his wife, Katie, who was the 1954 Women's World Champion, formed one of the hardest working husband-wife teams in the game. Archie served both as Secretary and as President of the NHPA and his activities included player, administrator, organizer, tournament manager, and master of ceremonies for many years.

PITCHING CHAMPIONSHIP HORSESHOES 196

RAYMOND B. HOWARD
Original Charter Member 1966

Raymond B. Howard, London, Ohio, published the *Horseshoe World* from 1920 until World War II. He served seven years as NHPA Secretary-Treasurer. His magazine was the greatest contribution in that it brought players all over the country together and provided monthly contact.

PUTT MOSSMAN
1967

Putt Mossman of Iowa won World Championships in 1924 and 1925. He manufactured a brand of shoe and developed the 1¼ turn to the point that a great many people thought he had invented it, and many referred to that turn as the "Mossman Twist." He was a showman, an exhibition pitcher, and stunt man who exposed the game to many all over the world.

GUY ZIMMERMAN
1967

Guy Zimmerman of Iowa and California was the 1954 World Champion. He pitched a perfect game World tournament play, won state championships in both Iowa and California and was considered one of the toughest competitors of his time.

HORSESHOE PITCHING'S HALL OF FAME 197

ELMER BELLER
1967

Elmer Beller of Bellflower, California, served 20 years as an NHPA official. He earned the title of "Mr. Horseshoes" by designing scoring devices, helping to run every World Tournament from 1949 to 1967, running tournaments in California and Arizona and in going out of his way to help a friend, especially if he were a horseshoe pitcher.

CASEY JONES
1968

Casey Jones was rated one of the top four pitchers in the game from 1935 through 1954, finishing as high as runnerup for the World Championship but never winning it. His 87.5% ringers for 31 games in 1948 stood as a World Record until 1968. He collected 16 Wisconsin state championships.

C. C. DAVIS
1968

C. C. Davis is a Kansas City carpenter. Considered one of the most colorful performers in the game he traveled widely doing trick pitching and exhibitions. Davis tied for the World Championship at the Chicago World Fair in 1933 and won five world championships outright. In 1928 he became the first player to hit 70% ringers for an entire tournament.

PITCHING CHAMPIONSHIP HORSESHOES

HARRY "POP" WOODFIELD
1968

Harry "Pop" Woodfield, Washington, D. C., served as NHPA Secretary from 1941 through 1948. He was editor of the only booklet in the game during the period, promoted the game extensively in the D. C. area and had the unique experience of helping the President of the United States, Harry Truman, to install a playing court at the White House.

CURT DAY
1969

Curt Day of Frankfort, Indiana, has to be one of the toughest pitchers the game has known. He won World Championships in 1966 and 1971 as well as 17 Indiana State Championships and a multitude of major tournament titles. As an indication of his consistency in the 1971 World Tournament during 35 games there were no ten consecutive shoes in which Curt had fewer than seven ringers.

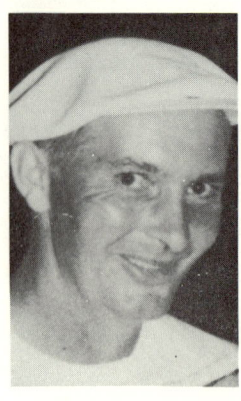

ELMER HOHL
1969

Elmer Hohl is a carpenter and farmer from Wellesley, Ontario, Canada. He won the World Championship in 1965, 1968, 1972, and 1973. His 88.5% ringers for the entire tournament in 1968 stands as the world record and included a perfect game. In fourteen years of World Tournament play he has never been below 5th place. He has been Canadian National Champion 12 times.

HORSESHOE PITCHING'S HALL OF FAME

ROBERT G. PENCE
1969

Robert G. Pence, Gary, Indiana, served as NHPA Secretary for fourteen difficult years. He has been instrumental in moving the World Tournament to different locations to insure the growth of the game, conducting the tournaments with a firm hand and working with local chapters. Bob was one of a group which introduced horseshoes to the Republic of South Africa. His pitching and his promotion of the game span four decades.

VICKI CHAPPELLE WINSTON
1970

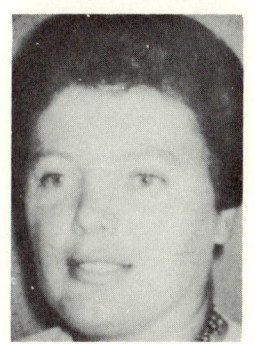

Vicki Chappelle Winston, LaMonte, Missouri, is the first woman inducted into the Hall of Fame. Winner of eight World Championships she is a good sport, rugged competitor and a master of the one and one-quarter turn. Pitching in 18 World Tournaments since her first in 1953 she has set many records.

ELLIS COBB
1970

Ellis Cobb, Aurora, Illinois, would have had to do nothing else but edit the *Horseshoe Pitchers' News Digest* since 1956 to earn his niche in the history of horseshoe pitching. He has been the Illinois state secretary since 1950 and manages the state championship meet each year. An outstanding pitcher he has played in the championship division of the world tournament three times with a tenth place finish in 1951. He served as the model for the horseshoe pitching figure on the trophies made by the major manufacturers.

PITCHING CHAMPIONSHIP HORSESHOES 200

BLAIR NUNAMAKER
1970

Blair Nunamaker, Cleveland, Ohio, won the World Championship in 1929 and held it until 1933. He won four Ohio championships and traveled from coast to coast giving exhibitions and stimulating interest in the game.

JIMMY RISK
1971

Jimmy Risk finished second for the World Championship but was never able to win it. Included in the titles he did win were eight Indiana state championships, but his great contribution to the game was his travel and exhibition pitching. With the USO he gave exhibitions for service men all over the globe.

LELAND MORTENSON
1971

Leland Mortenson, Des Moines, Iowa, was a promoter, organizer, tournament director, historian, and one of the moving spirits of the game since 1921. From 1936 to 1940 he conducted the Midwest Nationals and the 1940 World Tournament at Des Moines.

HORSESHOE PITCHING'S HALL OF FAME

FRED BRUST
1971

Fred Brust, Columbus, Ohio, won the World Championship in 1919, was one of the founding fathers in the NHPA, was the founder of the Ohio Horseshoe Manufacturing Company, and served as NHPA Vice-President.

JOHN GORDON
1971

John Gordon was a promoter, organizer, patron and sponsor of the game for many years. His chief contribution might have been the designing of the Gordon Spin On pitching shoe.

MRS. C. A. LANHAM
1971

Mrs. C. A. Lanham, Bloomington, Illinois, was a left-handed pitcher who won six Women's World Championships and completely dominated the game during the 1920s. Her combined seven-year record was sixty-nine wins and four losses.

GEORGE MAY
1972

George May, Akron, Ohio, won 1920 and 1923 World Championships. He is credited with perfecting the "open shoe," and is at least the first man to effectively use it in tournament play. It made a shambles of the 1920 tournament and revolutionized the game.

CARL STEINFELDT
1972

Carl Steinfeldt, Rochester, New York, finished second in the 1964 World Tournament and has averaged 80% ringers in twelve tournaments in which he played. He shares the world record of 15 consecutive four-deads and has won 18 New York state titles.

RALPH FORSSTROM
1972

Ralph Forsstrom, Hampden, Massachusetts, spent 40 years organizing and promoting horseshoe pitching in New England. He held state and regional offices during many of those years and helped run the 1965, 1968, and 1972 World Tournaments.

DALE DIXON
1973

Dale Dixon, Des Moines, Iowa, participated in national events for fifty years, won eleven Iowa state championships and constantly played in the World Championship Class A division. He designed a brand of pitching shoe, portable pitching courts, and promoted the game.

FRANK STINSON
1973

Frank Stinson, Minneapolis, Minnesota, won the World Junior Championship in 1924, won the Minnesota state championship eight times and played in the World Championships 36 times.

RALPH DYKES
1973

Ralph Dykes, Lombard, Illinois, served as President of the NHPA, devised qualifying and scoring devices and methods of making a smooth operation out of the World Tournament and has promoted the game in every area for many years.

12
State Champions

The records vary widely from state to state. Some states keep records in great detail, others do not. Some have been organized for many years, others for only a few.

In this chapter the state champions are listed as far back as they can be accurately ascertained. Wherever the figures are available on games won, games lost, shoes pitched, ringers, and ringer percentage, they have been listed.

Following each state are state records in those states where such records are kept.

Those who are statistic bugs can spend many pleasant hours studying these lists. It is fun to trace the rise in ringer percentage in each state or in the performance of some of the champions who keep winning. It is interesting to notice the wide variation in the number and caliber of pitchers from state to state.

Among the interesting items I have found are these:
1. A man who won state championships under two names. Lee Rose, 1934 Michigan champion, and Lee Jacobs, 1944 and 1955 Michigan champion, are one and the same man.
2. Men who have held the championship in more than one state. Ted Allen won titles in three states, Colorado,

Oregon and California. John Clingan won in both Pennsylvania and in Florida, Joe Dubie in Montana and Georgia, Guy Zimmerman in California and Iowa, Bob West in North Dakota and Oregon, and P. D. Riley in Texas and New Mexico.
3. A father and son winning state championships: W. F. Towne, an Oklahoma champ is the father of Tom Towne a New Mexico champ; Frank Jackson is the father of Hansford Jackson, both of whom won Iowa titles.
4. Ted Allen winning Colorado titles 46 years apart in 1922 and 1968.
5. In two states, Washington and Minnesota, the highest tournament percentages being pitched by players who did not win the tournament in the year when the record was set. The same could be said of a World Tournament, when in 1948 Casey Jones set the world record percentage of 87.5% and lost.

The list is endless.

Alabama

Year	Name of Champion	Won	Lost	Shoes Pitched	Ringers	Ringer Percentage
1920–1930	C. A. Grant					
1930–1963	No organized play.					
1964	Ottie W. Reno	6	0	408	256	62.7
1965	Ottie W. Reno	5	0	310	162	52.2
1966	Ottie W. Reno	3	0	198	96	48.5
1967	Ottie W. Reno	7	0	418	233	55.7
1968	Ottie W. Reno	5	0	250	133	53.2
1969	Ottie W. Reno	5	0	294	164	55.8
1970	Ottie W. Reno	8	1	640	394	61.6
1971	Ottie W. Reno	5	0	360	240	66.7
1972	Ottie W. Reno	7	0	362	218	60.2
1973	Ottie W. Reno	7	0	506	298	58.9

PITCHING CHAMPIONSHIP HORSESHOES

STATE RECORDS

Name of Record	Record Holder	Year Set	Record
Highest ringer percentage, Qualifying	Ottie W. Reno	1971	74%
Most points, Qualifying	Ottie W. Reno	1971	246
Highest R%, one game	Ottie W. Reno	1972	90%
(27 of 30 vs Carlton West at Calera)			
Highest R%, one tournament	Ottie W. Reno	1971	66.7
Most consecutive doubles, game	Ottie W. Reno	1971	11

Alaska

Year	Name of Champion	Won	Lost
1965	Bjarne June		
1966	Bjarne June		
1969	Paul Toole	7	0

Arizona

Year	Name of Champion	Won	Lost	Ringer Percentage
1926	S. N. Pullins			
1927	James O. Lecky			
1928	James O. Lecky			
1929	James O. Lecky			
1930	James O. Lecky			
1931	James O. Lecky			
1932	James O. Lecky			
1933	James O. Lecky			
1934	James O. Lecky			
1935	James O. Lecky			
1936	James O. Lecky			
1937	James O. Lecky			
1938	James O. Lecky			
1939	James O. Lecky			
1940	James O. Lecky			
1941	James O. Lecky			
1942	James O. Lecky			
1943	James O. Lecky			
1944	James O. Lecky			
1945	James O. Lecky			
1946	James O. Lecky			
1947	James O. Lecky			
1948	James O. Lecky			

(Continued)

STATE CHAMPIONS

1949	Stanley DeLeary			
1950	Stanley DeLeary			
1951	Stanley DeLeary			
1952	Stanley DeLeary			
1953	Stanley DeLeary			
1954	Stanley DeLeary	11	0	68.4
1955	Stanley DeLeary			
1956	Stanley DeLeary			
1957	Art Kamman	9	0	58.7
1958	Stanley DeLeary			
1959	Stanley DeLeary			
1960	Art Kamman	7	0	54.5
1961	Art Kamman	7	0	57.7
1962	Giff Thompson	9	0	64.0
1963	Art Kamman	7	0	67.0
1964	Art Kamman	9	0	70.3
1965	Art Kamman	7	0	71.4
1966	Art Kamman	7	0	71.3
1967	Art Kamman	5	0	74.1
1968	Art Kamman	5	0	81.0
1969	Art Kamman	7	0	73.3
1970	Roger Vogel	5	0	76.5
1971	Art Kamman	5	0	71.8
1972	Art Kamman	5	0	70.5
1973	Art Kamman	5	0	70.4

STATE RECORDS

Name of Record	Record Holder	Year Set	Record
Highest Ringer Percentage, Qualifying	Glen Crandell	1965	85.0
Most points, qualifying	Glen Crandell	1965	266
Highest Ringer Percentage,	Art Kamman	1968	81.0

Arkansas

Year	Name of Champion
1958	Floyd Toole
1970	Jimmie Riggs

California

Year	Name of Champion	Won	Lost	Shoes Pitched	Ringers	Ringer Percentage
1920	Billy Crick, Sr.					
1921	W. R. Bradfield					
1922	G. J. Milligan					
1923	Robert Nunn					
1924	Robert Nunn					

(Continued)

PITCHING CHAMPIONSHIP HORSESHOES

1925	Robert Nunn					
1926	Dean Brown					
1927	S. L. Hiatt					
1928	Dean Brown					
1929	Walter Krowel					
1930	Merle Stoner					
1931	Fernando Isais	11	0	664	435	65.5
1932	Fernando Isais	12	1	664	435	65.5
1933	Fernando Isais	15	0	996		80.3
1934	Ted Allen					
1935	Ted Allen					
1936	Lowell Gray					
1937	Fernando Isais					
1938	Dean Brown					
1939	Dean Brown					
1940	Fernando Isais	11	0	914	728	79.6
1941	Fernando Isais					
1942	Guy Zimmerman					
1943	Guy Zimmerman					
1944	Guy Zimmerman					
1945	Guy Zimmerman					
1946	Guy Zimmerman					
1947	Guy Zimmerman					
1948	Guy Zimmerman					
1949	Guy Zimmerman	11	0	710	616	86.7
1950	Guy Zimmerman	11	0	628	529	84.2
1951	Don Titcomb	10	1			79.3
1952	Fernando Isais	11	0			79.6
1953	Fernando Isais	11	0			78.8
1954	Guy Zimmerman	11	0			82.2
1955	Don Titcomb	11	0	698	529	76.0
1956	Don Titcomb	11	0	746	583	78.1
1957	Don Titcomb	10	1	698	553	79.2
1958	Don Titcomb	11	0	704	541	76.8
1959	Jim Weeks	11	0	742	563	75.9
1960	Don Titcomb	13	2	1010	780	77.2
1961	Don Titcomb	13	0	836	615	73.6
1962	Gerald Schneider	13	2			76.9
1963	Bill Blexrude	12	1	912	663	72.7
1964	Bill Fraser	13	2	1150	810	70.4
1965	Bill Blexrude	10	3	948	640	67.5
1966	Gerald Schneider	14	1	1216	942	77.4
1967	Don Titcomb	13	0			76.7
1968	Gerald Schneider	13	0			76.6
1969	John Walker	12	1			71.8
1970	John Walker	15	1	1044	836	80.0
1971	John Walker	14	1	944	691	73.2
1972	Gerald Schneider	15	1	1170	891	76.1
1973	Gerald Schneider	15	1	1088	761	69.9

STATE CHAMPIONS

STATE RECORDS

Name of Record	Record Holder	Year Set	Record
Highest ringer percentage, game	Fernando Isais	1952	100.0
Highest ringer percentage, tournament	Guy Zimmerman	1949	86.7
High ringer percentage, qualifying	Gerald Schneider	1968	90.0
Most points, qualifying	Gerald Schneider	1968	280

Colorado

Year	Name of Champion	Won	Lost	Shoes Pitched	Ringers	Ringer Percentage
1921	H. C. Grier					
1922	Ted Allen					
1923	Ira Allen					
1924	Ted Allen					46.0
1925	Ted Allen					
1926	Ira Allen					48.0
1927	Ted Allen					49.0
1928	Ted Allen					53.0
1929	Ted Allen					
1930	Ted Allen			406	245	60.0
1931	Ted Allen					
1932	Frank Wilson	20	3	1388	772	55.6
1933	Frank Wilson	15	0	776	475	61.2
1934	Robert Decker	12	3	1028	598	58.1
1935	Marvin Clayberg					
1936	John Oakey	11	4	984	577	58.6
1937	Marvin Clayberg	14	1	932	607	65.1
1938	Robert Decker	15	0	822	531	64.4
1939	Robert Decker	14	1			66.9
1940	Ralph Carr	14	1	994	617	62.0
1941	Orville Lauer	14	2	1020	698	68.4
1942	Robert Decker	15	1	860	591	68.7
1943	Ted Allen	7	0	404	315	77.8
1944	Ralph Carr	12	2	994	665	67.0
1945	Ralph Carr	14	1	958	578	60.3
1946	Robert Bowman					
1947	Ralph Carr	12	2			59.0
1948	Robert Bowman	10	1	744	466	62.6
1949	Jimmie Davis—Eino Tiilikaimen, Co-champs					
1950	Eino Tiilikainen	11	1	818	570	69.6
1951	Gerald Labbe	11	0	596	416	70.9
1952	Richard Allen	10	2	678	446	65.7

(Continued)

Year	Name of Champion	Won	Lost	Shoes Pitched	Ringers	Ringer Percentage
1953	Eino Tiilikainen	11	0	697	454	65.0
1954	Richard Allen	9	1	678	446	65.7
1955	Earl Graves	13	0	750	542	72.7
1956	Earl Graves	12	1	728	518	71.1
1957	Robert Bowman	9	2	654	394	60.2
1958	Gerald Labbe	11	0	558	394	70.6
1959	Harvey Ochsner	13	1	820	519	63.2
1960	Gerald Labbe	10	1	572	396	69.2
1961	Gerald Labbe	11	0	480	347	72.1
1962	Gerald Labbe	9	1			
1963	Harvey Ochsner	11	0			59.7
1964	Harvey Ochsner	12	2			63.2
1965	Roy Radcliffe	13	1			61.7
1966	Dick Wetherbee	13	0			66.3
1967	Dick Wetherbee	10	1			67.1
1968	Ted Allen	9	0			66.6
1969	Bill Thomas	11	0			54.7
1970	Dick Wetherbee	9	0			65.7
1971	Dick Wetherbee	7	0			69.5
1972	Roger Vogel	8	1			69.8
1973	Roger Vogel	11	0			74.0

Connecticut

Year	Name of Champion	Won	Lost	Shoes Pitched	Ringers	Ringer Percentage
1928	W. T. Cowles					
1929	Sam Lane					
1930	Sam Lane					
1931	Sam Lane					
1932	Sam Lane	11	2			
1933	Guido Georgetti	11	0	597	255	42.7
1934	Guido Georgetti					
1935	Irving Wood	10	1	712	350	49.0
1936	William Crofut	9	2	626	335	53.5
1937	Sam Lane	10	1	610	357	58.6
1938	William Crofut	7	2	590	348	59.0
1939	William Crofut	9	0	584	377	64.4
1940	William Crofut	8	1	518	333	64.2
1941	William Crofut	8	1	538	324	60.2
1942-1947 (no tournament held)						
1948	Guido Georgetti	10	1	688	383	55.6
1949	James Bessey, Jr.	9	2	628	372	59.2
1950	Dwight Smith	11	0	494	286	57.8
1951	Dwight Smith	9	2	612	386	63.0
1952	Walter Bagley	9	2	568	290	51.0

(Continued)

STATE CHAMPIONS

Year	Champion	Won	Lost			
1953	Walter Bagley	9	0	550	328	59.6
1954	Dwight Smith	10	1	660	402	60.9
1955	Ralph Hillburn	11	0	622	274	44.1
1956	Ralph Hillburn	11	0	722	413	57.2
1957	Ralph Hillburn	8	1	512	258	50.3
1958	Willie Paradis	8	1	566	305	53.9
1959	Clarence Lavers	7	2	550	299	54.3
1960	John Dudek	11	4	966	568	58.8
1961	Willie Paradis	5	0	324	215	66.3
1962	Willie Paradis	5	0	268	185	69.0
1963	Dominic Majewski	4	1			55.1
1964	Dominic Majewski	4	1	326	171	52.0
1965	Sherm Green	5	0	276	187	69.0
1966						
1967	Don Weik					
1968	Sherm Green	5	0			70.0
1969	Don Weik	4	1			74.1
1970	Norman Rioux	9	0			72.4
1971	Norman Rioux	4	1			66.8
1972						
1973	Norman Rioux	6	1			72.3

STATE RECORDS

Name of Record	Record Holder	Year Set	Record
Highest ringer percentage, one game	Willie Paradis	1960	81.8
Highest ringer percentage, one tournament	Don Weik	1969	74.1

District of Columbia

Year	Name of Champion	Won	Lost	Shoes Pitched	Ringers	Ringer Percentage
1929	Charles A. Fort					
1930	Harry Saunders					
1931	John Gourvenac					
1932	Hubbard Quantrille					
1933	Harry Saunders					
1934	Harry Saunders					
1935	William V. Moore					
1936	William V. Moore					
1937	Harry Saunders					

(Continued)

PITCHING CHAMPIONSHIP HORSESHOES 212

Year	Name	W	L	SP	R	%
1938	Irwin Carlberg					
1939	Irwin Carlberg					
1940	Clare Lacy					72.3
1941	Irwin Carlberg					
1942	Irwin Carlberg	14	1	832	602	72.3

1943 to date – No further District of Columbia tournaments have been held after the 1942 tournament. In 1966 the tournament was incorporated into the Metropolitan Washington, D. C. tournament which encompasses part of some adjoining states as well as the District of Columbia.

1967	Clayton Henson	5	0
1968	Clayton Henson	5	0
1969	Clayton Henson	5	0

RECORDS

Name of Record	Record Holder	Year	Record
Most points qualifying	Clare Lacy	1940	247
Highest percentage qualifying	Clayton Henson	1969	78.0
	Clare Lacy	1940	78.0
Highest percentage tournament	Clare Lacy	1940	72.3
	Irwin Carlberg	1942	72.3
Highest percentage game	Irwin Carlberg	1942	84.0

Metropolitan Washington, D. C.

Year	Name of Champion	Won	Lost	Shoes Pitched	Ringers	Ringer Percentage
1929	Millard Peake	11	2			
1930	Harry F. Saunders	11	0			
1931	Harry F. Saunders	11	1			
1932	Clayton C. Henson	11	1			
1933	Clayton C. Henson	11	1			
1934	Clayton C. Henson	11	0			
1935	Raymond L. Frye	11	1			
1936	William V. Moore	11	3			
1937	Raymond L. Frye	11	1			
1938	Harry F. Saunders	11	3			
1939	Clayton C. Henson	11	2			
1940	Clayton C. Henson	11	0			
1941	Clayton C. Henson	11	2			
1942	Clayton C. Henson	15	0	708	559	79.0

1943–1965 Clayton C. Henson – During these years no tournaments were held but Clayton C. Henson defended and won all challenge matches against worthy challengers and retained the title every year.

Year	Name of Champion	Won	Lost	Shoes Pitched	Ringers	Ringer Percentage
1966	Clayton C. Henson	5	0			
1967	Clayton C. Henson	5	0			
1968	Clayton C. Henson	5	0			
1969	Clayton C. Henson	5	0			
1970	Ray Thielke	5	0			
1971	Ray Thielke	5	0			
1972	Cecil Monday	5	0			67.9
1973	Dale Carson	5	0			68.4

STATE CHAMPIONS

RECORDS

Name of Record	Record Holder	Year Set	Record
High ringer percentage, qualifying	Clayton C. Henson	1942	81.0
Most points, qualifying	Clayton C. Henson	1942	254
High ringer percentage, tournament	Clayton C. Henson	1942	79.0
High ringer percentage, game	Clayton C. Henson	1942	87.0

Florida

Year	Name of Champion	Won	Lost	Shoes Pitched	Ringers	Ringer Percentage
1960	Charles Stevens	7	0			60.8
1961	John C. Davis	5	2	450	272	60.4
1962	John Clingan	9	0			62.1
1963	John Rademacher	9	0	618	369	59.7
1964	John Rademacher	8	1	604	350	57.9
1965	George Schummer	8	1	486	284	58.4
1966	John Rademacher	7	0	436	280	64.2
1967	John Clingan	7	0	366	255	69.7
1968	John Rademacher	6	1	670	493	73.6
1969	John Rademacher	7	0	424	267	63.0
1970	John Rademacher	8	0	426	322	75.6
1971	William Riley	7	0	534	332	62.2
1972	John Rademacher	7	0	396	274	69.2
1973	John Rademacher	6	1			

STATE RECORDS

Name of Record	Record Holder	Year Set	Record
High ringer percentage, game	John Rademacher	1968	87.2
Highest game by a loser	Gene Rademacher	1968	76.7
Most 4-deads, game	John & Gene Rademacher	1968	18
High ringer percentage, qualifying	John Rademacher		80.0
Most points, qualifying	John Rademacher		260

Georgia

Year	Name of Champion	Won	Lost		
1967	Joe Dubie				
1968	James Evans	7	0		
1969	James Evans	7	1		
1970	Dones Blackwell	5	0		
1971	Ira Walters	5	1		
1972	James Evans	11	0		50.0
1973	James Brooks	6	0		56.5

Idaho

Year	Name of Champion	Won	Lost	Shoes Pitched	Ringers	Ringer Percentage
1952	E. J. Wiley					
1953	E. J. Wiley					
1954	E. J. Wiley					
1955	E. J. Wiley					
1956	E. J. Wiley					
1957	E. J. Wiley	7	0			70.0
1958	E. J. Wiley					
1959	E. J. Wiley	7	0			
1960	E. J. Wiley	7	0			66.3
1961	E. J. Wiley	7	0			
1962	E. J. Wiley	6	1			
1963	E. J. Wiley	7	0			67.0
1964	E. J. Wiley					
1965	Dean Curry					
1966	Les Reighard	7	0	430	248	57.7
1967	Les Reighard	6	1			55.1
1968	Dean Curry					
1969	Dean Curry	5	1			54.3
1970	Walt Hastings	7	0			54.6
1971	Dean Curry	7	0			54.5
1972	Walt Hastings	8	0			54.4
1973	Clarence Cummins	5	1			63.8

STATE RECORDS

Name of Record	Record Holder	Year Set	Record
Highest ringer percentage qualifying	Jim Kosterman	1957	66.0
Most points qualifying	Jim Kosterman	1957	231
Highest ringer percentage, one game	E. J. Wiley	1960	86.6
Highest ringer percentage, one tournament	E. J. Wiley	1957	70.0

Illinois

Year	Name of Champion	Won	Lost	Shoes Pitched	Ringers	Ringer Percentage
1920	Joe Heskett					
1921	Joe Heskett					

(Continued)

STATE CHAMPIONS 215

1922	John Hogan					
1923	George Hilst					
1924	E. A. Torbett					
1927	Walter Torbett					
1928	Gaylord Peterson					
1929	C. R. Thompson					
1930	Milton Tate					
1931	Milton Tate	14	1			
1932	Joe Bennett	13	2			59.8
1933	Milton Tate	14	1	942	564	59.8
1934	Gaylord Peterson					71.0
1935	Ellis Griggs					
1936	Howard Collier					
1937	Milton Tate	14	1	1056	708	67.0
1938	William Moore	14	1			77.3
1939	Aden Swinehamer					
1940	Ellis Griggs	14	1	1028	736	71.6
1941	Paul Engersoll	14	1			73.3
1942-1945 (no tournament held—war years)						
1946	Earl Bomke					
1947	Earl Bomke					
1948	John Lindermeier					
1949	John Lindermeier					
1950	John Lindermeier					78.9
1951	Earl Bomke					
1952	Ellis Griggs					
1953	Truman Standard					
1954	Truman Standard	9	2			74.2
1955	John Lindermeier	9	2			74.2
1956	Truman Standard	10	1	860	678	78.8
1957	Ellis Griggs	10	1	720	553	76.8
1958	Arthur Dugle	11	0	792	647	81.6
1959	Ellis Griggs	9	2	790	593	75.1
1960	Frank Palka	10	1	814	594	72.9
1961	Ellis Griggs	10	1	840	652	77.6
1962	Art Dugle	11	0			79.0
1963	Art Dugle	10	1	804	604	75.1
1964	Ray Martin	10	1	836	683	81.6
1965	Ray Martin	9	2	796	560	79.0
1966	Ellis Griggs	11	0	796	589	72.7
1967	Ellis Griggs	10	1			78.6
1968	Ellis Griggs	10	1			73.7
1969	Lynn Lyman	9	2			69.3
1970	Ellis Griggs	10	1			
1971	Eldon Damarin	10	1			71.1
1972	Lester Miller	13	1			
1973	Ray Martin	11	0			

PITCHING CHAMPIONSHIP HORSESHOES 216

STATE RECORDS

Name of Record	Record Holder	Year Set	Record
Highest ringer percentage, one tournament	Arthur Dugle	1958	81.6
	Ray Martin	1964	81.6
Most shoes, one tournament	Milton Tate	1937	1056
Most ringers, one tournament	Ellis Griggs	1940	736
Highest percentage qualifying	Mel Utley	1968	82.0
Most points qualifying	Mel Utley	1968	261
High percentage game	Paul Ingersoll	1941	94.5

Indiana

Year	Name of Champion	Won	Lost	Shoes Pitched	Ringers	Ringer Percentage
1919	John Glakely					
1920	Vince Stevens					
1921	Ed Werner					
1922	George Atkinson					
1923	Vince Stevens					
1924	Lester Irey					
1925	George Randall					
1926	Jimmy Risk					
1927	Jimmy Risk					
1928	Jimmy Risk					
1929	Walter Lane					
1930	Jimmy Risk					
1931	Henry Pergal					
1932	Jimmy Risk					
1933	Jimmy Risk					
1934	Herb Trenkle					
1935	Jimmy Risk					
1936	Herb Trenkle					
1937	Arlo Harris	8	1	646	484	74.4
1938	Jim Cox					
1939	Jimmy Risk					
1940	Bill Neilson	9	0			76.2
1941	Herb Trenkle					
1942-1945 (No Tournament Held—War years)						
1946	Wayne Nelson					
1947	Wayne Nelson					

(Continued)

STATE CHAMPIONS

1948	Arlo Harris					73.0
1949	Graydon McFatridge	18	1	950	715	75.3
1950	Graydon McFatridge	15	0	1100	781	71.0
1951	Graydon McFatridge	14	1	1150	843	73.3
1952	Wayne Nelson	10	0			76.3
1953	Curtis Day	15	0	1002	771	77.1
1954	Wayne Nelson	11	2	922	694	75.3
1955	Curtis Day	13	0	958	734	76.6
1956	Gene Brumfield	12	1	964	740	76.8
1957	Curtis Day	14	1	970	742	76.5
1958	Ed Sharp	9	2	820	619	75.5
1959	Curtis Day	19	0	1228	1007	82.0
1960	Curtis Day	15	0	988	776	78.5
1961	Curtis Day	14	1	996	796	80.1
1962	Curtis Day	11	0			85.1
1963	Curtis Day	11	0			85.8
1964	Curtis Day	10	1			84.3
1965	Curtis Day	9	0	726	627	86.4
1966	Curtis Day	9	0			82.5
1967	Curtis Day	9	0			85.7
1968	Curtis Day	8	1	644	522	81.1
1969	Curtis Day	9	0	616	547	88.8
1970	Curtis Day	8	1			81.3
1971	Curtis Day	8	1			80.4
1972	Curtis Day	7	0			85.9
1973	Mark Seibold	8	1			79.3

STATE RECORDS

Name of Record	Record Holder	Year Set	Record
Highest percentage qualifying	Graydon McFatridge	1956	91.0
Most points qualifying (150 shoes)	Graydon McFatridge	1956	406
Highest percentage game	Gene Brumfield	1961	95.0
Highest percentage tournament	Curt Day	1969	88.8
Most shoes, game	Curt Day and Karl VanSant	1969	168
Most ringers, game	Curt Day	1969	150
Most ringers, tournament	Bill Neilson	1959	1084
Most shoes, tournament	Bill Neilson	1952	1444
Consecutive 4-deads	Harrison Maitlen Bill Neilson	1956	10

Iowa

Year	Name of Champion	Won	Lost	Shoes Pitched	Ringers	Ringer Percentage
1921	Frank Jackson					
1922	Frank Lundin					
1923	Frank Lundin					
1924	Putt Mossman					
1925	Putt Mossman					
1926	Putt Mossman					
1927	Frank Jackson					
1928	Frank Jackson					
1929	Putt Mossman					
1930	Frank Jackson					
1931	Hansford Jackson					
1932	Frank Jackson					
1933	Frank Jackson					
1934	Guy Zimmerman					
1935	John Garvey					
1936	Guy Zimmerman					
1937	Guy Zimmerman					
1938	Lyle Brown					
1939	Guy Zimmerman					
1940	Guy Zimmerman					
1941	Dale Dixon					
1942	Ted Harlan					
1943	Dale Dixon					
1944	Dale Dixon					
1945	Clifford Hansen					
1946	Dale Dixon					
1947	Harold Shaw					
1948	Harold Shaw					
1949	Harold Shaw					
1950	Dale Dixon					
1951	Harold Shaw					
1952	Dale Dixon	14	1			79.0
1953	Dale Dixon	10	0			
1954	Dale Dixon	16	2			70.8
1955	Dale Dixon	14	4			68.2
1956	Willard James					
1957	Earl Wiges	14	1			

(Continued)

STATE CHAMPIONS 219

Year	Name	Won	Lost	Pct
1958	Dale Dixon			
1959	Dale Dixon	15	0	72.4
1960	Francis Rogers	13	2	73.6
1961	Glen Henton	14	1	71.4
1962	Glen Henton	16	1	76.2
1963	Glen Henton	12	3	71.2
1964	Glen Henton	10	1	75.5
1965	Glen Henton			
1966	Glen Henton	11	1	76.6
1967	Glen Henton	11	0	71.1
1968	Art Hampton	11	0	73.8
1969	Art Hampton	11	0	76.8
1970	Art Hampton	12	2	72.5
1971	Art Hampton	10	1	70.6
1972				
1973	Glen Henton	10	1	68.6

Kansas

Year	Name of Champion	Won	Lost	Shoes Pitched	Ringers	Ringer Percentage
1920	Henry Daly					
1921	Henry Daly					
1922						
1923	Ed Brainine					
1924	Bert Duryee					
1929	Lloyd Woodward	10	1			60.0
1930	Bert Harriss	10	1			62.0
1931	Les McCollam	11	0			65.0
1932	Les McCollam	6	1			66.0
1933	Frank Phillips	6	1			63.0
1934	Bert Duryee	7	0	452	335	74.0
1935	Alvin Gandy	22	1	1362	959	70.0
1936	Frank Phillips	20	3			63.0
1937	Garold Brown	20	3	1244	813	65.0
1938	Alvin Gandy	22	1			70.0
1939	Alvin Gandy	10	1			72.0
1940	Alvin Gandy	11	0			75.0
1941	Alvin Dahlene	11	0			72.0
1942	Alvin Dahlene	11	0			77.0
1943	Garold Brown	7	0			63.0

(Continued)

PITCHING CHAMPIONSHIP HORSESHOES 220

Year	Champion	W	L	Pts For	Pts Ag	%
1944	Marines Tamboer	10	1			68.0
1945	Marines Tamboer	10	1			70.0
1946	Marines Tamboer	11	0			72.0
1947	Roland Kraft	5	2			70.0
1948	Roland Kraft	15	0			76.0
1949	Roland Kraft	14	1			73.0
1950	Marines Tamboer	14	1			70.0
1951	Marines Tamboer	14	1			70.0
1952	Marines Tamboer	15	0			73.0
1953	Marines Tamboer	14	1			73.0
1954	Marines Tamboer	15	0			74.0
1955	Roland Kraft	14	1			75.0
1956	Roland Kraft	15	0			74.0
1957	Roland Kraft	15	0			75.0
1958	Roland Kraft	(Retained Title—No Meet)				
1959	Roland Kraft	7	0			74.0
1960	Roland Kraft	7	0	428	313	73.0
1961	Roland Kraft	6	1			67.0
1962	Marines Tamboer	11	0	596	460	77.2
1963	Marvin Reheis	13	2			68.4
1964	Merlin Potts	13	2			64.7
1965	Marines Tamboer	9	0	632	435	68.8
1966	Merlin Potts	12	3	912	629	68.8
1967	Merlin Potts	15	0			68.9
1968	Merlin Potts	15	0			73.2
1969	Merlin Potts	15	0			76.1
1970	Merlin Potts	11	0			68.6
1971	Merlin Potts	10	1			72.7
1972	Merlin Potts	11	0			74.3
1973	Merlin Potts	11	0			78.5

STATE RECORDS

Name of Record	Record Holder	Year Set	Record
High ringer percentage, qualifying	Marines Tamboer	1970	90.0
Most points, qualifying	Marines Tamboer	1970	280
High ringer percentage, game	Roland Kraft	1952	94.1
High ringer percentage, tournament	Merlin Potts	1973	78.5
Most shoes, game	Roland Kraft and Alvin Dahlene	1938	120

Kentucky

Year	Name of Champion	Won	Lost	Shoes Pitched	Ringers	Ringer Percentage
1921	T. C. Story					
1922	E. M. Merchant					
1923	J. W. Netherton					
1924	W. P. Soete					
1925	Les Miller					
1926	Edward Beckman					48.9
1927	Sam B. Mattingly					
1928	Edward Beckman					
1929	Sam B. Mattingly					
1930	Lee Akers					
1931	Lee Akers					
1932	Mr. Young					
1933	George Moore					
1934	Mr. Young					
1935	Harry Henn					
1936	Harry Henn					
1937	George Moore	12	1	650	364	56.0
1938	George Moore	14	1	750	461	61.4
1939	Elmer McCoy					
1940	Elmer McCoy					
1941	Elmer McCoy	9	1			59.0
1942–1946	(no tournament held - War years)					
1947	James H. Johnson					
1948	James H. Johnson					
1949	James H. Johnson	5	0	400	330	82.5
1950	James H. Johnson	5	0	400	271	67.8
1951–1964	(no tournament held)					
1965	George Fraley					
1966	(No tournament held)					
1967	Howard Hamilton	10	1	668	357	53.4
1968	Lavern Hawkins	10	1	628	329	52.8
1969	Bill Henn	15	0	830	543	65.4
1970	Howard Hamilton	9	1			63.5
1971	Bill Henn	9	1			70.2
1972	Bill Henn	15	0			72.0
1973	Bill Henn	14	1			69.5

STATE RECORDS

Name of Record	Record Holder	Year Set	Record
High ringer percentage, game	James H. Johnson	1949	86.3
High ringer percentage, tournament	James H. Johnson	1949	82.5

PITCHING CHAMPIONSHIP HORSESHOES 222

Louisiana

O. S. Plott of Shreveport was recognized as Louisiana State Champion in 1927 when he played in the National Tournament at Duluth, Minnesota. Since that time he has been regarded as the champion. He has defended against several challengers in special matches but no state tournaments have been held with one exception. In 1929 the *Shreveport Times* staged the tournament and Plott won it with Billy Vosbury second.

Maine

Year	Name of Champion	Won	Lost	Shoes Pitched	Ringers	Ringer Percentage
1926	Mr. Cummings					
1927	Milton Bush					
1928	Guy Sturtevant					
1929	Guy Sturtevant					
1930	Guy Sturtevant					
1931	Charles Gerrish					
1932	Guy Sturtevant					
1933	Ralph Robinson					
1934	Ralph Robinson					
1935	Harold Goodier					
1936	Leonard Lombardi					68.2
1937	Ralph Robinson					60.3
1938	Harold Goodier	8	0			63.6
1939	Merrill Barnes	8	1	504	262	52.0
1940	Merrill Barnes	9	0	548	318	59.1
1941	Merrill Barnes	10	1			57.8
1942	Merrill Barnes					70.2
1943-1945 (no tournament held—war years)						
1946	Merrill Barnes					64.3
1947	Merrill Barnes	13	1			
1948	Carl Browning					
1949	George Noyes					
1950	Charles Gerrish	10	1			58.2
1951	Charles Gerrish	11	0			65.7
1952	Charles Gerrish	11	0			65.5
1953	Charles Gerrish	12	1			61.2
1954	Merrill Barnes	9	1			55.0
1955	Porter Clark	15	1			59.7

(Continued)

STATE CHAMPIONS

Year	Champion	Won	Lost	Pitched	Ringers	Percentage
1956	Porter Clark	6	1			64.0
1957	Charles Gerrish	11	0			63.7
1958	Joseph Davis	8	1			62.0
1959	Porter Clark	11	0			63.5
1960	Charles Gerrish	9	0			64.5
1961	Porter Clark	7	2			50.0
1962	N. Libbey	10	1	622	404	64.9
1963	Porter Clark	12	1	786	486	61.8
1964	Paul Tobey					
1965	William Libbey	9	0			62.2
1966	William Libbey	8	1			64.1
1967	Rene Sirois	9	0			58.1
1968	Albert Lord	7	0			64.3
1969	Albert Lord	9	1			66.1
1970						
1971	Porter Clark	4	1			57.1
1972	Paul Tobey	7	0			66.6
1973	Albert Lord	7	0			76.0

STATE RECORDS

Name of Record	Record Holder	Year Set	Record
High ringer percentage, game	Charles Gerrish	1960	79.4
High ringer percentage, tournament	Albert Lord	1973	76.0

Maryland

Year	Name of Champion	Won	Lost	Shoes Pitched	Ringers	Ringer Percentage
1929	Millard Peake					
1930	Millard Peake					
1931	Joseph Merryman					
1932	Joseph Merryman					
1933	Lee Fleshman					
1934	Lee Fleshman					
1935	Temple R. Jarrell					
1936	Temple R. Jarrell					
1937	Lee Fleshman					
1938	Lee Fleshman					
1939	Lee Fleshman					
1940	Lee Fleshman					

(Continued)

Year	Name of Champion	Won	Lost	Shoes Pitched	Ringers	Ringer Percentage
1941	Lee Fleshman					
1942	Clare Lacy	13	2	790	496	63.0
1943-1946	No tournament held					
1947	Dale Carson					
1948	Dale Carson					
1949	Dale Carson					
1950	Dale Carson					
1951	Dale Carson					
1952	Dale Carson					
1953	Dale Carson					
1954	Dale Carson					
1955	Dale Carson					
1956	Dale Carson					
1957	Dale Carson					
1958	Dale Carson					
1959	Dale Carson					
1960	Dale Carson					
1961	Jene Durham					
1962-1968	No tournament held					
1969	Dale Carson	7	0			69.1
1970	Dale Carson	7	1			69.7
1971	Dale Carson	7	0			67.5
1972	Dale Carson	7	0			72.2
1973	Raymond Thielke	7	0			61.7

Massachusetts

Year	Name of Champion	Won	Lost	Shoes Pitched	Ringers	Ringer Percentage
1933	James O'Shea					58.0
1934	James O'Shea	11	0	646	399	61.7
1935	James O'Shea					69.0
1936	Stanley DeLeary	11	0	748	454	60.7
1937	James O'Shea	11	0			81.6
1938	James O'Shea	9	0	534	433	81.2
1939	Stanley DeLeary					72.3
1940	James O'Shea					81.2
1941	James O'Shea	7	0	554	422	76.1
1942-1949	No tournament held					
1950	Donald Jackson	5	2			68.6
1951	Joseph Comeau					
1952	Edgar Landry	11	0			76.6

(Continued)

STATE CHAMPIONS 225

Year	Champion	Won	Lost	Shoes Pitched	Ringers	Percentage
1953	Edgar Landry					
1954	Joseph Comeau					
1955	Joseph Comeau					
1956	Edgar Landry					
1957	Edgar Landry	7	0	384	290	75.5
1958	Edgar Landry					
1959	Edgar Landry	9	0	496	354	70.9
1960	William Babinski	7	0	424	275	64.8
1961	Melvin Merritt	7	0	520	330	63.4
1962	Edgar Landry	7	0			70.2
1963	Joseph Comeau	8	1			73.1
1964	Edgar Landry	7	0	406	304	74.8
1965	Edgar Landry	6	1	452	335	74.1
1966	Edgar Landry	7	0			77.5
1967	Melvin Merritt	6	1	462	329	71.2
1968	Donald Kaddy	7	0	542	387	71.4
1969	Donald Kaddy	6	1			65.7
1970	Russ Sweeney	7	0			62.4
1971	Russ Sweeney	8	2			64.4
1972	Russ Sweeney	6	2			65.3
1973	Bernard Herfurth	6	2			66.1

STATE RECORDS

Name of Record	Record Holder	Year	Record
Highest percentage game	Edgar Landry	1957	93.0
Highest percentage tournament	James O'Shea	1937	81.6

Michigan

Year	Name of Champion	Won	Lost	Shoes Pitched	Ringers	Ringer Percentage
1923	Lewis Wilkes					
1924	Ralph Baxter					
1925	Ben Emerson					
1926	Frank Seals					
1927	Ed Walls					
1928	Ed Walls					
1929	Joe Latzko					
1930	Ed Walls					

(Continued)

1931	Ed Walls					
1932	Ed Walls and Jack Hoeksema (two tournaments held)					
1933	Ralph Baxter	10	1	740	440	59.5
1934	Lee Rose					
1935	Jim Skinner	18	1	1226	768	62.6
1936	Bob Hitt	25	2			68.4
1937	Bob Hitt					
1938	Bob Hitt					
1939	Joe Latzko					
1940	Joe Latzko					
1941	Joe Latzko	10	3			75.0
1942	Elmer Raab					
1943	Joe Latzko					
1944	Lee Jacobs					
1945	Joe Latzko					
1946	Joe Latzko					
1947	Joe Latzko					
1948	Joe Latzko					
1949	Joe Latzko					
1950	Joe Latzko					
1951	Joe Latzko					
1952	Jule Winters					
1953	Jule Winters					
1954	Joe Latzko					
1955	Lee Jacobs					
1956	Irwin Carlberg					
1957	Del Hallock					
1958	Ken Jensen	8	1			69.3
1959	Ken Jensen	8	0	584	405	70.8
1960	Alex Clark	8	0			70.8
1961	Ken Jensen	6	0			67.0
1962	Roy Smith	7	0			74.8
1963	Roy Smith	6	1			62.9
1964	Roy Smith	5	2			73.2
1965	Roy Smith	7	0			78.2
1966	Ken Jensen					69.0
1967	Roy Smith	12	1	782	590	75.4
1968	Roy Smith	11	0	696	542	77.8
1969	Roy Smith	13	1	914	718	78.6

Michigan Wolverine

1970	Roy Smith	10	1			71.3

(Continued)

STATE CHAMPIONS 227

1971	Gerald Maison	10	1		76.1
1972	Gerald Maison	10	1		73.1
1973	Roy Smith	10	1		72.2

Michigan Upper Peninsula

1970	Waino Huotari	6	1	57.0
1971	Waino Huotari	5	1	59.6
1972	Robert Paquette	7	0	56.4
1973	Ray Hill	7	0	62.0

STATE RECORDS

Name of Record	Record Holder	Year	Record
Highest percentage game	Roy Smith	1969	93.7
Highest percentage tournament	Roy Smith	1969	78.6
Consecutive four-deads	Roy Smith and Joe Holland	1969	6
Consecutive double ringers	Gerald "Doc" Maison	1968	19
High game, loser	Lee Jacobs	1943	77.4
Most doubles, one game	Robert Hitt	1938	38

Minnesota

Year	Name of Champion	Won	Lost	Shoes Pitched	Ringers	Ringer Percentage
1919	L. B. Allen					
1920	L. B. Allen					
1921	Fred Hay					
1922	R. M. Ransdell					
1923	R. M. Ransdell					
1924	Haakon Hauge					
1925	Haakon Hauge					
1926	Art Cummings					
1927	Fred Hay					
1936	Fred Hay	10	1	1040	726	70.0
1937	Garland Gable					
1938	Garland Gable (Retained title - no tournament held)					
1939	Frank Stinson	14	1			63.5
1940	Frank Stinson	15	0			67.3
1941	Frank Stinson	7	0			
1942–1943	No tournament held.					

(Continued)

PITCHING CHAMPIONSHIP HORSESHOES 228

Year	Champion	W	L			Pct.
1944	Haakon Hauge					
1945	Carl West	8	1			60.0
1946	Ron Cherrier	9	2			63.0
1947	Nels Peterson	10	2			61.6
1948	George Suess	12	2			
1949	Ron Cherrier	15	0			71.3
1950	Ron Cherrier	13	0			73.5
1951	Ron Cherrier	11	1	708	470	66.4
1952	Nels Peterson	15	0	826	517	62.6
1953	Ron Cherrier	14	0			69.9
1954	Ron Cherrier	15	0			67.0
1955	Ron Cherrier	6	1			67.7
1956	Ron Cherrier	11	0	608	414	67.8
1957	Ron Cherrier	11	0	592	417	70.4
1958	John Yernberg	9	2	686	364	53.0
1959	Ron Cherrier	9	2	680	417	61.0
1960	Howie Ganz	10	1	608	413	67.9
1961	Howie Ganz	10	1			70.0
1962	Andy Paglarini	9	2	746	473	63.4
1963	Hart Knutson	10	1			
1964	Andy Paglarini	15	0	940	604	64.3
1965	Frank Stinson	10	0			61.8
1966	Andy Paglarini	10	1			63.5
1967	Frank Stinson	11	0			72.8
1968	Andy Paglarini	10	1			74.1
1969	Frank Stinson	10	1			75.1
1970	Frank Stinson	11	0			72.0
1971	Frank Stinson	10	2			68.0
1972	Gust Magnuson	10	1			73.4
1973	Dale Lipovsky	6	1			64.5

STATE RECORDS

Name of Record	Record Holder	Year Set	Record
High ringer percentage, tournament	Andy Paglarini	1967	75.6
High ringer percentage, game	Frank Stinson	1971	86.2
High ringer percentage, qualifying	Gust Magnuson	1969	91.0
Most points, qualifying	Gust Magnuson	1969	282

Mississippi

Year	Name of Champion	Ringer Percentage
1969	John Norris	48.2

Missouri

Year	Name of Champion	Won	Lost	Shoes Pitched	Ringers	Ringer Percentage
1921	Tom Meager					
1922	Wash Baird					
1923	Wash Baird					
1924	Tom Meager					
1925	Tom Meager					
1926	Ed Wall					
1927	Ed Wall					
1928	Tom Meager					
1929	Tom Meager					
1930	Lawrence Robinson					
1931	Lefty Steinman					
1932	Jack Erwin					
1933	Lawrence Robinson					
1934	C. C. Davis	7	0	436	272	62.3
1935	C. C. Davis	15	0			72.0
1936	Gene Wors	14	1	892	548	61.4
1937	Jimmie Denny	14	1	952	641	67.3
1938	Paul Lattray	14	1	942	682	72.3
1939	Oscar Bozick	15	0			72.2
1940	Bob Bales	15	0			76.0
1941	Joe Wors	14	1			70.9
1942	Bob Bales					66.3
1943-1945	No tournament held					
1946	Jack Erwin					71.0
1947-1948	No tournament held					
1949	John Elkins					65.1
1950	John Elkins	7	0			67.2
1951	W. D. Wommack	6	1			63.3
1952	John Elkins	7	0			73.0
1953	John Elkins	6	1			70.3
1954	Art Schroeder	10	1			59.4
1955	Earl Winston	10	1			66.4
1956	John Elkins	10	1			61.4
1957	Paul Lattray	9	2			69.5
1958	David Baker	10	1			69.8
1959	William Kempfe	11	0			73.1

(Continued)

PITCHING CHAMPIONSHIP HORSESHOES

1960	John Elkins	9	2	63.1
1961	Bob Bales	9	2	64.9
1962	Paul Lattray	10	1	75.5
1963	Paul Lattray	10	1	74.4
1964	Paul Lattray	11	0	78.9
1965	Paul Lattray	11	0	71.2
1966	David Baker	10	1	74.0
1967	David Baker	10	1	74.4
1968	David Baker	10	1	74.5
1969	David Baker	10	1	74.7
1970	Lilliard Pinion	11	0	66.8
1971	David Baker	15	0	77.6
1972	David Baker	15	0	76.2
1973	David Baker	14	1	71.9

STATE RECORDS

Name of Record	Record Holder	Year	Record
Highest percentage qualifying	Paul Lattray	1967	93.0
Most points qualifying	Paul Lattray	1967	282
Highest percentage game	Bob Bales	1941	100.0
Highest percentage tournament	Paul Lattray	1964	78.9
Most shoes, game	David Baker and Frank Baker	1954	110
Youngest state champion	Jack Erwin	1932	16

Montana

Year	Name of Champion	Won	Lost	Shoes Pitched	Ringers	Ringer Percentage
1923	R. R. Frazier					
1924	A. G. Bussard					
1925	Joe Dubie					
1926	Joe Dubie					
1927	Joe Dubie					
1928	Joe Dubie					
1929	Joe Dubie					
1930	Joe Dubie					
1931	Joe Dubie	7	0	378	151	39.9
1932	Joe Dubie					
1934	Joe Dubie					

(Continued)

STATE CHAMPIONS

1935	Joe Dubie					
1936-1958	No organized play					
1959	Carl M. Horn	6	1	386	192	49.7
1960	Carl M. Horn	9	0	544	301	55.3
1961	Carl M. Horn	6	1	416	232	55.7
1962	Phil Prescott	6	1	452	241	53.3
1963	Phil Prescott	7	0			58.7
1964	Walter McChesney	7	0	422	252	58.7
1965	Ira Jensen	7	0			52.1
1966	Ed Holmberg	8	0			60.0
1967	Phil Prescott	7	1			53.5
1968	Ira Jensen	7	1			52.5
1969	Phil Prescott	7	0			60.0
1970	Ed Holmberg	6	1			51.0
1971	Ed Holmberg	7	0			71.7
1972	Ed Holmberg	6	2			56.2
1973	Ed Holmberg	7	1			63.6

STATE RECORDS

Name of Record	Record Holder	Year Set	Record
High ringer percentage, tournament	Ed Holmberg	1971	71.7
High ringer percentage, game	Ed Holmberg	1971	77.6
High ringer percentage, qualifying	Ernie McChesney	1961	58.0
Most points, qualifying	Phil Prescott	1961	202
Most shoes, game	Ed Holmberg & Nat Clark	1969	104
Most ringers, game	Ed Holmberg	1969	74
Most 4-deads, game	Ed Holmberg & Nat Clark	1969	14
Most consecutive 4-deads	Ed Holmberg & Arn Mosness	1971	4
Most consecutive ringers	Nat Clark	1969	16
	Ed Holmberg	1973	16
Fewest shoes, game	Al Dige & Jack Belzer	1972	36
Highest game by loser	Arnie Mosness	1972	67.1

Nebraska

Year	Name of Champion	Won	Lost	Shoes Pitched	Ringers	Ringer Percentage
1924	Charles McClelland					

(Continued)

PITCHING CHAMPIONSHIP HORSESHOES

Year	Champion	Won	Lost			Ringer %
1927	Guy Uhlig					
1928	Guy Uhlig					
1929	Howard Robinson					
1930	Guy Uhlig					
1931	Sam Sommerhalter	14	2			
1932	Howard Robinson					
1933	Sidney Harris					
1934	Sam Sommerhalter					
1935	Sam Sommerhalter					
1936	Sam Sommerhalter					
1937	Sidney Harris					
1938	Sidney Harris					
1939	Sidney Harris					
1940	Sidney Harris					
1941	Sidney Harris					
1942-1952	(No tournament held)					
1953	Joe Foster	12	0			72.0
1954	Howard Robinson	8	0			72.0
1955	Howard Robinson	7	1			72.0
1956	Howard Robinson	8	0			72.0
1957	Donald McCance	9	0			64.0
1958	Howard Robinson	7	0			73.6
1959	Donald McCance	5	0			76.6
1960	Donald McCance	9	0	578	388	73.7
1961	Donald McCance	5	0			73.1
1962	Donald McCance	5	0			77.6
1963	Donald McCance	5	0			67.3
1964	Donald McCance	7	0			63.5
1965	Donald McCance	5	0			69.1
1966	Donald McCance	5	0			68.9
1967	Donald McCance	7	0			72.7
1968	Donald McCance	7	0			67.2
1969	Donald McCance	8	0			69.2
1970	Donald McCance	9	0			70.6
1971	Donald McCance	7	0			68.9
1972	Donald McCance	6	1			66.7
1973	Donald McCance	7	0			67.3

Nevada

Year	Name of Champion	Won	Lost	Ringer Percentage
1969	Cliff Jones	9	0	38.2

(Continued)

STATE CHAMPIONS 233

1970	Cliff Jones			
1971	Bill Richardson	7	0	51.1
1972	Boyce Miller	6	1	46.0
1973	Boyce Miller	6	1	49.0

New Hampshire

Year	Name of Champion	Won	Lost	Shoes Pitched	Ringers	Ringer Percentage
1935	James Guyett					50.0
1936	James Guyett					55.0
1937	James Guyett					60.0
1938	James Guyett					62.0
1939	James Guyett					65.0
1940	No record					
1941	James Guyett					70.0
1942-1945	(no tournament held					
1946	James Guyett					60.0
1947	Howard White					60.0
1948	Howard White					62.0
1949	James Guyett					65.0
1950	James Guyett					65.0
1951	Howard White					62.0
1952	Howard White					65.0
1953	James Guyett	11	0			67.0
1954	Howard White					58.0
1955	James Guyett					68.0
1956	Howard White					61.0
1957	Howard White	8	0			66.0
1958	Howard White					68.0
1959	Howard White	11	3			60.0
1960	Eddie Paquin					51.0
1961	George Buskey	6	1			61.0
1962	George Buskey	7	2			56.0
1963	George Buskey	8	1			50.9
1964	Don Pickering	7	0			60.5
1965	Don Pickering	8	1			61.4
1966	Don Pickering	10	0			66.6
1967	Art Wayne	9	0			65.5
1968						
1969	Walter Piletz	8	1			66.1

(Continued)

PITCHING CHAMPIONSHIP HORSESHOES

1970	Walter Piletz	9	0	68.9
1971	Walter Piletz	8	1	57.2
1972	H. Winters	8	3	61.7
1973	Walter Piletz	7	2	61.4

STATE RECORDS

Name of Record	Record Holder	Year Set	Record
Most state championships	William Kolb		12
Most consecutive championships	Lawrence Mahoney		7
Most ringers one game	Joe Zichella	1957	102
Most shoes one game	Joe Zichella and Dale Carson	1956	114
	Joe Zichella and Sol Berman	1957	114
Highest tournament average	Lawrence Mahoney	1940	73.6
Most 4-deads game	Joe Zichella and Dale Carson	1956	23
Most consecutive doubles	Joe Zichella	1956	16
Highest percentage game	John Fulton	1954	90.6
Highest percentage qualifying	William Kolb	1942	81.0

New Jersey

Year	Name of Champion	Won	Lost	Ringer Percentage
1933	Joe Puglise	9	0	36.9
1934	Lawrence Mahoney	9	0	58.0
1935	Lawrence Mahoney	9	0	58.4
1936	Lawrence Mahoney	9	0	67.2
1937	Lawrence Mahoney	9	0	71.5
1938	Lawrence Mahoney	9	0	73.5
1939	Lawrence Mahoney	9	0	67.8
1940	Lawrence Mahoney	9	0	73.6
1941	William Kolb	9	0	73.5
1942	Anthony Scolari	9	0	70.6
1943	No Tournament Held			
1944	No Tournament Held			
1945	No Tournament Held			
1946	No Tournament Held			
1947	Lawrence Mahoney			69.0

(Continued)

STATE CHAMPIONS 235

Year	Champion	Won	Lost	Pct
1948	Lawrence Mahoney			71.0
1949	Douglas Fogal			64.0
1950	William Kolb	7	1	67.0
1951	William Kolb	8	1	68.1
1952	William Kolb	10	1	66.2
1953	William Kolb	7	0	70.8
1954	William Kolb	9	0	63.8
1955	Sol Berman	9	3	63.0
1956	William Kolb	7	0	66.9
1957	Sol Berman	4	1	66.2
1958	Douglas Fogal			62.0
1959	William Kolb	3	0	67.5
1960	Lee Davis	5	0	68.0
1961	William Kolb	5	1	68.9
1962	William Kolb	5	0	
1963	William Kolb	4	0	55.6
1964	Walter Haring			
1965	Sol Berman	5	2	
1966	William Kolb			58.1
1967	Jack Giddes	5	0	67.2
1968	Jack Giddes	5	1	64.2
1969	Sol Berman	5	0	62.8
1970	Sol Berman	6	1	57.9
1971	Jack Giddes	7	0	70.8
1972	Jack Giddes	5	0	66.7
1973	Sol Berman	7	0	67.3

STATE RECORDS

Name of Record	Record Holder	Year Set	Record
High Ringer percentage, tournament	Larry Mahoney	1940	73.6
High ringer percentage, game	Jack Giddes	1972	94.4
Most consecutive doubles	Jack Giddes	1972	15

New Mexico

Year	Name of Champion	Won	Lost	Ringer Percentage
1939	Charles Curran			
1941	John Newell			
1961	P. D. Riley	9	0	54.9
1962	Joe Helms	7	0	60.8

(Continued)

Year	Champion	W	L	Pct
1963	Joe Helms	3	0	
	P. D. Riley	8	0	60.2

(In 1963 two state tournaments were held using the count-all and cancellation scoring systems respectively. Both winners listed)

Year	Champion	W	L	Pct
1964	Joe Helms	6	1	64.5
1965	P. D. Riley	5	0	58.2
1966	Glenn Tassell	6	1	64.7
1967	Tom Towne	7	0	62.4
1968	Joe Robertson	5	1	56.4
1969	Tom Towne	7	0	62.8
1970	Bobby McCharen	6	1	48.9
1971	P. D. Riley	8	0	64.2
1972	P. D. Riley	8	0	60.6
1973	Wayne Springfield	6	1	55.1

STATE RECORDS

Name of Record	Record Holder	Year Set	Record
High ringer percentage, tournament	Glenn Tassell	1965	65.4
Most points, qualifying (50 shoes)	Joe Helms	1963	133
High percentage, qualifying	Joe Helms	1963	84.0

New York

Year	Name of Champion	Won	Lost	Shoes Pitched	Ringers	Ringer Percentage
1921	David T. Leonard					
1922	G. E. Snyder					
1924	David T. Leonard	19	1			32.8
1925	David T. Leonard					38.4
1926	David T. Leonard					41.9
1927	David T. Leonard					47.3
1928	Harold Forbes	11	0			56.4
1929	Frank Niven					53.4
1930	Herbert Grant					49.2
1931	Robert Brown					50.1
1932	Robert Brown	28	2	1608	881	54.8
1933	Harold Seaman					64.8
1934	Don Bickerton					66.0
1935	Robert Brown					71.0
1936	Vito Feliccia					75.2

(Continued)

STATE CHAMPIONS

1937	(no tournament—Vito Feliccia retained title)					
1938	William Hamman					
1939	Carl Steinfeldt					
1940	Carl Steinfeldt					
1942	Tom Brownell					
1942-1947	(no tournament held—war years)					
1948	Tom Brownell					
1949	Vito Feliccia					73.8
1950	Carl Steinfeldt					72.2
1951	Carl Steinfeldt					72.1
1952	Carl Steinfeldt					78.5
1953	Tom Brownell					75.0
1954	Tom Brownell					79.1
1955	Tom Brownell					78.3
1956	Tom Brownell					76.1
1957	Carl Steinfeldt	14	1	952	717	76.5
1958	Carl Steinfeldt					76.1
1959	Anthony Natale	15	0	908	644	70.9
1960	Carl Steinfeldt	15	0			81.1
1961	Anthony Natale	15	0	910	716	78.7
1962	Carl Steinfeldt	9	0			82.2
1963	Steve Fenicchia	6	1			69.9
1964	Carl Steinfeldt	15	0			80.8
1965	Carl Steinfeldt	10	1			76.6
1966	Carl Steinfeldt	11	0			76.5
1967	Carl Steinfeldt	11	0			84.4
1968	Carl Steinfeldt	11	0			80.6
1969	Carl Steinfeldt	11	0			78.8
1970	Carl Steinfeldt	10	0			79.6
1971	Carl Steinfeldt	10	0			82.1
1972	Al Stockholm	10	1			76.7
1973	Carl Steinfeldt	11	0			87.5

STATE RECORDS

Name of Record	Record Holder	Year Set	Record
Highest ringer percentage, one game	Carl Steinfeldt		97.6
High ringer percentage, tournament	Carl Steinfeldt	1973	87.5
Most shoes, one game	Carl Steinfeldt & Tom Brownell		146
Most 4 dead, one game	Carl Steinfeldt & Tom Brownell		38

PITCHING CHAMPIONSHIP HORSESHOES

North Carolina

Year	Name of Champion	Won	Lost	Shoes Pitched	Ringers	Ringer Percentage
1922	E. Z. Jarrett					
1937	Wilson Hill					
1959	Walter A. King	11	0	672	446	66.4
1960	Woody Thomas	9	2	730	416	57.0
1961	Glynden Moore	11	1			70.0
1962	Melvin Howard					
1963	Melvin Howard	7	2	656	436	70.5
1964	Melvin Howard	11	0	748	524	70.2
1965	Darrell Eller	9	0			70.2
1967	James Scotten	7	2			
1968	Gurney York	7	1			59.7
1970	Gurney York	7	2			
1971	Walter King	8	1			

STATE RECORDS

Name of Record	Record Holder	Year	Record
Most points qualifying	Glendon Moore	1965	256
High percentage qualifying	Glendon Moore	1965	79.0

North Dakota

Year	Name of Champion	Won	Lost	Shoes Pitched	Ringers	Ringer Percentage
1922	H. D. Peters					
1923	H. D. Peters					
1924	H. D. Peters	6	0			
1925	L. O. Kelvsen					
1926	Wayne McGee	10	1		204	
1927	J. W. Burkhard	6	1			
1928	Art Engebretson	7	0		151	
1929	Art Engebretson	6	0		102	
1930	No Tournament					
1931	Art Engebretson	7	0		163	

(Continued)

STATE CHAMPIONS

1932	Art Engebretson	11	0	440	251	57.0
1933	Ernolf Roland	11	2	1010	434	42.9
1934	Otto Loseth	10	1		316	
1935	Morris Wold	9	3			
1936	Morris Wold	11	0			
1937	Harold Bomstad	11	2			
1938	Harold Bomstad	11	0			
1939	Bob West	11	0		353	
1940	Bob West	9	2			58.2
1941	Phil Prescott	14	1			
1942	Harold Bomstad	9	0			
1942	O. N. Nordland	7	0		142	
1944	Brown Williams	8	1			
1945	Clarence Nelson	7	2			
1946	Otto Loseth	9	0			
1947	Otto Loseth	9	0			
1948	Quentin Olsen	10	1			
1949	Bill Lybeck	10	1			
1950	Bill Lybeck	10	1		346	
1951	Bill Lybeck	8	1			
1952	Art Engebretson	10	1			
1953	Art Engebretson	10	1		307	
1954	Bob West	10	1		307	
1955	Otto Loseth	7	1		247	
1956	Art Engebretson	11	0	672	397	59.0
1957	Art Engebretson	10	1		419	
1958	Gene Lykken	10	1			61.0
1959	Art Engebretson	8	1	544	319	59.0
1960	Art Engebretson	9	0			65.0
1961	Art Engebretson	9	0	446	318	71.3
1962	Gene Lykken	9	0			64.3
1963	Art Engebretson	8	1			
1964	Art Engebretson	8	1			64.0
1965	Art Engebretson	9	0			60.0
1966	Wally Rislov	9	1			52.5
1967	Art Engebretson	8	1			66.7
1968	Art Engebretson	8	1			67.1
1969	Lee Sharff	8	1			56.0
1970	Lee Sharff	8	1			58.8
1971	Gene Lykken	9	0			62.5
1972	Jerry Black	8	1	532	363	68.2
1973	Harvey Peterson	7	0	472	288	61.0

PITCHING CHAMPIONSHIP HORSESHOES 240

STATE RECORDS

Name of Record	Record Holder	Year	Record
Highest qualifying percentage	Bill Lybeck	1955	70.0
Most points qualifying	Art Engebretson	1959	469
Highest percentage game	Art Engebretson	1932	81.2
Highest percentage tournament	Art Engebretson	1961	71.3

Ohio

Year	Name of Champion	Won	Lost	Shoes Pitched	Ringers	Ringer Percentage
1915	Charles Roy Cox					
1916	Frank Eachus					
1919	George May					
1921	Ira Wolf					
1922	Loren May					
1923	Loren May					
1924	Loren May					
1929	Harry Collins					
1930	Bert Duryee					
1931	Bert Duryee	23	1	1276	913	71.5
1932	Bert Duryee					
1933	Blair Nunnemaker					
1934	Blair Nunnemaker					
1935	Blair Nunnemaker					
1936	Blair Nunnemaker					
1937-1940	No tournaments held					
1941	Grover Hawley	15	0	1200	885	73.8
1943	Grover Hawley					
1944	Grover Hawley					
1945	Grover Hawley					
1946	John Sebek	15	0	750	601	80.1
1947	Robert Cash	13	2	750	550	73.3
1948	Ralph Lackey	18	1	912	695	76.2
1948	Russell Yaus—Second meet held in 1948. Both NHPA Sanctioned					
1949	Grover Hawley					
1950	Ralph Lackey	18	1			72.4
1951	Ralph Lackey	17	2			70.6
1952	Ralph Lackey	12	3	1042	733	70.3
1953	Paul Focht	24	1	1210	870	71.9

(Continued)

STATE CHAMPIONS

Year	Champion	Won	Lost	Shoes Pitched	Ringers	Ringer %
1954	Harold Reno	14	1	956	714	74.6
1955	Stan Manker	14	1	914	610	66.7
1956	Harold Reno	14	1	868	671	77.6
1957	Harold Reno	15	0	808	615	76.1
1958	Harold Reno	12	1	762	593	77.8
1959	Harold Reno	13	0	736	597	81.1
1960	Harold Reno	13	0	754	609	80.7
1961	Harold Reno	11	0	698	591	84.7
1962	Paul Focht	10	1	794	624	79.0
1963	Paul Focht	11	0	878	725	82.5
1964	Harold Reno	11	0	740	656	88.6
1965	Glenn Riffle	10	1	854	658	77.0
1966	Harold Reno	10	1	734	611	83.2
1967	Harold Reno	9	2	904	732	80.9
1968	James Knisley	12	1	972	792	81.4
1969	Harold Reno	10	1	890	721	81.0
1970	Wilbur Kabel	11	0	854	689	80.6
1971	Wilbur Kabel	11	0	722	583	80.8
1972	Donnie Roberts	10	1	922	751	81.5
1973	Wilbur Kabel	11	0	734	584	79.6

STATE RECORDS

Name of Record	Record Holder	Year Set	Record
High ringer percentage, tournament	Harold Reno	1964	88.6
High ringer percentage, game	Harold Reno	1960 & 1961	93.1
High ringer percentage, qualifying	Paul Focht	1972	93.0
Most points, qualifying	Paul Focht	1972	285
Most shoes, game	Wilbur Kabel & Donnie Roberts	1972	144

Oklahoma

Year	Name of Champion	Won	Lost	Shoes Pitched	Ringers	Ringer Percentage
1920-1930	Ralph Kelly Spencer					
1937	Albert Valentine	9	0			
1942	Ralph Randall	7	0			55.0

(Continued)

PITCHING CHAMPIONSHIP HORSESHOES

1943	Ralph Randall	7	0	338	184	54.4
1944	W. F. Towne					
1945	W. F. Towne					
1946	Ralph Randall					
1947	W. F. Towne					
1948	Loy Ross					
1949	Mr. Lee	8	1	468	236	50.4
1950	Ralph Randall	6	1	410	252	61.5
1951	Loy Ross	7	0	362	238	67.2
1952	Loy Ross	7	0	352	221	62.5
1953	Loy Ross	8	1	556	343	61.5
1954	Loy Ross	11	0	576	373	64.3
1955	Loy Ross	11	0			67.0
1956	Wallace Uhlig	8	0	318	216	68.0
1957	Wallace Uhlig	8	0	442	273	61.8
1958	Wallace Uhlig	7	0	378	256	67.7
1959	Charles Schrum	5	0	308	179	58.1
1960	Charles Schrum	4	1	528	300	56.8
1961	Andy Mogus	7	0	314	188	59.9
1962	Andy Mogus	6	1			65.6
1963	Andy Mogus	4	1			63.8
1964	Andy Mogus	4	1	236	157	66.5
1965	Andy Mogus	5	0	316	209	66.1
1966	Bill Muirheid	4	1			60.8
1967	Bill Muirheid	5	1			54.1
1968	Charles Schrum	4	1			62.2
1969	Andy Mogus	5	0			64.3
1970	Andy Mogus					57.2
1971	Charles Brewer	5	1			57.6
1972	Andy Mogus	7	0			62.2
1973	Andy Mogus	6	0			65.5

STATE RECORDS

Name of Record	Record Holder	Year Set	Record
Highest ringer percentage qualifying	Wallace Uhlig	1954	79.0
Most points qualifying	Wallace Uhlig	1954	255
Highest ringer percentage one game	Charles Schrum	1961	75.0
Highest ringer percentage one tournament	Wallace Uhlig	1956	68.0

(Continued)

STATE CHAMPIONS 243

Most shoes one tournament	Hardy Young	1954	704
Most ringers one game	Earl Wall	1961	51
Most ringers one tournament	Loy Ross	1954	373
Most shoes one game	Schrum vs Gerald Kahle	1961	82
Most 4 dead one game	Schrum vs Earl Wall	1961	5

Oregon

Year	Name of Champion	Won	Lost	Shoes Pitched	Ringers	Ringer Percentage
1923	R. R. Chapman					
1924	W. H. Hayden					
1925	W. H. Hayden					
1926	W. H. Hayden					
1927	W. H. Hayden					
1928	Henry McGrew					45.5
1929	W. H. Hayden					
1930	Henry Graham					
1931	Leon Jenkins					
1932	Ted Allen					71.5
1933	Hilmer Pell					61.0
1934	Otto Johnson					72.4
1935	Otto Johnson					
1936	Otto Johnson					
1937	W. H. Hayden					
1938	Hilmer Pell					
1939	Hilmer Pell					59.6
1940	W. H. Hayden					61.0
1941	Cletus Chapelle					
1942	Lee Wright					
1943	Cletus Chapelle					
1944	Prescott Kaufman					
1945	Otto Johnson					
1946	Ray Parker					
1947	Cletus Chapelle					
1948	Roy Getchell					
1949	Irving Schaumburg					
1950	Cletus Chapelle					
1951	Roy Getchell					
1952	Roy Getchell					
1953	Roy Getchell					

Year	Champion	W	L	SP	R	%
1954	Bryant Hampton					
1955	Bryant Hampton					
1956	Eldon Harvey					
1957	Bob West	9	0	584	428	73.3
1958	Bob West	7	0	470	366	77.9
1959	Bob West	7	0	428	324	75.7
1960	Bob West	8	1	714	528	73.9
1961	Eldon Harvey	5	1			
1962	Bob West	7	0	568	404	71.1
1963	Eldon Harvey	7	0			73.2
1964	Lauren Hill	7	1	636	454	71.4
1965	Lowell Davis					72.9
1966	Bob West	6	1	458	331	72.4
1967	Bob West	6	1	468	368	78.6
1968	Bob West	9	0	594	456	76.7
1969	Bob West	9	0	580	460	80.3
1970	Bob West	9	0			84.6
1971	Bob West	9	0			79.7
1972	Bob West	11	0	652	530	81.2
1973	Jim Burke	11	0	914	692	75.7

STATE RECORDS

Name of Record	Record	Year Set	Record Holder
High ringer percentage, qualifying (50 shoes)	142 pts.	1962	Barney Hampton
High ringer percentage, one game	90.5	1969	Bob West
High ringer percentage, one tournament	80.3	1969	Bob West

Pennsylvania

Year	Name of Champion	Won	Lost	Shoes Pitched	Ringers	Ringer Percentage
1922	Roy Fouriner					
1927	Merwin George					
1931	George Curry					
1933	Stewart Straw					
1934	Steve Menrchik					
1935	John Fulton					
1936	John Fulton					

(Continued)

STATE CHAMPIONS

1937	George Curry	10	1			68.3
1938	John Fulton					
1940	John Fulton					69.0
1942-1946 (no tournament held)						
1947	John Fulton					
1948	Ivan Lute					
1949	John Fulton					75.0
1950	John Clingan					66.3
1951	John Fulton					70.4
1953	John Fulton	6	1			72.5
1954	John Fulton	7	0			75.9
1955	John Fulton	6	1			72.0
1956	James Ohler					
1957	James Ohler	8	1			74.4
1958	James Ohler					
1959	James Ohler	16	1	1000	718	71.8
1960	John Fulton	14	1	1018	769	75.6
1961	James Ohler	18	1			76.1
1962	James Ohler	13	2			74.5
1963	James Ohler	15	0			79.9
1964	Jim Solomon	15	0			81.2
1965	Al Zadroga	15	0			78.5
1966	Dan Kuchcinski					82.7
1967	Dan Kuchcinski	15	0			82.3
1968	Oscar Engle	14	1			75.6
1969	Al Zadroga	13	0			78.6
1970	Clyde Martz	15	0			81.6
1971	Buck Engle	15	1			80.2
1972	Al Zadroga	14	1			81.6
1973	Clyde Martz	14	1			81.6

STATE RECORDS

Name of Record	Record Holder	Year Set	Record
Highest percentage, tournament	Dan Kuchcinski	1966	82.7
Highest percentage, game	Jim Solomon	1963	95.0

Rhode Island

Year	Name of Champion	Won	Lost	Ringer Percentage
1925	Albert Hudson			40.8
1926	John Potter			45.6
1927	Howard Hutchens			51.3
1928	John Kilpeck			50.4
1929	George Clairess			53.7
1930	John Kilpeck			51.6
1931	Howard Huchens			54.0
1932	Howard Huchens			53.9
1933	Howard Huchens			55.2
1934	Howard Huchens			60.7
1935	Pete Heroux			67.3
1936	Kenneth Hurst	6	1	69.1
1937	Kenneth Hurst			71.3
1938	Kenneth Hurst			73.5
1939	Kenneth Hurst	9	0	72.6
1940	Kenneth Hurst			75.8
1947	Pete Heroux			65.2
1948	Pete Heroux			64.1
1949	Pete Heroux			67.7
1950	Roy Pearson			64.2
1951	Roy Pearson			66.3
1952	Pete Heroux	6	1	68.3
1953	Roy Pearson			65.0
1954	Pete Heroux	7	0	67.2
1955	Pete Heroux			69.8
1956	H. Al Bourgeois			58.3
1957	Leo Lacroix			60.2
1958	Leo Lacroix			59.7
1959	H. Al Bourgeois	6	1	58.9
1960	H. Al Bourgeois			61.6
1961	H. Al Bourgeois	7	0	60.6
1962	H. Al Bourgeois	8	1	58.7
1963	George Collard	7	0	68.0
1964	H. Al Bourgeois	6	1	69.2
1965	George Collard	7	0	73.8
1966	No tournament held			
1967	H. Al Bourgeois			74.1
1968-69	No tournament held			
1970	H. Al Bourgeois			
1971	H. Al Bourgeois	6	0	58.9
1972	H. Al Bourgeois			
1973	Ray Rylands	7	0	52.6

STATE CHAMPIONS

STATE RECORDS

Name of Record	Record Holder	Year Set	Record
Highest percentage tournament	Kenneth Hurst	1940	75.8
Youngest state champion	Kenneth Hurst	1936	14

South Carolina

Year	Name of Champion	Won	Lost	Ringer Percentage
1970	Marshall Bryant	8	1	60.2
1971	Bill Gibby	7	0	47.5

South Dakota

Year	Name of Champion	Won	Lost	Shoes Pitched	Ringers	Ringer Percentage
1924	Frances Jones					
1925	Frances Jones					
1926	Verne Erickson					
1927	Verne Erickson					
1929	William Curts					
1930	Frances Jones					
1931	Joe Sauco					
1932	Pete Olson					
1933	H. M. Christensen					
1934	Leigh Dunker	9	2			
1935	Leigh Dunker	11	0			
1936	Leigh Dunker (No games. All entrants pitched 100 shoes)					77.0
1937	George Paulson	10	1	732	345	47.0
1938	Leigh Dunker	10	1	572	345	60.3
1939	Leigh Dunker	11	0	536	351	65.4
1940	Leigh Dunker	15	0	673	480	71.2
1941	Arnold Christensen	23	0			59.1
1942	Leigh Dunker	19	0	862	581	67.3
1943	Leigh Dunker (Retained Title—No Meet—World War II)					
1944	Leigh Dunker (Retained Title—No Meet—World War II)					
1945	Leigh Dunker (Retained Title—No Meet—World War II)					

(Continued)

PITCHING CHAMPIONSHIP HORSESHOES

1946	Leigh Dunker	16	0	703	480	68.0
1947	Leigh Dunker	15	0	704	413	58.5
1948	Leigh Dunker	(Retained Title—No Meet Held)				
1949	Leigh Dunker	(Retained Title—No Meet Held)				
1950	Leigh Dunker	9	0	384	255	66.5
1951	Leigh Dunker					
1952	Leigh Dunker	9	0			
1953	Glen Morris	13	0			
1954	Leigh Dunker	7	0	312	214	68.5
1955	Leigh Dunker	7	0	326	197	60.0
1956	Leigh Dunker	9	0	452	310	68.4
1957	Lloyd Swartwout	11	0	688	457	66.4
1958	Leigh Dunker	10	0	508	331	65.0
1959	Lloyd Swartwout	11	0	658	399	60.0
1960	Leigh Dunker	11	0	608	406	67.0
1961	Leigh Dunker	10	1	616	397	64.4
1962	Walter Finkbohn	11	0			64.5
1963	Leigh Dunker	12	0			64.0
1964	Arnold Christensen	7	1			63.8
1965	Arnold Christensen	9	2			61.8
1966	Arnold Christensen	11	0			62.9
1967	Leigh Dunker	11	0			64.9
1968	Walter Finkbohn	11	1			59.3
1969	Lloyd Swartwout	15	0			71.1
1970	Leigh Dunker	10	1			62.3
1971	Leigh Dunker	8	1			70.5
1972	Leigh Dunker	9	0			71.1
1973	Leigh Dunker	9	0			73.1

STATE RECORDS

Name of Record	Record Holder	Year Set	Record
Highest ringer percentage, qualifying	Leigh Dunker	1940	84.0
Highest ringer percentage, game	Leigh Dunker	1940	87.0
High ringer percentage, tournament	Leigh Dunker	1973	73.1
Most ringers, game	Leigh Dunker	1960	72
Most four-deads, game	Leigh Dunker and Lloyd Swartwout	1960	15
Most consecutive four-deads	Leigh Dunker and Lloyd Swartwout	1960	5

STATE CHAMPIONS

Tennessee

Year	Name of Champion	Won	Lost	Shoes Pitched	Ringers	Ringer Percentage
1924	H. R. Baker					49.5
1925	Asa G. Atnip					
1926	J. L. Amos					
1927	J. L. Amos					
1928	J. L. Amos					
1934	Miff Nave					
1935	Miff Nave					
1936	Miff Nave					
1937	Miff Nave					
1945	Temple Jarrell					
1946	John LeBow					
1958	O. D. LeBow					
1959	O. D. LeBow					
1960	Charles Fortenberry					
1961	Charles Fortenberry					
1962	Rogers Norwood					
1963	Charles Fortenberry	6	0			76.3
1964	Charles Fortenberry	6	1			68.5
1965	Charles Fortenberry					73.3
1966	Rogers Norwood	5	0			71.8
1967	Rogers Norwood					71.3
1968	Charles Jarnigan	5	0			73.8
1969	James Burns	11	0	768	589	76.6
1970	James Burns	11	0	742	568	76.6
1971	James Burns	10	1	662	496	74.9
1972	Harley McCamey	10	1	606	421	69.9
1973	Rogers Norwood	9	2	596	440	73.8

STATE RECORDS

Name of Record	Record Holder	Year Set	Record
High ringer percentage, tournament	James Burns	1969	76.6
High ringer percentage, game	James Burns	1972	90.0
Most shoes, game	James Burns & Rogers Norwood	1969	118
Fewest shoes, game	James Burns & Clyde Kersey	1970	30
Most ringers, game	James Burns	1969	94
Most 4-deads, game	Harley McCamey & Dexter Stallings	1973	19
Most consecutive 4-deads	Harley McCamey & Dexter Stallings	1973	7

PITCHING CHAMPIONSHIP HORSESHOES 250
Texas

Year	Name of Champion	Won	Lost	Ringer Percentage
1923	B. E. Strode			
1924	B. E. Strode			
1937	Shirley Donnell			
1938	Ralph Travis			
1939	Ralph Travis			
1940	Ralph Travis			
1941	Ralph Travis			
1942	Louis Mettlach			
1943	Louis Mettlach			
1944	B. E. Sipple			
1945	E. J. McFarland			
1946	E. J. McFarland			
1947	E. J. McFarland			
1948	E. J. McFarland			
1949	E. J. McFarland	5	0	58.9
1950	E. J. McFarland			
1951	E. J. McFarland			
1952	E. J. McFarland			
1953	E. J. McFarland			
1954	E. J. McFarland	9	1	57.2
1955	E. J. McFarland	9	0	61.0
1956	E. J. McFarland			
1957	E. J. McFarland	11	0	61.5
1958	P. D. Riley			
1959	Marvin Burgess	8	1	
1960	Matt Bowers	9	1	45.6
1961	Marvin Burgess	5	1	43.1
1962	J. W. Cash	6	1	43.2
1963	Marvin Burgess	3	0	
1964	Marvin Burgess	3	1	37.3
1965	Marvin Burgess	6	0	62.5
1966	Marvin Burgess	6	0	54.0
1967	Marvin Burgess	5	1	58.1
1968	Jim Woodson	8	2	54.0
1969	Marvin Burgess	8	1	54.5
1970	Marvin Burgess	9	1	47.8
1971	Bob Graham	10	1	61.6
1972	Ed McFarland	7	1	63.2
1973	Rod Hatton	10	0	63.0

Utah

Year	Name of Champion	Won	Lost	Shoes Pitched	Ringers	Ringer Percentage
1927	J. Waymarr					
1928	J. L. Healy					
1929	J. Webb					
1930	Ed Ramshaw					
1931	Mr. Mitchell					
1932	Oscar Hunsaker					
1933	George Greener	9	0	522	348	66.6
1934	Willard Anderson					
1935	Arthur Thomas	10	0			75.0
1936-1939	(no tournament held)					
1940	Art Dittman					
1941	William Brinkley					
1942	Bruce Walters					
1943	Leo Rollick					
1944	Ed Beardsley					
1945	Cherry Bennett					
1946	Ray Ohlms					
1947	Bruce Walters					
1948	Ray Ohlms					
1949	Ray Ohlms					
1950	Ray Ohlms					
1951	Ray Ohlms					
1952	Ray Ohlms					
1953	Ray Ohlms					
1954	Ray Ohlms					
1955	Clive Wahlin					
1956	Clive Wahlin					
1957	Clive Wahlin	15	0			78.2
1958	Clive Wahlin					
1959	Clive Wahlin	7	0			77.0
1960	Clive Wahlin					
1961	Milton Tate	7	0			72.4
1962	Clive Wahlin	5	0			
1963	Clive Wahlin	7	0			80.0
1964	Roger Parsons	11	0	410	331	80.7
1965	Clive Wahlin					
1966	Clive Wahlin	5	0			70.1
1967	Clive Wahlin	11	0			77.2

(Continued)

PITCHING CHAMPIONSHIP HORSESHOES 252

1968	Clive Wahlin	10	1	662	434	65.6
1969	Alma Madsen	10	1	768	451	58.7
1970	Alma Madsen	9	2			53.8
1971	Elwood Scott	11	1			55.9
1972	Clive Wahlin	8	0			68.5
1973	Clive Wahlin	11	0			71.6

Vermont

Year	Name of Champion	Won	Lost	Shoes Pitched	Ringers	Ringer Percentage
1939	Maynard Brown	11	0			56.0
1940	Frank Baker	11	0			49.0
1941	Fred Butler	11	0			60.0
1942	Fred Butler	11	0			62.0
1943	Fred Butler	11	0			65.0
1944	Fred Butler	Retained Title—No tournament				
1945	Fred Butler	Retained Title—No tournament				
1946	Fred Butler	10	1			60.0
1947	Maynard Brown	10	1			54.0
1948	Maynard Brown	10	1			58.0
1949	Ted Saasville	10	1			54.0
1950	Maynard Brown	11	0			62.0
1951	Maynard Brown	11	0			67.5
1952	Maynard Brown	11	0			65.0
1953	Maynard Brown	10	1			67.8
1954	Maynard Brown	11	0			69.3
1955	Fred Butler					50.9
1956	Maynard Brown					62.2
1957	Roland Fisher	8	1			57.2
1958	Fred Butler	8	1			56.2
1959	Fred Butler					58.5
1960	Fred Butler					62.5
1961	Fred Butler	7	0			58.5
1962	Fred Butler	7	0			52.2
1963	Fred Butler	6	1			55.3
1964	Fred Butler	6	1			
1965	Maynard Brown	7	0			70.6
1966	Maynard Brown	6	1			66.5
1967	Lewis "Pete" Prouty	7	0	450	287	63.6
1968	Lewis "Pete" Prouty	7	0	408	260	63.7
1969	Maynard Brown	7	0			59.7

(Continued)

STATE CHAMPIONS 253

1970	Maynard Brown	6	1			55.9
1971	Robert Chapman	7	1			54.3
1972	Lewis "Pete" Prouty	7	0			67.1
1973	Lewis "Pete" Prouty	7	0			67.7

STATE RECORDS

Name of Record	Record Holder	Year	Record
High ringer percentage, game	Maynard Brown	1951	83.3
High ringer percentage, tournament	Maynard Brown	1965	70.6
Most 4-deads, game	Maynard Brown and Fred Butler		9

Virginia

Year	Name of Champion	Won	Lost	Shoes Pitched	Ringers	Ringer Percentage
1929	Alex Kirchner	11	0			
1930	Clayton C. Henson	11	0			
1931	Charles C. Darr	11	0			
1932	Clayton C. Henson	11	0			
1933	George C. Thompson	11	0			
1934	Raymond L. Frye	11	0			
1935	Raymond L. Frye	11	0			
1936	Clayton C. Henson	11	0			
1937	Raymond L. Frye	11	0			72.0
1938	Clayton C. Henson	11	0			
1939	Clayton C. Henson	11	0			
1940	Clayton C. Henson	11	0			76.4
1941	Clayton C. Henson	11	0			
1942	Clayton C. Henson	15	0	708	559	79.0
1943	Clayton C. Henson					
1944	Clayton C. Henson					
1945	Clayton C. Henson					
1946	Clayton C. Henson					
1947	Clayton C. Henson					
1948	Clayton C. Henson					
1949	Clayton C. Henson					
1950	Raymond L. Frye					
1951–1956	No tournaments held.					
1957	J. B. Barnes					
1958	Robert Toney					
1959	W. R. Flaherty	11	1			52.2

(Continued)

CLAYTON C. HENSON
Virginia

Clayton C. Henson of Virginia is one of the all time greats of horseshoe pitching. Henson won the Virginia State Title 15 times and the Metropolitan Washington D. C. title 34 times. His 79% ringers for the 15 game round robin in the 1942 state tournament is still the state record. He tied for ninth in the World Tournament in 1941, served as an NHPA officer and has pitched many exhibitions. The 1974 season is his 52nd year of organization play.

STATE CHAMPIONS 255

Year	Champion	W	L	Shoes	Ringers	Pct
1960	W. M. Owen					
1961	Robert Toney	14	1	818	445	54.4
1962	L. E. Templeton	15	0	772	507	68.3
1963	Cecil Monday	13	2	866	569	65.7
1964	Robert Toney	11	1	634	436	68.8
1965	Robert Toney	9	0	406	295	72.7
1966	Robert Toney	14	0			65.0
1967	Cecil Monday	11	0	710	512	72.1
1968	Frank Monday	14	1			63.9
1969	Charles Price	13	0	796	560	70.4
1970	Cecil Monday	11	0	616	418	67.9
1971	Cecil Monday	15	0			71.3
1972	Cecil Monday	13	0	800	595	74.4
1973	Cecil Monday	14	1	904	673	74.4

STATE RECORDS

Name of Record	Record Holder	Year Set	Record
High ringer percentage, tournament	Clayton C. Henson	1942	79.0
High ringer percentage, game	Charles Price	1972	87.5
High ringer percentage, qualifying	Tommie Ballowe	1971	82.0
Most points, qualifying	Tommie Ballowe	1971	262
Most shoes, game	Jack Walker & Doc Good	1972	110
Most shoes, tournament	Charles Price	1969	1054
Most ringers, game	Tommie Ballowe	1967	83
Most ringers, tournament	Charles Price	1969	760
High percentage game by loser	Frank Monday	1973	75.0

Washington

Year	Name of Champion	Won	Lost	Shoes Pitched	Ringers	Ringer Percentage
1925	Floyd Sayre	21	2	1168	599	51.3
1926	Floyd Sayre					62.0
1927	Floyd Sayre					64.0
1928	Henry Tessandore	21	2	1340	687	53.3
1929	Ray Ashcraft	18	2	1138	615	54.0
1930	Ray Ashcraft	15	0	900	506	56.2
1931	Floyd Sayre	15	0	704	486	69.0
1932	Floyd Sayre	14	1	934	633	67.8
1933	Roy Getchell	14	1	838	546	65.1

(Continued)

PITCHING CHAMPIONSHIP HORSESHOES

1934	Roy Getchell	12	3	926	635	68.5
1935	Lewis Getchell	23	8	1458	1007	69.1
1936	Harold Oakes					62.7
1937	Prescott Kaufman	13	2	916	611	65.2
1938	Prescott Kaufman	14	1	950	599	63.0
1939	Oscar Lee	13	2	918	537	59.0
1940	Prescott Kaufman	13	0	706	517	73.2
1941	Charles Davis	8	3	694	403	56.8
1942-1944 (no tournament held)						
1945	Lewis Getchell	13	2			61.0
1946	Lewis Getchell	15	0			70.0
1947	Prescott Kaufman	15	0			67.0
1948	Lewis Getchell	12	3			67.1
1949	John Monasmith	13	2	964	622	64.5
1950	Lewis Getchell	13	2			66.2
1951	Lewis Getchell	15	0			71.2
1952	John Monasmith	14	1			70.7
1953	John Monasmith	15	0			78.1
1954	John Monasmith	14	1			70.2
1955	John Monasmith	15	0			74.7
1956	John Monasmith	14	1			73.5
1957	John Monasmith	15	0			78.7
1958	John Monasmith	15	0			76.5
1959	Ed Fishel	15	0			78.2
1960	John Monasmith	15	1	881	707	80.2
1961	John Monasmith	15	0	822	659	80.1
1962	John Monasmith	15	0	874	709	80.2
1963	Ed Fishel	15	0	930	712	76.6
1964	John Monasmith	15	0	872	703	80.6
1965	John Monasmith	15	0	852	650	76.3
1966	Henry Knauft	13	1	1002	804	80.2
1967	John Monasmith	14	0	960	776	80.8
1968	John Monasmith	13	1	916	714	77.9
1969	Henry Knauft	12	2	1000	751	75.1
1970	Henry Knauft	14	0	840	657	78.2
1971	Henry Knauft	14	0	856	650	75.9
1972	Henry Knauft	14	0	904	697	77.1
1973	Joe Krug	13	1	940	710	75.5

STATE RECORDS

Name of Record	Record	Year Set	Record Holder
Highest ringer percentage, qualifying	91.0	1964	Henry Knauft

STATE CHAMPIONS 257

Most points, qualifying	280	1964	Henry Knauft
Highest ringer percentage, one game	97.2	1966	John Monasmith
Highest ringer percentage, one tournament	84.0	1966	John Monasmith
Most shoes, one game	124	1961	Monasmith & Fishel
		1966	Monasmith & Knauft
Most shoes, one tournament	1340	1928	Henry Tessandore
Most ringers, one game	105	1966	Henry Knauft
Most ringers, one tournament	820	1967	Ed Fishel
Most 4 dead, one game	34	1966	Monasmith & Knauft
Most consecutive doubles	25	1973	Henry Knauft

West Virginia

Year	Name of Champion	Won	Lost	Shoes Pitched	Ringers	Ringer Percentage
1931	Emmett Van Pelt					
1935	Ralph Maddox	9	0	422	237	56.0
1936	Grover Anderson	9	0	446	264	59.0
1937	Grover Anderson	9	0	494	297	60.0
1938	Grover Anderson	9	0	466	304	65.0
1939	Grover Anderson	9	0	518	342	66.0
1940	Grover Anderson	9	0	538	367	68.0
1941	Grover Anderson	8	1	376	204	54.0
1942-1945 (no tournament held)						
1946	Grover Anderson	9	0	508	300	59.5
1947	Grover Anderson	9	1	562	367	65.5
1948	Ralph Maddox	7	0	354	227	64.0
1949	Arner Lindquist					
1950	Arner Lindquist					
1951	Ralph Maddox	9	0			70.8
1952	Ralph Maddox	8	1			69.7
1953	Arner Lindquist	8	1			65.6
1954	Ralph Maddox	11	0			63.2
1955	Ralph Maddox	9	0			70.7
1956	Arner Lindquist	8	0			66.5
1957	Arner Lindquist	10	1			58.7
1958	Ralph Maddox					
1959	Ralph Maddox	8	1			
1960	Ralph Maddox	11	0			76.2

(Continued)

Year	Name	W	L	Pct
1961	Ralph Maddox	10	1	74.1
1962	Ralph Maddox	9	0	76.4
1963	Andy Deem	9	0	75.0
1964	Ralph Maddox	15	0	78.0
1965	Ralph Maddox	11	0	81.0
1966	Andy Deem	10	0	74.8
1967	Ralph Maddox	9	0	75.7
1968	Howard Shriver	9	0	78.7
1969	Howard Shriver	8	1	72.5
1970	Ralph Maddox	9	0	78.5
1973	Frank Boggess	10	1	64.8

STATE RECORDS

Name of Record	Record	Year Set	Record Holder
Highest ringer % qualifying	87.0	1966	Andy Deem
Highest qualifying score	272	1966	Andy Deem
Highest ringer % one tournament	81.0	1965	Ralph Maddox

Wisconsin

Year	Name of Champion	Won	Lost	Shoes Pitched	Ringers	Ringer Percentage
1923	Ed Mitchell					
1924	Seymour Johnson					
1925	Floyd Billings					
1926	Harvey Elmerson					
1927	Harvey Elmerson					
1928	Harvey Elmerson					
1929	Harvey Elmerson					
1930	Harvey Elmerson					
1931	Harvey Elmerson	11	0	570	398	69.8
1932	Harold Sheets					
1933	Harold Sheets					
1934	Harvey Elmerson					
1935	Casey Jones					
1936	Casey Jones	15	0			
1937	Casey Jones					
1938	Casey Jones	11	0	1020	845	82.8
1939	Casey Jones					
1940	Casey Jones					

(Continued)

STATE CHAMPIONS

1941	Harvey Elmerson					
1942	Casey Jones	10	1	680	491	72.2
1943	Harvey Elmerson					
1944	Casey Jones					
1945	Casey Jones					85.2
1946	Casey Jones					
1947	Mike Barachy					
1948	Casey Jones					
1949	Tommy Bartlen					
1950	Casey Jones	15	0			
1951	Casey Jones					
1952	Casey Jones					
1953	Tommy Bartlen	10	1			69.7
1954	Casey Jones					
1955	Earl Ramquist					
1956	Carl Pfeffer					
1957	Tommy Bartlen	10	1			
1958	Carl Pfeffer					
1959	Tommy Barlen	11	0			56.9
1960	Ed Schimek					
1961	Casey Jones	9	2			67.0
1962	Ed Schimek	11	0			
1963	Ed Schimek	9	2			
1964	Wally Saeger	10	1			
1965	Tommy Bartlen	9	2			
1966	Carl Joppe					
1967	Tommy Bartlen	9	2			56.4
1968	Bill Glass	11	0			69.4
1969	Bill Glass	10	1			67.6
1970	Bill Glass	10	1			73.5
1971	Bill Glass	8	1			73.6
1972	Ralph Maylahn	6	0			73.1
1973	Harold Sheets	6	1			65.4

STATE RECORDS

Name of Record	Record Holder	Year Set	Record
High ringer percentage, tournament	Casey Jones	1945	85.2
High ringer percentage, qualifying	Casey Jones	1942	90.0
Most points, qualifying	Casey Jones	1942	278

PITCHING CHAMPIONSHIP HORSESHOES 260

Wyoming

Year	Name of Champion	Won	Lost	Shoes Pitched	Ringers	Ringer Percentage
1931	Harold Pence					50.0
1932	Clarence Carlson					
1933	Clarence Carlson					
1934	Clarence Carlson					
1935	Clarence Carlson	12	0			60.4
1936	L. W. Forsyth	6	0			52.7
1937	Jack Jones	6	0	370	161	43.5
1938	Merle C. Palmer	6	1	400	186	46.5
1939	Shell Patton	9	2			60.1
1940	Merle C. Palmer	11	0	678	442	65.1
1941	Merle C. Palmer	5	1	366	225	61.8
1942	Merle C. Palmer	6	0	404	232	57.7
1943	Merle C. Palmer	Retained title—No Meet—World War II				
1944	Merle C. Palmer	Retained title—No Meet—World War II				
1945	Merle C. Palmer	Retained title—No Meet—World War II				
1946	Shell Patton	12	2			57.2
1947	John Rutz	11	2			56.7
1948	Merle C. Palmer	7	0	404	240	60.8
1949	Merle C. Palmer	7	0	354	236	67.2
1950	Merle C. Palmer	8	1	450	323	71.8
1951	Merle C. Palmer	7	0	302	196	64.9
1952	Merle C. Palmer	11	0	562	350	62.3
1953	Merle C. Palmer	5	1	302	197	47.8
1954	Merle C. Palmer	14	1	724	434	59.9
1955	Merle C. Palmer	11	0	588	374	63.6
1956	Merle C. Palmer	10	3	780	485	62.2
1957	Merle C. Palmer	11	1	680	447	65.7
1958	Shell Patton	7	0			60.0
1959	Merle C. Palmer	9	1	752	495	65.8
1960	Merle C. Palmer	10	2	792	503	63.5
1961	L. W. Forsyth	8	2			62.0
1962	Shell Patton	9	1			62.6
1963	Merle C. Palmer	9	1	634	434	68.6
1964	Lee Laughlin	9	1	648	373	57.6
1965	Ted Chase	7	0	416	222	53.4
1966	Nestor Miller	12	2	802	414	51.6
1967	Merle C. Palmer	12	2	820	530	64.9
1968	Nestor Miller	11	2	696	391	56.2
1969	Lee Laughlin	8	2	650	358	55.1

(Continued)

STATE CHAMPIONS

1970	Merle C. Palmer	8	0	622	355	57.1
1971	Merle C. Palmer	11	1	650	395	60.8
1972	Merle C. Palmer	9	1	538	321	59.7
1973	Lavern J. German	6	2	592	251	42.4

STATE RECORDS

Name of Record	Record Holder	Year Set	Record
High ringer percentage, tournament	Merle C. Palmer	1950	71.8
Most shoes, game	W. H. Arnold and Nestor Miller	1968	94
Most state championships	Merle C. Palmer	1972	24
Most consecutive state championships	Merle C. Palmer	1957	10

13

World Tournament Records

Frank Jackson, sometimes called the Father of Horseshoes or the Grand Old Man of Horseshoes, claimed that he was Champion of the World 13 times. Jackson was born in 1870 in Iowa. He had this much in common with Satchel Paige, the great Negro baseball pitcher; he was born too soon. Jackson was born before horseshoe pitching was properly organized and was 39 years old before the first tournament was held that had any semblance of being a world meet. By the time the NHPA came into being, Frank was 51. In addition to his world titles, Jackson put horseshoe pitching on the map, so to speak, by touring the country with his sons, putting on exhibitions. The tales of Jackson's feats, his adjustment to all rule changes, and his domination of the game during his prime years made him a legend. Jackson retired from horseshoes in 1935 at the age of 65.

The first so-called World Tournament was held at Bronson, Kansas, in 1909. It was staged by the promoter of a colt show in connection with his show and it is impossible to tell how widely this meet was advertised. At any rate, Frank Jackson won this meet and was awarded a championship belt. While no records are available, it is fairly certain that Jackson defended his title in 1910, 1911, 1912, 1913 and 1914 in tournaments held in Kansas.

He won the first official World Tournament sanctioned by the Grand League of the American Horseshoe Pitchers' Association in 1915 at Kansas City, Kansas. His record was 24 victories and one defeat.

No meets were held in 1916, 1917 or 1918, but Jackson retained his title.

In 1919 a tournament was held in St. Petersburg, Florida, and for the first time the stakes were 40 feet apart as they are now. Fred Brust of Columbus, Ohio, who later established the Ohio Horseshoe Company, won the meet with a 53-1 record. It was following this tournament that representatives from 25 states formed the National League of Horseshoe and Quoit Pitchers.

Under the direction of this organization the 1920 tournament was held, again in St. Petersburg. It was at this meet that George May of Akron, Ohio, pitched the "open shoe" with consistency for the first time. He averaged slightly over 50 percent and was undefeated in 24 games. A summer version of the world tournament was held in the same year at Akron, Ohio, and Frank Jackson climbed back to the top of the heap.

At Williams Park in St. Petersburg in February of 1921 Charles Bobbit of Lancaster, Ohio, won the title with a 20-1 record. The winner of the summer tournament in that year again was Frank Jackson.

By this time the National Horseshoe Pitchers' Association had been formed and the playing rules had been set up substantially as they are today.

All meets since that time have been played according to the NHPA rules and under its sanction. Women's meets have been held in conjunction with the men since 1920, and in 1951 a Junior Division was begun. Champions in all three divisions are listed at the end of this chapter.

The ringer percentages show that the champions have become increasingly proficient. No champion since 1940 has been able to win with less than 82 percent ringers.

All these champions were great pitchers, and I can see no point in praising each one separately. However, the prolonged domination of the game from 1933 to the present time by two men, Ted Allen and Fernando Isais, cannot be passed up. These two men held the title between them for 27 years, with the lone exception of 1954, when Guy Zimmerman won the crown.

Allen won ten titles and held the crown five years in which no meet was held. Allen has played in every tournament since 1933 and holds many of the world's pitching records. When his pitching is combined with his all-around contribution of the game—exhibition pitching, promotion, articles—Allen may well be the greatest figure to cross the horseshoe pitching stage.

So far as the method of play in the present tournaments is concerned, the only man sure of a berth is the defending champion. He is the only man who does not have to qualify. The championship class is made up of 36 men, the defending champion and the 35 highest qualifiers. No title, whether it be the championship of a state or a foreign country, entitles one to a berth in the tournament. Any person who can pay a modest entry fee and who can pitch enough points to get in the top 35 can get in the big show. The lowest qualifier must plan to throw 500 points with 200 shoes and a few have missed Class A with that score.

The prize money involved is an interesting subject. On page 265 is the prize money set up for the 1973 meet.

$12,569.00
CASH PRIZE LIST FOR THIS 1973 WORLD TOURNAMENT

MENS CHAMPIONSHIP	MENS CLASS 'B'	MENS CLASS 'C'	MENS CLASS 'D'	WOMENS CHAMPIONSHIP
1 – – $1,000.00	1 $ 60.00	1 – $ 35.00	1 – $ 22.00	1st – – – $250.00
2 – – – 600.00	2 – – 55.00	2 – – 34.00	2 – – 21.00	2nd – – – 100.00
3 – – – 500.00	3 – – 54.00	3 – – 33.00	3 – – 21.00	3rd – – – 75.00
4 – – – 450.00	4 – – 53.00	4 – – 32.00	4 – – 20.00	4th – – – 60.00
5 – – – 400.00	5 – – 52.00	5 – – 32.00	5 – – 20.00	5th – – – 50.00
6 – – – 350.00	6 – – 51.00	6 – – 31.00	6 – – 19.00	6th – – – 45.00
7 – – – 300.00	7 – – 50.00	7 – – 31.00	7 – – 19.00	7th – – – 40.00
8 – – – 250.00	8 – – 50.00	8 – – 30.00	8 – – 19.00	8th – – – 35.00
9 – – – 225.00	9 – – 49.00	9 – – 30.00	9 – – 19.00	Total $655.00
10 – – – 200.00	10 – – 49.00	10 – – 30.00	10 – – 18.00	
11 – – – 180.00	11 – – 48.00	11 – – 29.00	11 – – 18.00	SENIOR AND INTERMEDIATE MEN
12 – – – 160.00	12 – – 48.00	12 – – 29.00	12 – – 18.00	
13 – – – 150.00	13 – – 47.00	13 – – 29.00	13 – – 18.00	
14 – – – 140.00	14 – – 47.00	14 – – 28.00	14 – – 17.00	CLASS 'A'
15 – – – 130.00	15 – – 46.00	15 – – 28.00	15 – – 17.00	1st – – – $150.00
16 – – – 120.00	16 – – 46.00	16 – – 28.00	16 – – 17.00	2nd – – – 80.00
17 – – – 110.00	17 – – 45.00	17 – – 27.00	17 – – 17.00	3rd – – – 70.00
18 – – – 100.00	18 – – 45.00	18 – – 27.00	18 – – 16.00	4th – – – 60.00
19 – – – 90.00	19 – – 44.00	19 – – 27.00	19 – – 16.00	5th – – – 50.00
20 – – – 80.00	20 – – 44.00	20 – – 27.00	20 – – 16.00	6th – – – 45.00
21 – – – 79.00	21 – – 43.00	21 – – 26.00	21 – – 16.00	7th – – – 40.00
22 – – – 78.00	22 – – 43.00	22 – – 26.00	22 – – 15.00	8th – – – 35.00
23 – – – 77.00	23 – – 42.00	23 – – 26.00	23 – – 15.00	Total $530.00 ea.
24 – – – 76.00	24 – – 42.00	24 – – 25.00	24 – – 15.00	
25 – – – 75.00	25 – – 41.00	25 – – 25.00	25 – – 15.00	WOMEN, SENIOR AND INTERMEDIATE MEN
26 – – – 74.00	26 – – 41.00	26 – – 25.00	26 – – 15.00	
27 – – – 73.00	27 – – 40.00	27 – – 25.00	27 – – 14.00	
28 – – – 72.00	28 – – 40.00	28 – – 24.00	28 – – 14.00	CLASS 'B'
29 – – – 71.00	29 – – 39.00	29 – – 24.00	29 – – 14.00	1st – – – $ 30.00
30 – – – 70.00	30 – – 39.00	30 – – 24.00	30 – – 14.00	2nd – – – 25.00
31 – – – 69.00	31 – – 38.00	31 – – 23.00	31 – – 14.00	3rd – – – 24.00
32 – – – 68.00	32 – – 38.00	32 – – 23.00	32 – – 14.00	4th – – – 23.00
33 – – – 67.00	33 – – 37.00	33 – – 23.00		5th – – – 22.00
34 – – – 66.00	34 – – 37.00	34 – – 22.00		6th – – – 21.00
35 – – – 65.00	35 – – 36.00	35 – – 22.00		Total $145.00 ea.
36 – – – 64.00	36 – – 36.00	36 – – 22.00		
TOTAL $6,679.00	TOTAL $1,615.00	TOTAL $982.00	TOTAL $543.00	WOMEN, SENIOR AND INTERMEDIATE MEN

CLASS 'C'

1st – – – $ 20.00
2nd – – – 18.00
3rd – – – 17.00
4th – – – 16.00
5th – – – 15.00
6th – – – 14.00

Total $100.00 ea.

75 TROPHIES WILL BE AWARDED

A COLLEGE SCHOLARSHIP CERTIFICATE will be presented to the JUNIOR WORLD CHAMPION in the BOYS and GIRLS division.

Additional Trophy Awards in All Classes

The amount of prize money awarded at the World Horseshoe Tournament is a nominal amount by comparison to prize money in other sports. The winner does not win enough money to pay the expenses of bringing his family to the tournament for a week or ten days and certainly does not win enough to justify the practice and competition needed to win such an event.

There are two views on the subject. One is that every effort should be made to increase the amount of prize money and to get the top pitchers to fight for it. Another view is that horseshoe pitching is one of the few remaining true sports and that the absence of prize money keeps it on a hobby basis with the accent on competition, and sportsmanship. When Wally Shipley was elected President of the NHPA in 1973, one of his pledges was to work for more prize money. His election may reflect the fact that the delegates around the nation lean toward a concerted effort to get more prize money into the game. If so, this is a distinct change of attitude from the rank and file NHPA pitcher of the past.

World Horseshoe Pitching Records

Established in the annual World & National Tournament
MEN'S DIVISION

Complete Tournament

Ringer pct, 35 games	88.5	Elmer Hohl, Wellesley, Ont., Can.	1968
Total ringers	2903	Ralph Maddox, Poca, W. Va.	1964
Double ringers	1173	Ralph Maddox, Poca, W. Va.	1964
Shoes pitched	3586	John Rademacher, Plant City, Fla.	1968

Single Game, Individual

Ringer pct, winner	100.0	Elmer Hohl, Wellesley, Ont., Can.	1968
		Guy Zimmerman, Danville, Calif.	1948
Ringer pct, loser	89.7	Ray Martin, Philo, Ill.	1965
Ringers, winner	175	Glen Henton, Maquoketa, Iowa	1965
Ringers, loser	174	Ray Martin, Philo, Ill.	1965
Double ringers, winner	80	Glen Henton, Maquoketa, Iowa	1965
Double ringers, loser	77	Ray Martin, Philo, Ill.	1965
Consecutive ringers	72	Ted Allen, Boulder, Colo.	1951
Shoes, shortest game winner	22	Roland Kraft, Lecompton, Kan.	1941

(Continued)

World Horseshoe Pitching Records

Single Game, Both Players

Longest game, shoes pitched	194	Glen Henton & Ray Martin	1965
Ringer pct.	91.15	Paul Focht, Dayton, Ohio & Marvin Craig, Parker, Ind.	1965
Total ringers	349	Glen Henton & Ray Martin	1965
Double ringers	157	Glen Henton & Ray Martin	1965
Cancelled ringers	316	Glen Henton & Ray Martin	1965
"Four Deads"	63	Glen Henton & Ray Martin	1965
Consecutive "Four Deads"	15	Carl Steinfeldt, Rochester, N. Y. & Elmer Hohl, Wellesley, Ont., Can.	1964

Qualifying, 200 Shoes

Total Points	572	Elmer Hohl, Wellesley, Ont., Can.	1968
Ringers	187	Ted Allen, Boulder, Colo.	1955
Double ringers	87	Harold Reno, Sabina, Ohio	1966
Ringers, 100 shoes	97	Don Titcomb, Los Gatos, Calif.	1958

WORLD TOURNAMENT RECORDS 269

World Horseshoe Pitching Records
Established in the annual World & National Tournament
Intermediate Division
Men between 60 & 65

Complete Tournament, 7 Games

Ringer pct.	72.8	Francis Winetrout, Lummi Island, Wash.	1968
Total ringers	377	Dale Dixon, Des Moines, Iowa	1969
Double ringers	127	Dale Dixon, Des Moines, Iowa	1969
Shoes pitched	564	Dale Dixon, Des Moines, Iowa	1969

Single Game, Individual

Ringer pct., winning player	88.2	Francis Winetrout, Lummi Island, Wash.	1968
Ringer pct., losing player	73.5	Dale Dixon, Des Moines, Iowa	1969
Ringers, winner	76	Francis Winetrout, Lummi Island, Wash.	1969
Ringers, loser	75	Dale Dixon, Des Moines, Iowa	1969
Double ringers, winner	28	Francis Winetrout, Lummi Island, Wash.	1969
Double ringers, loser	28	Dale Dixon, Des Moines, Iowa	1969
Consecutive ringers	16	Francis Winetrout, Lummi Island, Wash.	1968
	16	Earl Grable, Dimondale, Mich.	1969
	16	Abe Austin, Oak Park, Ill.	1970
	16	Art Holter, Minneapolis, Minn.	1970

Single Game, Both Players

Ringer pct.	74.0	Francis Winetrout & Dale Dixon	1969
Total ringers	151	Francis Winetrout & Dale Dixon	1969
Double ringers	56	Francis Winetrout & Dale Dixon	1969
Cancelled ringers	120	Francis Winetrout & Dale Dixon	1969
"Four Deads"	16	Francis Winetrout & Dale Dixon	1969
Consecutive "Four Deads"	6	Frank Kilinsky, Pittsburgh, Pa. & Wayne Winston, Lamonte, Mo.	1967
Longest game, shoes pitched		Dale Dixon & Les Cameron, Lewiston, Maine	1971

Qualifying, 100 Shoes

Total points	251	Abe Austin, Oak Park, Ill.	1970
Total ringers	77	Abe Austin, Oak Park, Ill.	1970
Double ringers	31	Abe Austin, Oak Park, Ill.	1970

SENIORS DIVISION, Men over 65

Shoes pitched	508		

Complete Tournament, 7 Games
	Joseph Wilkinson, Akron, Ohio	1961
	John Paxton, Ottumwa, Iowa	1966
	John Paxton, Ottumwa, Iowa	1966
	Harry Page, Waterloo, Iowa	1966

Single Game, Individual
Ringer pct., winner	81.2	John Paxton, Ottumwa, Iowa	1967
Ringer pct., losing player	70.4	Henry F. Franke, Centralia, Ill.	1972
Ringers, winner	71	Ray Miller, Springfield, Ohio	1972
Ringers, loser	69	Henry F. Franke, Centralia, Ill.	1972
Double ringers, winner	24	Ray Miller, Springfield, Ohio	1972
Double ringers, loser	25	Henry F. Franke, Centralia, Ill.	1972
Consecutive ringers	22	Virgil Huffman, Poneto, Ind.	1968

Single Game, Both Players
Longest game, shoes pitched	100	Virgil Huffman & Ray Miller	1969
Ringer pct.	72.5	H. O. Maxwell & Joe Wilkinson	1960
Total ringers	140	Henry F. Franke & Ray Miller	1972
Double ringers	49	Henry F. Franke & Ray Miller	1972
Cancelled ringers	110	Henry F. Franke & Ray Miller	1972
"Four Deads"	13	Henry F. Franke & Ray Miller	1972
Consecutive "Four Deads" (tied)	5	Harold Tuttle & Walt Horner	1964

Qualifying 100 Shoes
Total points	261	Dale Carson, Baltimore, Md.	1971
Total ringers	81	Dale Carson, Baltimore, Md.	1971
Double ringers	34	Dale Carson, Baltimore, Md.	1971

The Men's World Champions

Year	Name of Champion, Home Town	Played at	Won	Lost	Ringer Percentage
1909	Frank Jackson, Kellerton, Iowa	Bronson, Kansas	24	1	97 R
1915	Frank Jackson, Kellerton, Iowa	Kansas City, Kansas	53	1	367 R
1919	Frank Brust, Columbus, Ohio	St. Petersburg, Florida	23	0	430 R
1920 W	George May, Akron, Ohio	St. Petersburg, Florida			850 R
1920 S	Frank Jackson, Kellerton, Iowa	Akron, Ohio			
1921 W	Charles Bottitt, Lancaster, Ohio	St. Petersburg, Florida	20	1	493
1921 S	Frank Jackson, Kellerton, Iowa	Minneapolis, Minnesota			391 R
1922 W	Charlie Davis, Columbus, Ohio	St. Petersburg, Florida			448 R
1922 S	Frank Lundin, New London, Iowa	Des Moines, Iowa	14	1	424 R
1923 W	Harold Falor, Akron, Ohio	St. Petersburg, Florida	29	0	55.3
1923 S	George May, Akron, Ohio	Cleveland, Ohio	14	1	60.0
1924 W	Charlie Davis, Columbus, Ohio	Lake Worth, Florida	22	0	57.9
1924 S	Putt Mossman, Eldora, Iowa	Minneapolis, Minnesota	23	0	62.5
1925	Putt Mossman, Eldora, Iowa	Lake Worth, Florida	53	2	67.6
1926	Frank Jackson, Kellerton, Iowa	St. Petersburg, Florida	24	6	61.4
1927 W	Charlie Davis, Columbus, Ohio	St. Petersburg, Florida	29	4	69.2
1927 S	Charlie Davis, Columbus, Ohio	Duluth, Minnesota	30	3	64.8
1928	Charlie Davis, Columbus, Ohio	St. Petersburg, Florida	28	1	70.2
1929	Blair Nonnamaker, Cleveland, Ohio	St. Petersburg, Florida	13	1	69.5
1933	Ted Allen, Boulder, Colorado	Chicago, Illinois	20	3	73.5
1934	Ted Allen, Boulder, Colorado	Los Angeles, California			73.9
1935	Ted Allen, Boulder, Colorado	Moline, Illinois	21	2	75.5

(Continued)

The Men's World Champions

Year	Champion	City			
1940	Ted Allen, Boulder, Colorado	Des Moines, Iowa	29	2	82.4
1941	Fernando Isais, Los Angeles, California	Des Moines, Iowa	23	0	82.9
1946	Ted Allen, Boulder, Colorado	Des Moines, Iowa	22	1	83.9
1947	Fernando Isais, Los Angeles, California	Murray, Utah	34	1	83.2
1948	Fernando Isais, Los Angeles, California	Milwaukee, Wisconsin	29	2	84.2
1949	Fernando Isais, Los Angeles, California	Murray, Utah	34	1	83.3
1950	Fernando Isais, Los Angeles, California	Murray, Utah	34	1	83.5
1951	Fernando Isais, Los Angeles, California	Murray, Utah	35	0	85.7
1952	Fernando Isais, Los Angeles, California	Murray, Utah	34	1	83.5
1953	Ted Allen, Boulder, Colorado	Murray, Utah	34	1	83.2
1954	Guy Zimmerman, Danville, California	Murray, Utah			84.8
1955	Ted Allen, Boulder, Colorado	Murray, Utah			86.5
1956	Ted Allen, Boulder, Colorado	Murray, Utah			83.4
1957	Ted Allen, Boulder, Colorado	Murray, Utah	12	1	85.1
1958	Fernando Isais, Los Angeles, California	Murray, Utah	13	0	84.3
1959	Ted Allen, Boulder, Colorado	Murray, Utah	35	0	84.4
1960	Don Titcomb, Los Gatos, California	Muncie, Indiana	33	2	84.9
1961	Harold Reno, Sabina, Ohio	Muncie, Indiana	34	1	83.9
1962	Paul Focht, Dayton, Ohio	Greenville, Ohio	32	3	81.8
1963	John Monasmith, Yakima, Washington	South Gate, California	32	3	82.3
1964	Harold Reno, Sabina, Ohio	Greenville, Ohio	32	3	84.1
1965	Elmer Hohl, Wellesley, Ontario	Keene, New Hampshire	32	3	84.6
1966	Curt Day, Frankfort, Indiana	Murray, Utah	16	1	86.1

1967	Dan Kuchcinski, Erie, Pennsylvania	Fargo, North Dakota	34	1	84.4
1968	Elmer Hohl, Wellesley, Ontario	Keene, New Hampshire	35	0	88.5
1969	Dan Kuchcinski, Erie, Pennsylvania	Erie, Pennsylvania	35	0	84.7
1970	Dan Kuchcinski, Erie, Pennsylvania	South Gate, California	34	1	84.9
1971	Curt Day, Frankfort, Indiana	Middlesex, New Jersey	35	0	85.0
1972	Elmer Hohl, Wellesley, Ontario, Canada	Greenville, Ohio	33	2	86.0
1973	Elmer Hohl, Wellesley, Ontario, Canada	Eureka, California	32	3	83.5

Other Tournament Divisions

Only 36 players compete in the Men's championship division, but many more outstanding pitchers compete in other divisions. Many fine pitchers who have poor qualifying rounds will play in the B, C, and D classes as well as many enthusiastic young players who are seeking the experience of playing in the big show. An intermediate class is set up for those players age 62–65 who cannot stand the long grind of the other classes or who fail in their attempt to qualify for them. A Senior Division is set up for the pitchers who are older than 65. There are also classes for Junior Boys, Junior Girls, and Women, which are taken up in other chapters.

These classes are very important, not only to provide many others with a chance to participate but to attract many others to the championship competition as well. Although I realize the work which would accompany such an attempt, I personally look forward to the day when every person who signs an entry and pitches a qualifying round would be able to compete in some class.

CLASS "B" CHAMPS

Year	Champion Home Town	R %
1935	Bob Bales, Kansas City, Mo.	68.3
1951	Roy Getchell, Tigard, Ariz.	60.5
1952	Harry Page, Waterloo, Iowa	55.4
1953	Milt Tate, Peoria, Ill.	58.5
1954	Harry Dolan, Fontana, Calif.	53.4
1955	Vigil Taylor, Greencastle, Ind.	74.8
1956	Sam Somerhalder, Ruskin, Nebr.	63.7
1957	Harry Page, Waterloo, Iowa	66.0
1958	Gene Mendenhall, Noblesville, Ind.	61.9
1959	O. S. Plott, Shreveport, La.	63.3
1960	Wilbur Kabel, New Madison, Ohio	75.9
1961	Bill Porter, Levittown, Pa.	73.5
1962	Steve Fenicchia, Rochester, N. Y.	68.9
1963	Floyd Toole, Pine Bluff, Ark.	74.8
1964	Ed Landry, Fall River, Mass.	78.4
1965	Walt Wilhoite, Lebanon, Ind.	62.3
1966	Dave Baker, Wentworth, Mo.	71.2
1967	Jim Knisley, Bremen, Ohio	71.1
1968	Roy Smith, Muskegon, Mich.	78.3
1969	Hugh Rogers, Cedar Falls, Iowa	79.8
1970	Harold Anthony, Arcanum, Ohio	73.1
1971	Wilbur Kabel, New Madison, Ohio	78.4
1972	Ross Stevenson, Calgary, Alberta, Canada	73.4
1973	Rod Hatton, San Antonio, Texas	64.8

WORLD TOURNAMENT RECORDS 275

CLASS "C" CHAMPS

Year	Champion Home Town	R %
1961	Harold Wolfe, Cedarville, Ohio	62.6
1962	Arner Lindquist, Morgantown, W. Va.	61.5
1963	John Walker, Chula Vista, Calif.	58.9
1964	Roger Norwood, Knoxville, Tenn.	74.4
1965	Don Kaddy, Fitchburg, Mass.	66.0
1966	Dick Backer, Salt Lake City, Utah	65.3
1967	Hartman Knutson, St. Paul, Minn.	63.3
1968	Abe Austin, Oak Park, Ill.	64.2
1969	Rich Maroni, Arnoud, Pennsylvania	71.5
1970	Henry Durr, Los Angeles, California	69.6
1971	Jack Rainbow, Monaca, Pennsylvania	70.0
1972	Bill Henn, Bellevue, Kentucky	70.6
1973	Barry Chapelle, Portland, Oregon	60.2

CLASS "D" CHAMPS

Year	Champion Home Town	R%
1971	Bill Kolb, Bellville, New Jersey	58.7
1972	Ed Curran, Paris, Kentucky	77.8
1973	Stan Hilton, Burbank, California	52.9

SENIOR DIVISION CHAMPS

Year	Champion Home Town	R %
1960	W. O. Maxwell, Hicksville, Ohio	62.4
1961	Joe Wilkinson, Akron, Ohio	72.6
1962	Joe Wilkinson, Akron, Ohio	61.5
1963	Ralph Navarro, South Gate, Calif.	56.0
1964	Harold Tuttle, Youngstown, Ohio	65.4
1965	Harold Tuttle, Youngstown, Ohio	64.0
1966	John Paxton, Ottumwa, Iowa	69.4
1967	John Paxton, Ottumwa, Iowa	67.2
1968	John Paxton, Ottumwa, Iowa	65.4
1969	John Paxton, Ottumwa, Iowa	68.5
1970	John Paxton, Ottumwa, Iowa	66.2
1971	Stan Manker, Martinsville, Ohio	67.2
1972	Ray Miller, Springfield, Ohio	69.0
1973	Ray Miller, Springfield, Ohio	62.5

INTERMEDIATE DIVISION CHAMPS

Year	Champion Home Town	R %
1967	Wayne Winston, Lamonte, Mo.	58.1
1968	Francis Winetrout, Lummi Island, Wash.	72.8
1969	Francis Winetrout, Lummi Island, Washington	68.5
1970	Art Holter, Minneapolis, Minnesota	64.8
1971	Art Holter, Minneapolis, Minnesota	59.3
1972	Abe Austin, Oak Park, Illinois	68.6
1973	Ralph Randall, Barstow, California	72.4

PITCHING CHAMPIONSHIP HORSESHOES

1961 World Tournament

MEN'S CLASS A CHAMPIONSHIP SUMMARY

Place	Name	W	L	%
1.	Harold Reno, Ohio	34	1	83.8
2.	Ted Allen, Colorado	32	3	82.4
3.	Ralph Maddox, West Virginia	30	5	80.9
4.	Elmer Hohl, Ontario, Canada	30	5	80.7
5.	Curtis Day, Indiana	28	7	83.1
6.	Floyd Toole, Arkansas	28	7	81.9
7.	Paul Focht, Ohio	28	7	80.3
8.	Bob West, Oregon	28	7	79.1
9.	Gene Brumfield, Indiana	26	9	80.4
10.	Roger Vogel, Illinois	23	12	72.3
11.	Graydon McFatridge, Indiana	22	13	76.0
12.	Floyd Fowler, Indiana	20	15	75.6
13.	Wilbur Kabel, Ohio	20	15	75.1
14.	Clarence Bellman, Indiana	20	15	73.2
15.	Herb Pinch, Pennsylvania	19	16	72.7
16.	Ray Martin, Illinois	18	17	72.8
17.	Jim Johnson, Kentucky	18	17	70.0
18.	Dale Dixon, Iowa	17	18	70.2
19.	Marvin Craig, Indiana	16	19	68.2
20.	Art Dugle, Illinois	15	20	70.5
21.	Walt Horner, Indiana	15	20	70.0
22.	Rod Hatton, Indiana	14	21	69.8
23.	Earl Wiges, Iowa	13	22	70.0
24.	Bill Sollars, Ohio	13	22	67.6
25.	Francis Rogers, Iowa	12	23	69.6
26.	Leland Wiges, Iowa	12	23	67.5
27.	Ron Cherrier, Minnesota	12	23	66.8
28.	Earl Winston, Missouri	11	24	70.8
29.	Steve Fenicchia, New York	11	24	67.5
30.	Jack Stout, Illinois	11	24	68.4
31.	Irwin Carlberg, Michigan	9	26	66.0
32.	Stan Manker, Ohio	9	26	65.4
33.	Howard Bryant, Ohio	7	28	64.5
34.	Karl Van Sant, Indiana	5	30	63.5
35.	Hugh Tooley, Illinois	3	32	60.2
36.	Harold McFatridge, Indiana	0	35	53.9

1962 World Tournament

CHAMPIONSHIP SUMMARY

	Won	Lost	R%
Paul Focht, Ohio	32	3	81.8
Curt Day, Indiana	31	4	81.8
Elmer Hohl, Canada	30	5	83.2
Harold Reno, Ohio	30	5	81.7
Ted Allen, Colo.	30	5	80.5
Ralph Maddox, W. Va.	29	6	80.0
Wilbur Kabel, Ohio	27	8	79.4
Glen Henton, Iowa	23	12	77.5
Art Dugle, Illinois	23	12	77.4
Roger Vogel, Illinois	23	12	76.9
Carl Steinfeldt, N. Y.	22	13	79.4
Ray Martin, Illinois	22	13	78.4
Marines Tamboer, Kan.	22	13	76.3
Bill Pentilla, Ohio	21	14	75.7
Kenneth Jensen, Mich.	21	14	75.0
Floyd Toole, Ark.	20	15	78.5
Floyd Fowler, Indiana	20	15	75.6
Al Zadroga, Penna	18	17	74.6
Gene Brumfield, Ind.	17	18	72.6
Truman Standard, Ill.	16	19	70.5
Jum Johnson, Ky.	15	20	74.6
Marvin Craig, Ind.	14	21	71.2
William Porter, Pa.	13	22	72.4
Andy Deem, W. Va.	12	23	70.1
Herb Pinch, Pa.	11	24	71.8
Harry Sibert, Ohio	11	24	69.8
Gene Mendenhall, Ind.	11	24	65.5
Graydon McFatridge, Ind.	10	25	70.8
Dale Dixon, Iowa	10	25	70.7
John Stimac, Ind.	10	25	68.8
Earl Winston, Mo.	10	25	68.3
Chas. Fortenberry, Tenn.	8	27	65.0
Bob May, Indiana	7	28	66.2
Harold Wolfe, Ohio	7	28	60.8
Lee Bennett, Ohio	4	31	62.7
Howard Robinson, Neb.	Forfeited		

1963 World Tournament

CHAMPIONSHIP SUMMARY

	Won	Lost	R%
John Monasmith, Wash.	32	3	82.3
Elmer Hohl, Canada	31	4	81.8
Carl Steinfeldt, N. Y.	29	6	79.9
Harold Reno, Ohio	29	6	78.9
Paul Focht, Ohio	29	6	78.8
Don Titcomb, Calif.	27	8	79.6
Ted Allen, Colo.	27	8	78.5
Fernando Isais, Calif.	27	8	78.0
Marines Tamboer, Kansas	25	10	77.7
Jerry Schneider, Calif.	23	12	76.8
Art Dugle, Illinois	23	12	74.1
Ralph Maddox, W. Va.	22	13	78.1
Jim Johnson, Ohio	22	13	75.4
Henry Knauft, Wash.	21	14	76.7
Glen Henton, Iowa	21	14	75.5
Wilbur Kabel, Ohio	21	14	75.0
Wellington Taylor, Iowa	19	16	71.3
Jim Weeks, Calif.	18	17	74.9
Frank Stinson, Minn.	17	18	70.6
Ira Allen, Calif.	16	19	73.6
Clive Wahlin, Utah	15	20	75.5
Homer Moefield, Calif.	15	20	71.8
Marvin Craig, Ind.	15	20	71.5
Earl Winston, Mo.	14	21	71.6
Charles Merrell, Calif.	11	24	67.8
Dale Dixon, Iowa	11	24	67.2
Harold Shatto, Wash.	11	24	65.9
Lee Bennett, Ohio	11	24	65.2
Andrew Paglarini, Minn.	9	26	65.3
Ned Shaver, Calif.	8	27	68.8
Bill Blexrude, Calif.	8	27	67.7
Henry Harper, Calif.	7	28	61.3
A. A. Austin, Illinois	7	28	60.9
Don Peterson, Calif.	5	30	62.8
Charles Stephens, Fla.	4	31	62.2
Roger Vogel, Illinois	Forfeited		

WORLD TOURNAMENT RECORDS

1964 World Tournament

CHAMPIONSHIP SUMMARY

Name and State	Won	Lost	R%
Harold Reno, Sabina, Ohio	32	3	84.1
Carl Steinfeldt, Rochester, N.Y.	30	5	83.3
Glen Henton, Maquoketa, Iowa	29	6	83.9
Elmer Hohl, Wellesley, Ontario	29	6	83.9
Curt Day, Frankfort, Indiana	28	7	84.4
Ray Martin, Philo, Illinois	28	7	82.9
Floyd Toole, Pine Bluff, Ark.	28	7	82.0
Al Zadroga, Elizabeth, Penna.	26	9	81.0
Ralph Maddox, Poca, West Va.	25	10	83.5
Paul Lattray, Webster Grove, Mo.	25	10	81.1
John Monasmith, Yakima, Wash.	24	11	80.0
Ted Allen, Boulder, Colorado	23	12	80.9
Henry Knauft, Spokane, Wash.	23	12	80.4
Ed Fishel, Neilton, Washington	22	13	78.8
Glen Riffle, Dayton, Ohio	21	14	75.5
Marines Tamboer, Wichita, Kan.	20	15	79.2
Clive Wahlin, Salt Lake City, Utah	20	15	76.1
Wilbur Kabel, New Madison, Ohio	18	17	78.7
Herb Pinch, Sharon, Pennsylvania	17	18	73.8
Jim Solomon, Uniontown, Penna.	16	19	78.4
Marvin Craig, Parker, Indiana	15	20	75.5
Floyd Fowler, Greencastle, Ind.	15	20	74.8
Bob May, Glenwood, Indiana	14	21	75.0
Lee Bennett, Middletown, Ohio	13	22	72.2
Don Owens, Summitville, Indiana	13	22	72.1
Joe Carmack, Lecoma, Missouri	11	24	74.1
Dick Carpenter, Union City, Ind.	11	24	73.2
Chas. Fortenberry, Knoxville, Tenn.	10	25	72.1
Jim Johnson, Cincinnati, Ohio	9	26	71.5
Frank Stinson, Minneapolis, Minn.	9	26	70.5
Dale Dixon, Des Moines, Iowa	8	27	70.9
Homer Moefield, Long Beach, Calif.	6	29	66.6
Well Taylor, Grand River, Iowa	5	30	68.0
Arn Lindquist, Morgantown, W. Va.	5	30	67.8
Nelson Vogel, Manito, Illinois	2	33	64.0
Art Dugle, Chicago, Illinois	Forfeited		

PITCHING CHAMPIONSHIP HORSESHOES 280
1965 World Tournament

CHAMPIONSHIP SUMMARY

	W	L	%
Elmer Hohl, Wellesley, Ont. Can.	32	3	84.6
Ray Martin, Illinois	31	4	85.3
Floyd Toole, Arkansas	31	4	84.5
Curt Day, Indiana	29	6	86.0
Paul Focht, Ohio	29	6	83.3
Carl Steinfeldt, New York	28	7	84.0
Jim Solomon, Pennsylvania	27	8	83.7
Harold Reno, Ohio	27	8	83.2
Ralph Maddox, West Virginia	27	8	80.8
Dan Kuchcinski, Pennsylvania	27	8	79.3
Ted Allen, Colorado	26	9	78.0
Sam Sutton, Pennsylvania	22	13	76.1
Glen Henton, Iowa	21	14	80.9
Roy Smith, Michigan	20	15	75.6
Marines Tamboer, Kansas	19	16	79.0
Bob May, Indiana	19	16	78.6
Glenn Riffle, Ohio	19	16	74.5
Frank Stinson, Minnesota	18	17	76.6
Joe Carmack, Missouri	18	17	76.5
Hugh Rogers, Iowa	17	18	74.8
John Fulton, Pennsylvania	15	20	74.6
Leonard Lenigar, Ohio	15	20	70.1
Bob Toney, Virginia	14	21	72.8
Marvin Craig, Indiana	14	21	72.1
Roger Vogel, Illinois	14	21	68.0
Herb Pinch, Pennsylvania	12	23	66.7
Wes Kuchcinski, Pennsylvania	9	26	69.5
Francis Winetrout, Washington	9	26	62.7
Tony Sauro, New York	8	27	68.5
Jack Giddes, New Jersey	8	27	64.2
Ray Miller, Ohio	6	29	65.8
Arner Lindquist, West Virginia	6	29	61.2
Terry Earley, New York	5	30	68.3
Lee Bennett, Ohio	3	32	61.0
Lee Jacobs, Michigan	3	32	56.3
Jim Johnson, Ohio	2	33	57.8

1966 World Tournament

CHAMPIONSHIP SUMMARY

	W	L	%
Curt Day, Frankfort, Ind.	16	1	86.6
Dan Kuchcinski, Erie, Penna.	13	4	81.6
Henry Knauft, Spokane, Wash.	13	4	79.4
Ray Martin, Philo, Ill.	11	6	82.8
Elmer Hohl, Wellesley, Ont., Can.	11	6	82.3
Paul Focht, Dayton, Ohio	11	6	81.9
Fernando Isais, Los Angeles, Calif.	10	7	80.1
Floyd Toole, Little Rock, Ark.	9	8	79.4
Harold Reno, Sabina, Ohio	9	8	78.8
Jim Solomon, Uniontown, Penna.	8	9	80.3
Gary Farnsworth, Bloomington, Ill.	8	9	79.3
Ralph Maddox, Poca, W. Va.	8	9	79.3
Wilbur Kabel, New Madison, Ohio	6	11	77.1
Harold Anthony, Arcanum, Ohio	6	11	76.7
Floyd Fowler, Greencastle, Ind.	5	12	77.0
Frank Stinson, Minneapolis, Minn.	5	12	75.9
Marines Tamboer, Wichita, Kan.	3	14	72.4
Jerry Schneider, Bell, Calif.	2	15	78.1

PITCHING CHAMPIONSHIP HORSESHOES 282

1967 World Tournament

CHAMPIONSHIP SUMMARY

	W	L	%
Danny Kuchcinski, Erie, Pa.	34	1	84.4
Curt Day, Frankfort, Ind.	32	3	81.4
Ray Martin, Philo, Ill.	32	3	81.0
Elmer Hohl, Wellesley, Ont., Can.	28	7	80.5
Paul Focht, Dayton, Ohio	26	9	76.1
John Monasmith, Yakima, Wash.	25	10	79.1
Harold Reno, Sabina, Ohio	25	10	75.5
Carl Steinfeldt, Rochester, N.Y.	24	11	79.1
Henry Knauft, Spokane, Wash.	23	12	76.3
Floyd Toole, Little Rock, Ark.	23	12	74.8
Frank Stinson, Minneapolis, Minn.	23	12	73.7
Al Zadroga, Elizabeth, Pa.	22	13	74.6
Ellis Griggs, Plainville, Ill.	22	13	74.5
Harold Anthony, Arcanum, Ohio	20	15	72.1
Jim Solomon, Uniontown, Pa.	19	16	74.0
Bob West, McMinnville, Ore.	19	16	73.5
Ted Allen, Boulder, Colo.	19	16	72.0
Red Henton, Maquoketa, Iowa	18	17	75.2
Dave Baker, Wentworth, Mo.	18	17	73.9
Ed Fishel, Neilton, Wash.	18	17	71.6
Hugh Rogers, Cedar Falls, Iowa	17	18	72.3
Ronnie Simmons, South Gate, Calif.	17	18	72.1
Ralph Maddox, Poca, W. Va.	14	21	73.2
Melvin Utley, Chicago, Ill.	14	21	70.7
Merlin Potts, Leonardville, Kan.	14	21	68.7
Andy Paglarini, Hibbing, Minn.	12	23	68.8
John Walker, Chula Vista	12	23	68.8
Sam Sutton, Washington, Pa.	10	25	70.2
Stan Manker, Martinsville, Ohio	10	25	69.3
Floyd Fowler, Greencastle, Ind.	8	27	67.7
L. Anderson, San Francisco, Calif.	8	27	62.3
Abe Carmack, Lecoma, Mo.	7	28	65.3
Roy Radcliffe, Denver, Colo.	5	30	62.3
Jean Howard, Selah, Wash.	5	30	62.1
Bob Williams, Cement City, Mich.	4	31	61.1
Francis Rogers, Waverly, Iowa	3	32	64.5

1968 World Tournament

CHAMPIONSHIP SUMMARY

	W	L	%
1. Elmer Hohl, Wellesley, Ont., Canada	35	0	88.5
2. James Knisley, Bremen, Ohio	31	4	82.8
3. Dan Kuchcinski, Erie, Penn.	30	5	82.3
4. Ray Martin, Philo, Ill.	29	6	84.2
5. Carl Steinfelt, Rochester, N. Y.	28	7	82.8
6. Paul Focht, Dayton, Ohio	25	10	81.9
7. Harold Reno, Sabina, Ohio	25	10	80.2
8. Gerald Schneider, Pico Rivera, Calif.	24	11	80.1
9. Ross Stevenson, Baden, Ont., Canada	23	12	77.8
10. Ellis Griggs, Plainville, Ill.	22	13	77.6
11. Al Zadroga, Elizabeth, Penn.	22	13	77.5
12. John Rademacher, Plant City, Fla.	21	14	79.9
13. Frank Stinson, Minneapolis, Minn.	21	14	79.4
14. David Baker, Wentworth, Mo.	20	15	78.4
15. Ralph Maddox, Poca, W. Va.	19	16	79.0
16. Ron Simmons, Downey, Calif.	19	16	75.6
17. James Solomon, Uniontown, Penn.	17	18	77.3
18. Hugh Rogers, Cedar Falls, Ia.	17	18	75.8
19. Glen Henton, Maquoketa, Ia.	16	19	79.2
20. Stan Manker, Martinsville, Ohio	16	19	75.1
21. Howard Shriver, Wadestown, W. Va.	15	20	77.8
22. Marvin Craig, Parker, Ind.	15	20	76.1
23. Harold Anthony, Arcanum, Ohio	15	20	75.6
24. Wilbur Kabel, New Madison, Ohio	14	21	77.5
25. Roger Vogel, Manito, Ill.	14	21	76.9
26. Ron Kuchcinski, Erie, Penn.	14	21	74.7
27. Floyd Fowler, Greencastle, Ind.	14	21	72.9
28. Steve Fenicchia, Rochester, N. Y.	11	24	75.3
29. Delbert Wright, Columbia City, Ind.	11	24	71.9
30. Dale Dixon, Des Moines, Ia.	10	25	72.2
31. Ted Allen, Boulder, Colorado	10	25	71.3
32. Karl Van Sant, Cayuga, Ind.	9	26	74.3
33. Wes Kuchcinski, Erie, Penn.	6	29	70.9
34. Don Kaiser, Clayton, Michigan	5	30	66.2
35. Clair Bruce, New Wilmington, Penn.	4	31	70.1
36. Al Bourgeois, West Barrington, R. I.	3	32	64.5

PITCHING CHAMPIONSHIP HORSESHOES 284

1969 World Tournament

CHAMPIONSHIP SUMMARY

	W	L	%
Danny Kuchcinski, Erie, Pa.	35	0	84.7
Elmer Hohl, Wellesley, Ont., Can.	33	2	86.4
Ray Martin, Philo, Ill.	30	5	85.8
Curt Day, Frankfort, Ind.	30	5	85.3
Roy Smith, Muskegon, Mich.	28	7	79.2
Frank Stinson, Minneapolis, Minn.	27	8	79.1
Al Zadroga, Elizabeth, Pa.	24	11	79.6
Ralph Maddox, Poca, W. Va.	23	12	80.2
Paul Focht, Dayton, Ohio	23	12	79.8
Clair Bruce, New Wilmington, Pa.	23	12	78.9
Jim Knisley, Bremen, Ohio	23	12	78.1
Oscar Engle, Pittsburgh, Pa.	22	13	79.1
Clyde Martz, Pittsburgh, Pa.	21	14	75.6
Clarence Bellman, Bremen, Ind.	20	15	78.9
Anthony, Arcanum, Ohio	20	15	75.5
Ted Allen, Boulder, Colo.	20	15	75.4
Merlin Potts, Leonardville, Kan.	17	18	76.1
Stan Manker, Martinsville, Ohio	17	18	74.0
Wilbur Kabel, New Madison, Ohio	16	19	77.6
Steve Fenicchia, Rochester, N. Y.	18	19	75.6
Jerry Schneider, Rosemead, Calif.	15	20	75.3
Floyd Toole, Little Rock, Ark.	14	21	76.3
Glenn Riffle, Dayton, Ohio	14	21	72.8
Jim Solomon, Uniontown, Pa.	13	22	75.8
Dale Carson, Baltimore, Md.	13	22	71.8
Jack Stout, Melrose Park, Ill.	12	23	74.4
John Rademacher, Plant City, Fla.	12	23	72.9
Howard Shriver, Wadestown, W. Va.	11	24	70.4
Ginger Natale, Rochester, N. Y.	10	25	71.9
Ronnie Simmons, Norwalk, Calif.	8	27	73.2
Joe Carmack, Lecoma, Mo.	8	27	71.9
Ron Kuchcinski, Erie, Pa.	8	27	70.1
Andy Paglarini, Hibbing, Minn.	7	28	70.7
Bob Williams, Cement City, Mich.	7	28	68.2
Bob Dean, McGaheysville, Va.	5	30	69.6
Ken Jensen, St. Joseph, Mich.	5	30	66.2

1970 World Tournament

CHAMPIONSHIP SUMMARY

	Won	Lost	R%
Dan Kuchcinski, Pennsylvania	34	1	84.9
Elmer Hohl, Canada	32	3	84.1
Bob West, Oregon	30	5	81.6
Henry Knauft, Washington	28	7	81.2
John Walker, California	27	8	78.7
Wilbur Kabel, Ohio	27	8	78.1
Glen Henton, Iowa	26	9	76.3
David Baker, Missouri	24	11	75.6
Glen Riffle, Ohio	24	11	73.8
Clyde Martz, Pennsylvania	23	12	78.4
Merlin Potts, Kansas	23	12	74.3
Jesse Gonzales, California	22	13	76.5
Jerry Schneider, California	21	14	76.6
Ronnie Simmons, California	21	14	75.0
Fernando Isais, California	21	14	73.4
Roy Smith, Michigan	20	15	75.9
Jim Knisley, Ohio	20	15	72.1
Gerald Maison, Michigan	16	19	72.3
Ted Allen, Colorado	15	20	72.1
Art Kamman, Arizona	15	20	71.9
Floyd Toole, Arkansas	15	20	71.8
Frank Stinson, Minnesota	15	20	70.1
Andy Paglarini, Minnesota	14	21	72.9
Stan Manker, Ohio	14	21	70.6
John Rademacher, Florida	13	22	71.8
James Ostrander, Michigan	12	23	67.5
Jonas Snyder, California	12	23	67.2
Ansil Copeland, Ohio	11	24	68.7
Ralph Randall, California	10	25	64.7
Jack Stout, Illinois	9	26	69.6
Curt Bestul, Wisconsin	8	27	68.0
Ned Shaver, California	8	27	64.5
Ed McFarland, California	7	28	64.6
Dale Dixon, Iowa	6	29	60.4
John Pratt, California	4	31	63.4
Monty Latino, California	3	32	62.0

PITCHING CHAMPIONSHIP HORSESHOES 286
1971 World Tournament

CHAMPIONSHIP SUMMARY	Won	Lost	R%
Curt Day, Indiana	35	0	85.0
Elmer Hohl, Canada	31	4	83.9
John Walker, California	29	6	81.7
Mark Seibold, Indiana	28	7	78.9
Clyde Martz, Pennsylvania	27	8	80.0
Harold Reno, Ohio	27	8	78.3
Ray Martin, Illinois	25	10	80.4
Bob West, Oregon	25	10	80.2
Dan Kuchcinski, Indiana	25	10	80.0
Gerald Maison, Michigan	25	10	78.2
Jim Knisley, Ohio	23	12	78.6
David Baker, Missouri	23	12	78.4
Paul Focht, Ohio	21	14	78.0
Merlin Potts, Kansas	20	15	77.0
Ronnie Simmons, California	20	15	77.0
Roger Vogel, Illinois	20	15	75.5
Al Zadroga, Pennsylvania	19	16	76.4
John Rademacher, Florida	19	16	75.6
Ralph Maddox, West Virginia	17	18	75.4
Clair Bruce, Pennsylvania	16	19	73.1
Roy Smith, Michigan	16	19	72.0
Ansil Copeland, Ohio	15	20	70.9
Harold Anthony, Ohio	14	21	74.3
Sam Sutton, Pennsylvania	13	22	73.7
Karl Van Sant, Indiana	11	24	72.7
Steve Fenicchia, New York	11	24	71.4
Marvin Craig, Indiana	11	24	71.1
Abe Austin, Illinois	11	24	67.8
Jim Solomon, Pennsylvania	10	25	67.4
Jack Giddes, New Jersey	9	26	71.3
Frank Stinson, Minnesota	9	26	68.9
Ted Allen, Colorado	7	28	69.5
Rich Maroni, Pennsylvania	7	28	64.9
Andy Paglarini, Minnesota	6	29	67.6
Burl Taylor, Indiana	5	30	66.1
Jerry Schneider, California	Forfeit		

WORLD TOURNAMENT RECORDS

1972 World Tournament

CHAMPIONSHIP SUMMARY	Won	Lost	R%
Elmer Hohl, Canada	33	2	86.0
Curt Day, Indiana	33	2	83.5
Mark Seibold, Indiana	32	3	81.8
Bob West, Oregon	30	5	83.4
Dan Kuchcinski, Indiana	29	6	81.8
Glen Henton, Iowa	28	7	83.6
Jesse Gonzales, California	26	9	80.8
Harold Reno, Ohio	25	10	79.6
Henry Knauft, Washington	23	12	80.7
Wilbur Kabel, Ohio	23	12	77.2
Alan Stockholm, New York	22	13	77.7
Carl Steinfeldt, New York	21	14	78.1
Al Zadroga, Pennsylvania	20	15	77.0
Harold Anthony, Ohio	19	16	77.6
Gerald Maison, Michigan	19	16	77.0
Merlin Potts, Kansas	19	16	74.7
Clair Bruce, Pennsylvania	18	17	78.0
Frank Stinson, Minnesota	17	18	76.0
John Rademacher, Florida	16	19	77.2
Paul Focht, Ohio	15	20	73.4
Dale Carson, Maryland	14	21	73.9
Ansil Copeland, Ohio	14	21	72.4
Cecil Monday, Virginia	13	22	72.0
Karl Van Sant, Indiana	13	22	72.0
Chet Reel, Indiana	13	22	71.8
Jim Solomon, Pennsylvania	11	24	72.6
Stan Manker, Ohio	11	24	72.5
Jerry Black, North Dakota	10	25	70.0
Marines Tamboer, Kansas	10	25	70.0
Floyd Toole, Arkansas	9	26	71.0
Art Tyson, Connecticut	9	26	70.1
Ralph Maylahn, Wisconsin	9	26	69.3
Rogers Norwood, Tennessee	9	26	69.2
Ted Harris, Ohio	7	28	69.3
Andy Paglarini, Minnesota	7	28	68.7
Rich Maroni, Pennsylvania	3	32	63.0

PITCHING CHAMPIONSHIP HORSESHOES

1973 World Tournament

CHAMPIONSHIP SUMMARY	Won	Lost	R%
Elmer Hohl, Canada	32	3	83.5
Mark Seibold, Indiana	32	3	80.9
Bob West, Oregon	28	7	82.2
Wilbur Kabel, Ohio	25	10	80.1
John Rademacher, Florida	25	10	77.4
Roger Vogel, Colorado	25	10	75.1
Glen Henton, Iowa	24	11	79.0
Paul Focht, Ohio	24	11	78.5
Jesse Gonzales, California	23	12	77.3
Norman Rioux, Connecticut	22	13	75.7
Dan Kuchcinski, Indiana	22	13	75.7
Al Stockholm, New York	22	13	74.1
Joe Krug, Washington	22	13	70.8
Merlin Potts, Kansas	21	14	75.7
Bill Henn, Kentucky	21	14	74.3
Henry Knauft, Washington	20	15	78.0
Jim Knisley, Ohio	20	15	74.9
Ansil Copeland, Ohio	20	15	73.0
Harold Anthony, Ohio	19	16	75.5
Jerry Schneider, California	18	17	75.3
Frank Stinson, Minnesota	17	18	71.9
Glen Riffle, Ohio	17	18	69.1
Art Tyson, Connecticut	16	19	69.7
Fred Lavett, California	15	20	71.7
Charles Killgore, Missouri	14	21	71.9
Stan Manker, Ohio	14	21	68.6
Jerry Black, North Dakota	13	22	70.5
Monte Latino, California	13	22	68.5
Harold Darnold, Iowa	9	26	67.7
Floyd Toole, Arkansas	9	26	65.6
James Burke, Oregon	8	27	66.6
Ronnie Simmons, California	6	29	64.3
Arthur Burch, Indiana	5	30	65.5
Ted Allen, Colorado	4	31	58.3
Elmer Harrison, Ohio	3	32	61.3
John Pratt, California	2	33	61.9

WORLD TOURNAMENT RECORDS 289

1973   Class B Summary

Rod Hatton, Texas	8	3	64.8
Edward Fishel, Washington	7	4	72.7
Herbert Criss, Washington	7	4	68.8
Al Richardson, Oregon	7	4	64.8
Sid Lash, Canada	6	5	68.7
Earl Winston, Missouri	6	5	66.1
Cletus Chapelle, Oregon	5	6	67.7
Russ DeHart, Indiana	5	6	66.7
Curt Bestul, Wisconsin	5	6	66.6
Eston Brown, California	5	6	62.4
Edward McFarland, Texas	3	8	62.8
James Ostrander, Michigan	2	9	63.3

1973   Class C Summary

Barry Chapelle, Oregon	10	1	60.2
Vic Joyner, Oregon	9	2	62.3
James Bustos, Colorado	9	2	54.3
Mate McBride, Utah	6	5	60.9
Jack Rainbow, Pennsylvania	6	5	59.0
Jim McCombs, Ohio	6	5	55.3
Jack Fahey, Kentucky	5	6	55.2
Ottie Reno, Ohio	5	6	52.5
Jim Douglas, California	5	6	50.4
Tom Webb, California	2	9	49.3
Gary Alexander, Washington	1	10	47.2
Clarence Giles, Utah	1	10	46.5

1973   Class D Summary

Stan Hilton, California	7	1	52.9
Orlean Clinton, Washington	6	2	50.8
Gene Rademacher, Florida	5	2	51.7
William Van Zanten, Arizona	3	4	47.5
Ronald Miller, Oregon	3	4	44.9
Albin Johnson, Washington	2	5	43.4
Jerry Moore, Connecticut	2	5	39.9
Roger Bolduc, Maine	1	6	39.1

14

Canadian Records

Since Elmer Hohl started pitching in the World Tournament in 1960 his record has been phenomenal. Four times he won the world championship, 1965, 1968, 1972, and 1973. In addition he has finished second five times, third twice, fourth twice and fifth once. He has never been under eighty percent ringers and in 1968 set the all time world record of 88.5% ringers for 35 games.

In addition to these titles Hohl has won most of the largest tournaments such as the Eastern National, the Greenville Classic, and has been the Canadian champion thirteen times.

Many other Canadian pitchers have distinguished themselves. Dean McLaughlin has won the Canadian championship twelve times including the 1973 title. Ross Stevenson won the 1965 Junior World Championship and in 1972 won the Class B Mens World Championship.

Most of the Canadian provinces have active chapters in the NHPA and players from the United States and Canada are playing more frequently in tournaments in both countries.

Records are not as plentiful as desired from the Canadian tournaments, but enough are included here to stimulate interest and so have been set aside in a separate chapter.

Canadian National Champions

Year	Name of Champion	Won	Lost	Ringer Percentage
1925	W. Struthers			
1926	W. Struthers			
1929	John Simmons			
1930	Fred Harburn			
1931	George Craggs			
1932	George Walwin			
1933	John Simmons			
1934	Robert Ferris			
1935	Robert Ferris			
1936	Fred Harburn			
1937	Fred Harburn			
1938	Dean McLaughlin			
1939	Fred Harburn			
1940-1948	No tournament held			
1949	Dean McLaughlin			
1950	Dean McLaughlin			79.6
1951	Walter Woodward	11	0	68.3
1952	Dean McLaughlin	11	0	68.8
1953	Walter Woodward	7	0	69.0
1954	Dean McLaughlin			
1955	Dean McLaughlin	11	0	83.3
1956	Dean McLaughlin	11	0	79.3
1957	Elmer Hohl	11	0	76.6
1958	Elmer Hohl	11	0	79.7
1959	Elmer Hohl	11	0	83.3
1960	Dean McLaughlin	5	0	91.6
1961	Elmer Hohl	8	0	82.0
1962	Elmer Hohl			
1963	Elmer Hohl	6	0	79.8
1964	Elmer Hohl			
1965	Elmer Hohl			
1966	Elmer Hohl			
1967	Dean McLaughlin	7	0	78.0
1968	Dean McLaughlin	11	0	81.2
1969	Dean McLaughlin	5	0	79.2
1970	Elmer Hohl			76.0
1971	Elmer Hohl	3	0	85.3
1972	Elmer Hohl	8	0	85.6
1973	Dean McLaughlin	7	0	78.9

PITCHING CHAMPIONSHIP HORSESHOES

Manitoba

Year	Name of Champion
1935	L. Orchard
1936	R. Myers
1937	Eddie Ballantyne
1938	Bert Snart
1939	Bert Snart
1940-1942	No tournament held
1943	Bert Snart
1944	Harry Phillips
1945	H. Ferguson
1946	Bert Snart
1947	Bert Snart
1948	Frank Park
1949	Bert Snart
1950	A. W. Smith
1951	Bert Snart
1952	Bert Snart
1953	Stan Giles
1954	Bert Snart
1955	Ted Lozanski
1956	Ted Lozanski
1957	William Crawford
1958	A. W. Smith
1959	A. W. Smith
1960	A. W. Smith
1961	A. W. Smith
1962	Sifton Rasmussen
1963	Ted Lozanski
1964	Ted Lozanski
1965	Roy McCann
1966	Lloyd Gemmel
1967	Ted Lozanski
1968	Ted Lozanski
1969	A. W. Smith
1970	A. W. Smith
1971	Lloyd Gemmell
1972	Ross Stevenson
1973	Lloyd Gemmell

Saskatchewan

Year	Name of Champion
1965	Fred Sorenson
1969	Lloyd Gemmell

Quebec

Year	Name of Champion	Won	Lost	Ringer Percentage
1959	Alex Gaudreau			
1960	Alex Gaudreau			
1961	Alex Gaudreau			
1962	Lucien Lambert			
1963	Constant Cote			
1964	Constant Cote	10	1	60.0
1965	Yvon Cloutier	17	1	
1966	Yvon Cloutier			
1967	Fernand Thibeault			
1968	Gillis Poirier			
1969	Fernand Thibeault	11	0	
1970	Fernand Thibeault			

ONTARIO

Year	Name of Champion	Won	Lost	R%
1971	Elmer Hohl	13	0	78.0

BRITISH COLUMBIA

1971	Sid Lash	4	0	67.7
1973	Sid Lash	5	1	67.3

NEW BRUNSWICK

1971	Wes Parlee
1972	Norman Gaudet

MARITIME

1971	Gordon McIsaac	46.7
1972	Gordon McIsaac	45.0
1973	Cyrus Gould	

This interesting old photograph shows the Championship Class which played at Vancouver, British Columbia on September 25, 1938. The title was won by Art Kindlan who is holding the plaque. This is the first tournament of record to decide a provincial champion. The participants, (left to right) are: McKenzie, Tom Nicholson, Joe Woods, Ed Hartley, Champion Art Kindlan, Andy Turriff, John Wallingham, Scott, Jimmy Porter and Rainford.

Pictured here are Charles Dupuis, President of the New Brunswick Horseshoe Players Association on the left, and Canadian Champion Dean McLaughlin, together for a clinic sponsored by the New Brunswick Department of Youth. The clinic was attended by 200 and commends the efforts of both men in promoting their sport.

WILLIAM MOUNTENAY
Bethune, Saskatchewan, Canada

He was one of the best in Canada during the late twenties and early thirties pitching about 80 percent in both tournament and exhibition play. Still active, Mountenay pitches about 50 percent ringers at 72 years of age.

DEAN McLAUGHLIN
12 times Canadian Champion. In 1960 McLaughlin hit the highest tournament on record with 91.6 percent ringers for five games to win the Canadian title and went on to win the North American title at Toronto.

Tips From Dean McLaughlin

When it comes to tips on playing horseshoes the one thing which stands out in my mind and seems to get me going on the right track is moving the head.

Since everything your body does is relayed through your head, it must be kept straight in line with the peg. Moving the head up and down during the swing is also moving the peg up and down or side to side as the case may be. Line up the peg and go through your swing keeping in mind that you will not move your head from the starting alignment. If you have to take a shorter back swing then try it, but first move up and make your step as close as you can to the foul line. This seems to work for me and I hope it will work for someone else.

When things aren't going well I paint my shoes white. This does two things:
1) You get a completely new feel of the shoe
2) Makes it easy to follow the shoe through the air to see what could be going wrong with the turn

Last but not least, if you miss the peg make sure you always miss on the left side. This is, of course, if you are a right handed pitcher using a clockwise turn. You will get a lot of ringers that have been tossed just a little too low or short that will grab the peg if played on the left side. The shoe opening is working toward the peg on the left and on the right the shoe is working away from the peg.

15

The Women

Participation in the women's division of horseshoe pitching has increased by leaps and bounds in recent years. Most states and open tournaments have separate classes for them. A few, like Vicki Winston and Cindy Dean, play frequently in the men's division because of a lack of competition.

With more participation has come a better caliber of play and more competition for the top pitchers.

Since they are permitted to pitch from 30 feet most women eagerly take advantage of the shorter distance. A few pitch from the men's distance of 40 feet. In any case they use the regulation court, merely moving up ten feet.

Occasional problems result from this because most courts are not built with 30 foot markings and oftentimes the standing surface is inferior. Couple with this a natural reluctance on the part of some men to play against women and a scarcity of women pitchers and you have a situation that calls for great patience.

The Women's World Champions

Year	Champion, Home Town	Played at	Won	Lost	Ringer Percentage
1920	Marjorie Voorhies, Asbury Park, New Jersey	Akron, Ohio	1	0	
1921	Mrs. J. R. Mathews, Minneapolis, Minn.	Minneapolis, Minnesota		0	
1922 W	Mrs. Mayme Francisco, Columbus, Ohio	St. Petersburg, Florida	3	0	
1922 S	Mrs. C. A. Lanhan, Bloomington, Illinois	Des Moines, Iowa	8	0	
1923 W	Mrs. Mayme Francisco, Columbus, Ohio	St. Petersburg, Florida	5	0	45.2
1923 S	Mrs. Mayme Francisco, Columbus, Ohio	Cleveland, Ohio	7	0	37.8
1924 W	Mrs. C. A. Lanhan, Bloomington, Illinois	Lake Worth, Florida	6	0	52.7
1924 S	Mrs. C. A. Lanhan, Bloomington, Illinois	Minneapolis, Minnesota	11	0	56.0
1925	Mrs. C. A. Lanhan, Bloomington, Illinois	Lake Worth, Florida	8	1	57.2
1926	Mrs. George Brouillette, Minneapolis, Minn.	St. Petersburg, Florida	14	1	43.2
1927 W	Mrs. George Brouillette, Minneapolis, Minn.	St. Petersburg, Florida	8	0	47.3
1927 S	Mrs. C. A. Lanhan, Bloomington, Illinois	Duluth, Minnesota	7	0	58.7
1928 S	Mrs. C. A. Lanhan, Bloomington, Illinois	St. Petersburg, Florida	9	0	54.9
1928 W	Mrs. Mayme Francisco, Columbus, Ohio	Rochester, New York	8	1	35.2
1929	Mrs. Mayme Francisco, Columbus, Ohio	St. Petersburg, Florida			54.9
1933	Caroline Schultz, Harvey, Illinois	Chicago, Illinois			73.8
1934	Caroline Schultz, Harvey, Illinois	Los Angeles, California			81.3
1935	Esther James, Hasting, Michigan	Moline, Illinois	5	0	63.6
1949	Anna Lindquist, Morgantown, W. Va.	Murray, Utah			
1950	Pat DeLeary, Phoenix, Arizona	Murray, Utah			51.2
1951	Sarah Byers, Portland, Oregon	Murray, Utah			44.3
1952	Sarah Byers, Portland, Oregon	Murray, Utah	7	0	53.5

PITCHING CHAMPIONSHIP HORSESHOES

Year	Champion	Location			
1953	Pat DeLeary, Phoenix, Arizona	Murray, Utah	9	0	35.7
1954	Katie Gregson, Crestline, California	Murray, Utah			
1955	Hazel Harris, Denver, Colorado	Murray, Utah			52.6
1956	Vicki Chapelle, Portland, Oregon	Murray, Utah	3	0	42.4
1957	Gertsie Lou Selby, Boulder, Colorado	Murray, Utah	4	0	51.8
1958	Vicki Chapelle, Portland, Oregon	Murray, Utah	4	0	52.8
1959	Vicki Chapelle, Portland, Oregon	Murray, Utah	5	1	54.1
1960	Esta McKee, Roy Center, Indiana	Muncie, Indiana	5	0	54.9
1961	Vicki Chapelle Winston, La Monte, Missouri	Greenville, Ohio	7	0	65.3
1962	Sue Gillespie, Portland, Indiana	South Gate, California	5	1	58.6
1963	Vicki Chapelle Winston, LaMonte, Missouri	Greenville, Ohio	7	0	81.3
1964	Sue Gillespie, Portland, Indiana	Keene, New Hampshire	6	1	75.9
1965	Sue Gillespie, Portland, Indiana	Murray, Utah	6	1	72.5
1966	Vicki Chapelle Winston, LaMonte, Missouri	Fargo, North Dakota	7	0	73.6
1967	Vicki Chapelle Winston, LaMonte, Missouri	Keene, New Hampshire	7	0	74.9
1968	Lorraine Thomas, Lockport, New York	Erie, Pennsylvania	7	0	79.6
1969	Vicki Chapelle Winston, LaMonte, Missouri	South Gate, California	7	0	72.0
1970	Ruth Hangen, Buffalo, New York	Middlesex, New Jersey	7	0	73.4
1971	Ruth Hangen, Buffalo, New York	Greenville, Ohio	7	0	76.6
1972	Ruth Hangen, Buffalo, New York	Eureka, California	7	0	79.6
1973	Ruth Hangen, Buffalo, New York				

Women's Division—World Records

COMPLETE TOURNAMENT, 7 GAMES

Ringer pct.	81.3	Sue Gillespie, Portland, Ind.	1964
Total ringers	383	Caroline Schultz, Harvey, Ill.	1934
Double ringers	154	Vicki Winston, LaMonte, Mo.	1969
Shoes Pitched	542	Vicki Winston, LaMonte, Mo.	1969
		Caroline Lankhorst, Keene, N. H.	1969

SINGLE GAME, INDIVIDUAL

Ringer pct., winning player	95.0	Ruth Hangen, Getzville, N. Y.	1973
Ringer pct., losing player	81.0	Ruth Hangen, Buffalo, N. Y.	1969
Ringers, winner	81	Vicki Winston, LaMonte, Mo.	1969
	81	Lorraine Thomas, Lockport, N. Y.	1973
Ringers, loser	81	Ruth Hangen, Buffalo, N. Y.	1969
Doubles, winner	33	Lorraine Thomas, Lockport, N. Y.	1973
Doubles, loser	34	Ruth Hangen, Buffalo, N. Y.	1969
Consecutive ringers	30	Sue Gillespie, Portland, Ind.	1964

SINGLE GAME, BOTH PLAYERS

Most shoes pitched	104	Lorraine Thomas, Lockport, N. Y. & Opal Reno, Lucasville, Ohio	1973
Ringer pct.	81.0	Vicki Winston and Ruth Hangen	1969
Total ringers	162	Vicki Winston and Ruth Hangen	1969
Double ringers	66	Vicki Winston and Ruth Hangen	1969
Cancelled ringers	130	Lorraine Thomas and Opal Reno	1973

(Continued)

Women's Division—World Records

Most four-deads	21	Lorraine Thomas and Opal Reno	1973
Consecutive four-deads	5	Sue Gillespie and Vicki Winston	1964
	5	Sue Gillespie and Anna Lindquist	1962
	5	Ruth Hangen and Cindy Dean	1970
	5	Helen Roberts and Ruth Hangen	1972
	5	Ruth Hangen and Lorraine Thomas	1973

QUALIFYING. 100 SHOES

Total points	266	Esther James, Hastings, Mich.	1935
Ringers	86	Esther James, Hastings, Mich.	1935
Doubles	34	Sue Gillespie, Portland, Ind.	1964
	34	Lorraine Thomas, Lockport, N. Y.	1972

LORRAINE THOMAS
1968 World Champion

World Tournament Action
Lorraine Thomas is firing here on the Keene, New Hampshire courts on her way to the 1968 World Championship. Her opponent is Ruth Hangen. Lorraine's shoe, a flip, can be seen in mid-air. On the court to her left walking away from the camera is Vicki Winston and on the court to her right wearing gloves is Cindy Dean, a fast rising star from Virginia.

Vicki Chapelle Winston

Vicki Chapelle Winston of LaMonte, Missouri, is one of the greatest if not the greatest female horseshoe pitcher the game has known. As the current world champion she reigns as the First Lady of Horseshoes.

Vicki's father, Cletus Chapelle of Oregon, was pitching tournament horseshoes before she was born. Vicki grew up with a horseshoe in her hand.

Father Chapelle was a four time champion of the state of Oregon and served as both a state and national officer for many years. To retain the flavor of the game in her household, Vicki married Earl Winston, 1955 champion of Missouri. They have one child.

Over the years Vicki has developed a flawless pitching style using a one and one-quarter turn.

See page 286 for a brief summary of her World Tournament competition:

VICKI CHAPELLE WINSTON
8 Times World Champion

PITCHING CHAMPIONSHIP HORSESHOES

Year	Won	Lost	Ringer Percentage	Comment
1953	3	4		Age 14, Finished 5th
1954	4	1		3rd after 3-way play-off for 1st
1955	Illness prevented play			
1956	7	0	52.2	1st World Title
1957	Did not compete			
1958	4	0	60.9	2nd World Title
1959	4	0	52.8	3rd World Title
1960	3	3	38.8	4th place (New Bride)
1961	5	0	54.9	4th World Title
1962	3	4	53.8	5th place
1963	5	1	58.6	5th World Title
1964	6	1	64.0	2nd place
1965	6	1	71.7	2nd place
1966	6	1	72.5	6th World Title
1967	7	0	73.6	7th World Title
1968	6	1	69.4	2nd place
1969	7	0	79.6	8th World Title

Tips from Vicki Chapelle Winston

When it comes to giving pitching tips, I find myself at a little bit of a loss for words. What comes naturally for me may not be at all the way someone else should pitch. Horseshoe pitching, to my mind, is a very individualistic sport, and people aren't all going to do it the same way. You can put a horseshoe in someone's hand, show them the various turns, how to hold the shoe and approximately how to throw it. You can show them where to stand and as soon as you show them these basic things, anyone who has horseshoe tournament experience can name numerous people who pitch just the opposite of what you've told the pupil. With this thought in mind I can mention a few things that have helped me, but they may not necessarily help anyone else.

The first thing is to know the rules. I notice two main

infractions made by players who have been pitching horseshoe for many years. They are failure to observe the foul line and improper position while waiting for the opponent to pitch. The few inches you may gain by stepping over the foul line are not worth the damage to your reputation as a good sportsman. It is only common courtesy, besides being a rule, that you stand to the side and to the rear of your opponent while she is pitching. Observation of these two rules will add greatly to the enjoyment of the tournament by everyone.

We are now ready to play and one of the most important things is to dress comfortably. Wear shoes that are good walking shoes and fit well. I like sleeveless blouses so I am not hampered by any restraining sleeves or seams when I give a horseshoe a little extra "oomph" or follow through. Always wear slacks, or shorts if you have the proper figure. Any woman who has tried pitching in a dress or skirt has probably suffered the consequences.

For 30 foot pitching I like the 1¼ turn. When a young girl, I first learned the ¾ turn. In a few years my father had me try the 1¼. I feel sure I could never have achieved the same success with the ¾ turn that I've had with the 1¼. Brands of horseshoes make a very big difference. After borrowing a pair of a certain make just a week before the 1963 World Horseshoe Tournament, I won the tournament and have been using that make ever since. I have increased my percentage considerably by finding a horseshoe with the proper balance for my turn. Unfortunately, I now find myself unable to properly turn any other make of horseshoes, so must be sure I always have my own with me. (This has proved very embarrassing when shooting some publicity film and I found that my husband had driven off with my horseshoes. The performance was definitely not up to championship standards.) Viewers of recent World Horseshoe Tournaments have probably noticed the increase of the flip artists in the women's division. Although I wouldn't try this myself, they tell me it is completely natural for the 30 foot distance. I have also seen the 1¾ turn used, but this turn is just too difficult for the 30 foot distance.

The most major change in my career has been the change in my method of delivery. I changed from holding the shoe in front of my face to holding it at my side. This still did not feel quite natural and I added a couple of short arm swings to relieve tension and ready myself for the delivery. This certainly was a major factor in raising my ringer percentage. I try not to throw too high. A lower, more direct line seems to give me better accuracy. I do not crowd the lines, as I want to give the shoe room to turn. At home I practice at 31 feet, and as I do not take a four-foot step, I throw a little farther than the required distance. However, in tournaments I tend to move up a little as the tension seems to lower my delivery and I do not want any shoes falling short. I find that keeping my hand and fingers relaxed is also important. I also have a certain pattern for breathing as I go through the pitching motions. Experimentation will enable you to find what is natural for yourself. The important thing is to do everything the same each time. You've probably heard the expression that a certain player looks just like a machine. Well, that's what it takes. Only then will you be able to accomplish any great deal of accuracy.

Practice, of course, is the most important ingredient in readying yourself for competition. If at all possible, have a court at home, whether it be permanent or portable. It doesn't have to be fancy. Other pitchers have laughed at my dirt court and wooden platforms. However, it seems to get the job done and has helped tremendously in the three or four years I've had it. I found it was so easy to put off practice when I knew I would have to drive to a court and then spend a lot of time carrying water and digging up clay that someone else had left to harden in the sun. Now all I have to do is walk out the back door. We have very nearly put horseshoe pitching back into the barnyard. The interruptions from cats, dogs and chickens help greatly in learning to pitch under adverse conditions.

This brings me to my final point and that is concentration. I know of no way to calm the jittery nerves and the butterflys. They are still with me after 17 years of competitive pitching, so I try to ignore them by concentrating on the job at hand. You cannot win a tournament by looking into the stands to see where the family is sitting, or carrying on conversations with spectators. I found myself guilty of another error this past year. I was watching another game. All of a sudden my opponent had climbed about 20 points before I could regain my composure. It cost me dearly in percentage, which is important to me.

I like to have goals for which to strive. It makes me try just a little harder. Concentrate on the stake and nothing else. If your concentration is broken, stop and then get set again. We will all have times when a judge or another player runs behind the stake just as we're ready to pitch. You must learn to overcome these interruptions and not let them bother you. It isn't easy, but it can be done. When you ignore all outside noises, all motion and can see nothing but the stake, then you are ready to be a competitive horseshoe pitcher.

SUE GILLESPIE KUCHCINSKI

Sue Gillespie Kuchcinski

Sue Gillespie, pitching out of Portland, Indiana, won the women's World Championship three times, 1962, 1964 and 1965. Her 81.3 percent ringers in 1964 tied the all time record for a tournament. Her 93.3 percent game in 1964 and her 259 point qualifying round in 1964 still stand as world records.

In 1969 Sue married World Champion Dan Kuchcinski of Erie, Pennsylvania, and as a new bride did not compete in the 1969 tournament. However, she is busy helping Dan with his exhibitions and can be expected to return to competition at some future date.

Sue offers these pitching tips:

One should learn the fundamentals of the game and begin with a positive attitude. A turn should then be developed and each individual's form and style should be that which is comfortable and that which comes naturally.

One should be "psyched up" to pitch and always have the confidence that she can and will make ringers. This, of course, comes with concentrated practice. Timing, relaxation, and concentration are important to the game and when all of these things are put together improvement will be immense.

As for our exhibitions, we have appeared on national T.V. and have travelled throughout the United States performing for sport shows, fairs, clubs, etc. The act is that of trick shooting with horseshoe pitching and acrobatics being involved at the same time. We do hope to create a little more interest in the game with our performances.

RUTH HANGEN
New York State Champion
(Photo courtesy *Buffalo Evening News*)

Ruth Hangen

Ruth Hangen of Buffalo, New York, is the current women's world champion, having won four consecutive titles for 1970, 1971, 1972, and 1973, and is one of the most dedicated women now pursuing the championship. Ruth has these comments on the game.

The largest women's league in the world is in Lockport, New York, and almost all of them throw the flip. This is holding the shoe by the heel and releasing it so that it turns once and should ring the stake from a front, forward position. Although most consider this an unorthodox grip, I believe it to be the easiest and most reliable for women.

I wholeheartedly believe the main help in horseshoe pitching is complete concentration. To reach this point you must have the fundamentals of the game ingrained. This requires practice, practice, practice! I recommend at least two hours per day if you want to reach the championship area.

After you have learned the fundamentals and the best turn, grip and approach for you, the subconscious takes hold, and in competition, severe concentration leads to perfect timing. If the timing is there, accuracy occurs and you have perfected and conquered the game. To acquire this keep your eyes glued on the stake during all phases of delivery.

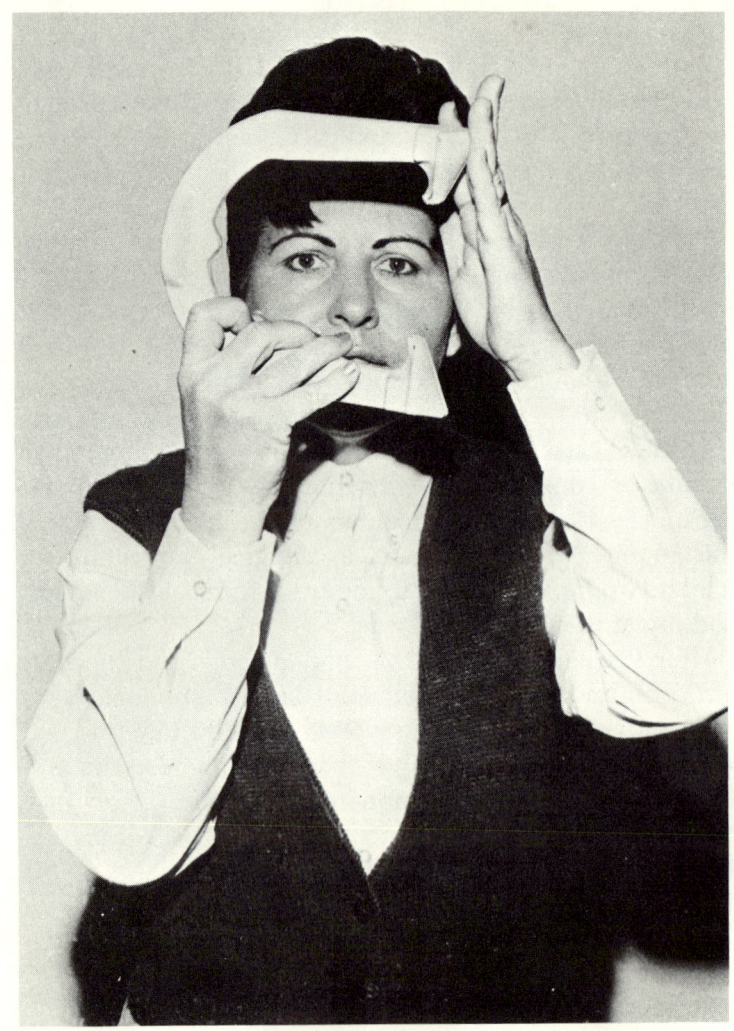

CINDY DEAN
1969 Virginia Champion

Comments from the Dean of Women, Cindy That Is, from McGaheysville, Virginia

I first became interested in pitching horseshoes in 1963 when my husband started entering tournaments in Virginia. He stayed on the courts most of the time so if I wanted to be with him it was pitch horseshoes or else. I started throwing the shoes back to him, then decided why waste this energy, might as well try to get ringers. Bob taught me the correct way to hold the shoe for a turn and a quarter and the rules of the game and in 1966 I entered my first tournament and loved every minute of it. Now it's in my blood.

It isn't just the thrill of winning but the challenge is always there. No matter how much I improve I know there is someone who can pitch better. My determination keeps me working hard, for I want to be able to pitch better than 80 percent, consistently. To date, my highest qualify has been 253 points with 78 percent ringers for 100 shoes.

Most of my pitching has been with the men as Virginia has very few ladies that are interested in the game. Even though I pitch from 30 feet it has no advantage, because I have to walk 20 feet farther each pitch than do the men and the games are usually longer, many of them over 100 shoes. One must have quite a bit of endurance to keep pace in a 16-man round robin.

Horseshoe pitching may come naturally to some but I must practice in order to coordinate my distance, speed and stride. Concentration is a must for me, so it makes no difference whether my opponent be male or female when I go on the court.

DOROTHY PINCH

Dorothy Pinch, Sharon, Pennsylvania, is 4th Vice President of the NHPA and one of many women dedicated to the game. Dorothy and her husband, Herb Pinch, have spent many years playing and promoting horseshoes.

THE WOMEN 317

CANADIAN NATIONAL CHAMPIONS

| 1972 | Jackie Sehn | 6 | 1 | 28.1 |
| 1973 | Jackie Sehn | 6 | 1 | 42.1 |

BRITISH COLUMBIA

| 1971 | June Moore | 4 | 1 | |

Women's State Champions

CALIFORNIA

Year	Name of Champion	Won	Lost	Shoes Pitched	Ringers	R%
1964	Esther Williams	3	0			
1965	Elsie Gregerson	5	0			43.3
1966	Elsie Gregerson	6	0			29.5
1967	Stella Gates	4	1			
1968	Flyorence Klees	5	0			37.4
1969	Pat Turner	3	0			
1970	Carrie Price	3	0	110	55	50.0
1971	Leona Anderson	5	0	170	85	50.0
1972	Leona Anderson	3	0	184	113	61.4
1973	Leona Anderson	11	0	472	259	54.9

STATE RECORDS

| High ringer percentage, tournament | Leona Anderson | 1972 | 61.4 |
| High ringer percentage, game | Leona Anderson | 1972 | 73.1 |

Year	Name of Champion	Won	Lost	Ringer Percentage
COLORADO				
1969	Esther Fouts			
1970	Emelie Arnold	4	0	
1971	Alice Abrams	3	1	

PITCHING CHAMPIONSHIP HORSESHOES 318

FLORIDA

1969	Opal Corbett	2	0	124	58	46.7
1970	Wanda Ditmer	2	0	142	88	62.0
1971	Opal Corbett	Retained title unchallenged				
1972	Opal Corbett	2	0	110	46	41.8
1973	Opal Corbett	Retained title unchallenged				

GEORGIA

1972	Mae Brooks	3	0	
1973	Brenda Turner	3	0	

INDIANA

1961	Esta McKee	5	0	
1963	Sue Gillespie			69.2
1967	Wanda Ditmer	3	0	55.3
1969	Bonnie Seibold	3	0	58.5
1970	Bonnie Seibold			50.0
1971	Carolyn Truman	3	0	55.6
1972	Bonnie Seibold	6	1	56.2
1973	Bonnie Seibold	4	1	62.5

IOWA

1965	Nancy Henton			
1967	Ruby Christensen			
1968	R. Bailey	3	1	42.6
1970	Mary Ann Kaiser	3	0	
1971	G. Robison	2	0	23.8
1973	Ruth Bailey	3	0	28.3

KENTUCKY

1968	Edith Hill	3	0	20.5
1969	Norma Johnson	5	0	33.4
1970	Christine Kelley	4	1	37.4
1971	Christine Kelley	3	0	50.0
1972	Christine Kelley	6	0	42.4
1973	Christine Kelley	6	0	50.3

MAINE

1966	Anita Patenaude	4	1	12.2

THE WOMEN 319

1967	Ada Smith	3	0	37.0
1968	Simone Thibeault	5	0	39.4
1969	Simone Thibeault	10	0	43.3
1970	Ona Pratt	7	1	40.8
1971	Ona Pratt	5	0	45.1
1972	Ona Pratt	5	0	51.1
1973	Alice Bonnevie	4	2	37.6

MANITOBA

1966	Phoabe Fraser
1967	Elsie Cook
1968	Fern Snart
1969	Fern Snart
1970	Helen Royalyea

MASSACHUSETTS

1964	Pamela Stowell	3	1	30.1
1966	A. Ducharme	4	1	43.1
1967	Rita Ducharme	3	0	48.7
1968	Rita Ducharme	2	0	59.4

1969–1970–1971 No women's classes held.

| 1972 | Deborah Michaud | 5 | 0 | 43.3 |
| 1973 | Deborah Michaud | Retained title—Unchallenged. | | | |

MICHIGAN

1961	Darlene Swanson	4	1	
1962	Dorothy Smith			
1965	Marge Buhler			
1967	Marge Buhler	4	1	44.0
1968	Dorothy Smith			
1969	Marge Buhler			

MICHIGAN WOLVERINE

1970	Marge Buhler	9	1	37.2
1971	Jean Swarthout	7	1	
1972	Jean Swarthout	5	0	52.9
1973	Irene Ostrander	5	0	51.6

PITCHING CHAMPIONSHIP HORSESHOES 320

MICHIGAN UPPER PENINSULA

1970	Bernice Huotari	3	0	36.0
1971	Bernice Huotari	4	0	38.0
1972	Pat Paquette	4	0	31.3
1973	Bernice Huotari	5	0	41.4

NEBRASKA

| 1972 | Margaret Fox | 3 | 0 | 35.8 |
| 1973 | Carolyn Schneider | 4 | 1 | 35.6 |

NEVADA

1969	Judy Cork	5	0	
1970	Gay Wilfon	5	0	21.0
1971	Gay Wilfon	5	0	24.3
1972	Marge Bower	4	1	20.2
1973	Gay Wilfon	4	1	29.0

NEW HAMPSHIRE

1966	A. Mason	5	0	23.1
1967	Caroline Lankhorst	5	1	46.7
1969	Caroline Lankhorst	7	0	65.5
1970	Beverly Jacques	5	1	59.2
1971	Beverly Jacques	6	0	54.3
1972	Debbie Pickering	3	1	50.6

NEW JERSEY

| 1973 | Jeanette Kemmerer | 7 | 0 | 39.3 |

NEW MEXICO

1968	Nancy Henson	6	0	26.8
1969	Nancy Henson	5	0	31.6
1970	Marilyn Hanes	5	0	15.5
1971	Marilyn Hanes	4	0	21.5
1972	Nancy Henson	5	0	43.6
1973	Betty Romero	4	1	23.2

THE WOMEN

NEW YORK

Year	Name	Won	Lost	Percentage
1963	Lorraine Thomas			37.0
1964	Lorraine Thomas	5	0	49.7
1965	Lorraine Thomas	5	0	60.5
1966	Lorraine Thomas	3	0	61.6
1967	Ruth Hangen	5	0	68.5
1968	Ruth Hangen	2	1	73.6
1969	Ruth Hangen	5	0	71.3
1970	Lorraine Thomas	3	0	80.9
1971	Ruth Hangen	2	0	57.9
1972	Lorraine Thomas	3	0	80.0
1973	Lorraine Thomas	3	0	68.7

STATE RECORDS

Name of Record	Record Holder	Year Set	Record
High ringer percentage, tournament	Lorraine Thomas	1970	80.9
High ringer percentage, game	Lorraine Thomas	1970	92.2

NORTH DAKOTA

Year	Name	Won	Lost	Percentage
1968	Mrs. Marcus Ihli			
1969	Sister Mary Stephen	3	1	13.8

OKLAHOMA

Year	Name	Won	Lost	Percentage
1963	Mrs. Don Renbarger	3	0	

OREGON

Year	Name	Won	Lost	Percentage
1964	W. Mitchel	3	0	
1965	Joan Williams	5	1	
1968	Judy Miller	3	0	21.6
1969	Edith Stafford	5	0	19.5

OHIO

Year	Name of Champion	Won	Lost	Shoes Pitched	Ringers	Ringer Percentage
1961	Kathryn Overman	3	0	176	40	22.7
1962	Barbara Lowery	8	1	426	225	52.8
1963	Ruth Bennett	5	0	256	161	62.9
1964	Ruth Bennett	5	0	232	151	65.0

PITCHING CHAMPIONSHIP HORSESHOES

1965	Ruth Bennett	Retained title—no meet				
1966	Ruth Bennett	3	0	118	63	53.5
1967	Ruth Bennett	5	0	198	131	66.1
1968	Ruth Bennett	3	0	138	86	62.3
1969	Katherine Harrison	3	0	164	72	43.9
1970	Katherine Harrison	3	0			50.0
1971	Katherine Harrison	5	0			49.7
1972	Opal Reno	4	1	262	169	64,5
1973	Opal Reno	5	0	294	207	70.4

Ohio State Records

Name of Record	Record Holder	Year	Record
High ringer percentage, tournament	Opal Reno	1973	70.4
Most shoes one game	Janet Reno & Avanelle Brown	1961	144

OREGON

1964	Wilma Mitchell			18.2
1965	Joan Williams			13.9
1966	Joan Williams			15.1
1967	Edith Stafford			19.6
1968	Judy Miller			21.6
1969	Geneva Frazier			25.0
1970	Geneva Frazier	3	0	32.7
1971	Phyllis Joyner	5	1	26.1
1972	Phyllis Joyner	5	0	37.0
1973	Fran Cooper	6	1	46.3

PENNSYLVANIA

Year	Name of Champion	Won	Lost	Ringer Percentage
1965	Opal Corbett			
1966	Opal Corbett			
1967	Opal Corbett			
1968	Opal Corbett			
1969	Opal Corbett			

THE WOMEN 323

1970	Mae Kilinsky	2	0	31.0
1971	Mae Kilinsky	2	0	26.8
1972	Mae Kilinsky	7	0	17.7

SOUTH DAKOTA

1968	Christine Finkbohm	5	0	31.7
1969	Christine Finkbohm	5	0	27.4
1970	Myrline Schliemann	7	0	42.7
1971	Myrline Schliemann	6	0	48.2
1972	Myrline Schliemann	6	0	45.7
1973	Myrline Schliemann	5	0	42.1

TEXAS

1969	Linda McGuffin	6	0	
1970	Linda McGuffin	8	0	
1971	K. McGuffin	5	0	
1972	M. Crawford	5	0	
1973	Nora Mann			

VERMONT

| 1972 | Syble Horton | | | |
| 1973 | Elizabeth Downer | 6 | 1 | 36.6 |

VIRGINIA

1966	Cindy Dean	4	0			37.1
1967	Cindy Dean	3	0			43.1
1968	Mary Monroe	4	0			48.2
1969	Cindy Dean	3	0			65.8
1970	Cindy Dean	Retained Title—Unchallenged				
1971	Cindy Dean	Retained Title—Unchallenged				
1972	Cindy Dean	4	0			65.6
1973	Cindy Dean	5	0	218	119	54.5

WASHINGTON

1966	P. Hansen	7	0	35.1
1967	Alice Rehard	6	1	40.2
1969	Mildred Kuhne	6	0	59.0

PITCHING CHAMPIONSHIP HORSESHOES 324

1970	Mildred Kuhne	6	0	282	163	57.8
1971	Mildred Kuhne	5	0	274	156	56.9
1972	Sarah Giacomini	6	1	404	219	54.2
1973	Debbie Woodman	6	1	444	246	55.4

STATE RECORDS

Name of Record	Record Holder	Year Set	Record
High ringer percentage, tournament	Mildred Kuhne	1969	59.0
High ringer percentage, game	Mildred Kuhne	1969	71.1
Most consecutive doubles	Shirley O'Brien	1973	6
Most ringers, game	Mildred Kuhne	1973	44
High game for both players	Debbie Woodman & Shirley O'Brien	1973	59.0
Most four-deads, game	Alice Rehard & Sarah Giacomini	1973	5

WEST VIRGINIA

1973	Connie Laudermilk	5	0

WISCONSIN

1969	S. Dollevolt	8	1	22.3
1970	Marion Ristau	5	1	21.4
1971	Marion Ristau	5	0	42.6
1972	D. Ebert	7	0	51.3

WYOMING

1962	Dorothy Miller	3	0			42.5
1963	Dorothy Miller					26.4
1964	Dorothy Miller	6	0			42.5
1965	Dessie Holliday	5	0			25.5
1966	Carol Ferguson	6	0			39.2
1967	Carol Ferguson	8	0	492	238	48.4
1968	Dessie Holliday	9	3	700	324	46.3
1969	Carol Ferguson	15	3	668	327	49.0
1970	Dessie Holliday	9	0	422	171	40.5
1971	Beverlee Holliday	10	0	562	116	20.6
1972	Dessie Holliday	6	3	610	298	48.9
1973	Dessie Holliday	6	0	352	127	38.9

THE WOMEN

STATE RECORDS

Name of Record	Record Holder	Year Set	Record
High ringer percentage, tournament	Carol Ferguson	1969	49.0
High ringer percentage, game	Carol Ferguson	1969	59.6
High ringer percentage, qualifying	Carol Ferguson	1969	49.0
Most shoes, tournament	Agnes Burns	1970	952
Most shoes, game	Agnes Burns & Beverlee Holiday	1970	110

QUEBEC

1965	Y. Cloutier
1966	Y. Cloutier

16

The Juniors

The Junior Division has been a part of horseshoes for a long time. Frank Stinson, 1969 Minnesota State Men's Champion, was crowned Junior World's Champion in 1924.

But in spite of the length of time that it has been recognized, the junior division did not receive much attention until recent years.

It is evident from the number of junior players of both sexes now taking part that this division is one of the brightest spots in the game. Not only do the juniors play hard, they become very accurate. The spectator interest in this division is good, too.

The age for juniors has been set at 17 and the pitching distance at 30 feet. Some players choose to start pitching from the men's distance of 40 feet. Others start at 30 and back up as they grow and become stronger. Some are never able to make the change successfully. That is to say that their ringer percentage drops so drastically that they do not continue to play the game on the same plane.

Many of the Junior World Champions go on to make their mark in the Men's Division. Mark Seibold won the

Indiana men's title in 1973 and tied Elmer Hohl for the 1973 men's world championship, losing in a play-off. Ross Stevenson won the 1972 men's class B world championship and Donnie Roberts won the 1972 Ohio men's title.

World Junior Champions

Year	Champion, Home Town	Won	Lost	Ringer Percentage
1924	Frank Stinson, Minnesota			
1951	Dave Louck, San Francisco, California	15	0	47.9
1952	Dave Louck, San Francisco, California			
1954	Byron Bowman, Murray, Utah			
1955	Byron Bowman, Murray, Utah			
1956	Bob Madsen, American Forks, Utah			
1957	Rodney Hilton, Murray, Utah			
1958	Billy Backer, Salt Lake City, Utah	9	0	
1959	Donnie Roberts, Lucasville, Ohio	7	0	55.9
1960	Hal Brown, Mulberry, Indiana	7	0	55.9
1961	Gary Roberts, Lucasville, Ohio	6	1	50.0
1962	Gary Roberts, Lucasville, Ohio	7	0	62.4
1963	Gary Roberts, Lucasville, Ohio	7	0	62.8
1964	Gary Roberts, Lucasville, Ohio	6	1	67.6
1965	Ross Stevenson, Bader, Ontario	7	0	65.1
1966	Mark Seibold, Huntington, Indiana	7	0	75.6
1967	Farron Eisemann, Riverton, Wyoming	6	1	73.6
1968	Farron Eisemann, Riverton, Wyoming	7	0	78.5
1969	Mark Seibold, Erie, Pennsylvania	7	0	83.7
1969	Mark Seibold, Huntington, Ind.	7	0	83.7
1970	Bill Holland, Indianapolis, Ind.			79.7
1971	Walter Ray Williams, Eureka, Cal.			86.3
1972	Walter Ray Williams, Eureka, Cal.			89.2
1973	Jeffrey Williams, Eureka, Cal.			85.5

THE JUNIORS 328

Complete Tournament, 7 Games

Ringer pct.	89.2	Walter Roy Williams, Eureka, Calif.	1972
Total ringers	533	Alvin Vinsant, Arcata, Calif.	1972
Double ringers	225	Walter Ray Williams, Eureka, Calif.	1972
Shoes pitched	648	Alvin Vinsant, Arcata, California	1972

Single Game, Individual

Ringer pct., winning player	96.9	Walter Ray Williams, Eureka, Calif.	1971
Ringer pct., losing player	84.2	Alvin Vinsant, Arcata, Calif.	1972
Ringers, winning player	133	Mark Seibold, Huntington, Ind.	1969
Ringers, losing player	125	Paul Day, Frankfort, Ind.	1969
Double ringers, winning player	59	Mark Seibold, Huntington, Ind.	1969
Double ringers, losing player	51	Paul Day, Frankfort, Ind.	1969
Consecutive ringers	40	Walter Ray Williams, Eureka, Calif.	1972

Single Game, Both Players

Longest game, shoes pitched	150	Mark Seibold & Paul Day	1969
Ringer pct.	87.1	Walter Ray Williams & Alvin Vinsant	1972
Total ringers	258	Mark Seibold & Paul Day	1969
Double ringers	110	Mark Seibold & Paul Day	1969
Cancelled Ringers	232	Mark Seibold & Paul Day	1969
"Four Deads"	43	Mark Seibold & Paul Day	1969
Consecutive "Four Deads"	10	Mike Weber & Mark Seibold	1970

Qualifying, 50 Shoes

Total points	141	Mark Seibold, Huntington, Ind.	1969
Ringers	46	Mark Seibold, Huntington, Ind.	1969
Double ringers	21	Mark Seibold, Huntington, Ind.	1969

THE BROTHERS WILLIAMS

Walter Ray "Deadeye" Williams, left, and Jeffrey Williams are brothers from Eureka, California. Walter Ray won the 1971 and 1972 World Junior titles setting an all time ringer percentage of 89.2% in 1972. He injured a hand before the start of the 1973 tournament but played anyway. Brother Jeffrey stepped in with a blistering 85.5% to keep the 1973 title in the family, a pace which could have won the title even with Walter Ray in top form. As a brother act they join Donnie and Gary Roberts as brothers who held the Junior World Championship and they appear set to dominate the division for several seasons.)

PITCHING CHAMPIONSHIP HORSESHOES 330

World Junior Girls Champions

Year	Champion, Home Town	Won	Lost	Shoes	Ringers	R%
1967	Bonita Seibold, Huntington, Ind.					29.1
1968	Carolyn Truman, Columbia City, Ind.	5	1			48.7
1969	Mary Lee, Brooklyn, N. Y.	6	0			50.1
1970	Peggy Smith, Muskegon, Michigan	4	2			32.0
1971	Jennifer Reno, Lucasville, Ohio	5	0	240	95	39.7
1972	Jennifer Reno, Lucasville, Ohio	5	0	246	147	59.8
1973	Rosemary Gibson, Centralia, Illinois	7	0			38.0

JENNIFER RENO

Jennifer Reno, Lucasville, Ohio, is the only girl to hold the World Junior Girls Championship twice, 1971 and 1972. Jennifer holds or shares seven world records including highest single game at 71.9% and highest single tournament at 59.8%.

THE JUNIORS 331

Girls' Division, Girls under 17

COMPLETE TOURNAMENT
Ringer Pct.	59.8	Jennifer Reno, Lucasville, Ohio	1972
Total ringers	155	Mary Lee, Brooklyn, N. Y.	1972
Double ringers	46	Jennifer Reno, Lucasville, Ohio	1972
Shoes pitched	418	Pat Thomas, Lockport, N. Y.	1967

SINGE GAME, INDIVIDUAL
Ringer Pct., winning player	71.9	Jennifer Reno, Lucasville, Ohio	1972
Ringer Pct., losing player	53.4	Mary Lee, Brooklyn, N. Y.	1972
Total ringers, winner	39	Delores Ducharme, Eastampton, Mass.	1968
Total ringers, loser	34	Peggy Smith, Muskegon, Mich.	1968
Double ringers, winner	13	Jennifer Reno, Lucasville, Ohio	1972
Double ringers, loser	8	Mary Lee, Brooklyn, N. Y.	1972
Consecutive ringers	10	Jennifer Reno, Lucasville, Ohio	1972

SINGLE GAME, BOTH PLAYERS
Most shoes pitched	94	Kathy Daniels & Roberta Lovelady	1973
Ringer pct.	59.5	Jennifer Reno and Mary Lee	1972
Total ringers	73	Delores Ducharme & Peggy Smith	1968
Double ringers	14	Muffie Woodman & Lynne Harison	1973
Cancelled ringers	46	Delores Ducharme & Peggy Smith	1968
		Jennifer Reno & Mary Lee	1972
Most four-deads	4	Lynne Harrison & Cathy Melling	1972

QUALIFYING, 50 SHOES
Total points	109	Carolyn Truman, Columbia City, Ind.	1968
Total ringers	33	Carolyn Truman, Columbia City, Ind.	1968
Double ringers	12	Carolyn Truman, Columbia City, Ind.	1968

PITCHING CHAMPIONSHIP HORSESHOES 332

Junior State Championships
Boys and Girls

ALABAMA

Year	Name of Champion	Won	Lost	Pitched	Ringers	Percentage
1969	Tommy Whisenant	7	0	350	95	27.0
1972	Jimmie Cleckler	7	0	350	88	25.0

Year	Champion	Won	Lost			Ringer Percentage
CALIFORNIA						
1964	Billy Seymour	3	0			47.5
1965	Harold Carden	6	0			46.7
1966	George Hughey	5	0			45.0
1967	Kevin Turner	7	0			
1968	Kevin Turner	3	0			50.0
1969	Kevin Turner	5	0			
1970	Walter Ray Williams	3	0	90	76	84.4
1971	Walter Ray Williams	5	0	164	147	89.6
1972	Walter Ray Williams	3	0	250	209	83.6
1973	Walter Ray Williams	5	0	284	250	88.0

California Junior Girls

1971	Debbi Williams	3	0	76	18	23.7
1972	Debbi Jensen	2	0	112	43	38.3
1973	Cindy Williams	3	0	242	35	14.5

STATE RECORDS

Name of Record	Record Holder	Year Set	Record
High ringer percentage, tournament	Walter Ray Williams	1971	89.6
High ringer percentage, game	Walter Ray Williams	1971	100.0

(Walter Ray Williams pitched two consecutive perfect games, each 20 of 20)

WALTER RAY "DEADEYE" WILLIAMS'S RECORDS

At age ten Walter Ray Williams, Jr., pitched in his first major tournament, the Western States Indoor Open, finishing second and averaging 33.3% ringers. The interest sparked by this tournament started him to practicing.

Later that same year, 1970, he was high qualifier at the World Tournament at South Gate, California, with 45 ringers out of 50 shoes good for 140 points. It was here that Erma Turner hung the name of "Deadeye" on him most appropriately.

Deadeye lost the 1970 tournament to Bill Holland, his only loss a 50–46 loss to Holland, but set world records with 644 shoes and 507 ringers while posting a 78.7% ringer average. In the 1970 California tournament he became the youngest champion at 10 and hit 84.4%.

In the 1971 Western States Indoor Open Williams posted a 5–0 record and averaged 85.2%. At Middlesex, New Jersey, he became the youngest World Champion at 11 winning all seven games with a record breaking 86.6% average. He also set a single game record hitting 31 of 32 for 96.9%.

During 1971 Deadeye pitched four perfect sanctioned NHPA games. Two of these came in the state meet, each 20 ringers out of 20 shoes against Chris Mohammed and Scott Mohammed. The other two came in the Northern California Junior Championships, 20 out of 20 against Gary Fontaine and 36 out of 36 against his brother Jeffrey Williams. For the tournament he hit 183 ringers out of 194 shoes for 94.3%.

In 1972 Deadeye defended his World Championship at Greenville, Ohio, winning all seven games with another record-breaking performance. His 496 ringers out of 556 shoes gave him a record 89.2% for the tournament, including a record 225 doubles, a record 40 consecutive ringers, and his combined game with Alvin Vinsant a record 87.1%.

When we point to the injury to Deadeye's hand at the site of the 1973 World Championship at Eureka, California, and to the fact that he fell to fourth place pitching with a splint on his pitching hand and posting a 78.4% average, it is not to take away from the magnificent performance put on by Jeffrey Williams in winning it. Jeffrey might have beaten a well Deadeye. Both will be back in top form for the 1974 meet at Keene, New Hampshire.

Suffice it to say that Deadeye returned to form to win the 1973 California title with 88% ringers. As of now he will have to rank as the greatest Junior pitcher ever.

BRITISH COLUMBIA

1969	John Hoffard			
1971	Louis Hoffard	4	0	30.3

CANADIAN NATIONAL CHAMPIONS

1972	Billy Zinger	5	0	38.0
1973	Stephen Hohl	4	0	44.4

COLORADO

1969	Bud Carl			
1970	Buddy Carl			
1971	Mike Roney	6	1	40.9

CONNECTICUT

1961	Gary Dunleary	7	0

THE JUNIORS

FLORIDA

1965	Wayne Warner	5	0		
1966	F. Statner	5	0		
1966	Frankie Statzer	5	0		
1967	Frankie Statzer	8	0		
1968	Larry Shelley	9	0		
1969	Frankie Statzer	6	0		
1970	Larry Shelley	3	0	148 59 39.9	

GEORGIA

1972	Tim Thomas	4	0
1973	Tim Thomas	5	1

ILLINOIS

1957	Gary Farnsworth	7	0	
1959	David Williams	7	0	
1960	David Hamilton	6	1	43.5
1965	David Hamilton	7	0	
1966	Steve Jenkins	7	0	45.8
1968	Russell Staker	7	0	
1969	Larry Staker	7	0	41.1
1971	Mike Stout	9	0	60.3
1972	Mike Stout			
1973	Mike Stout	5	0	

INDIANA

1957	Mike Cody	6	1	30.2
1959	Jim Atwell	6	1	
1967	Mark Seibold	3	0	80.5
1969	Mark Seibold			90.6
1970	Mark Seibold	5	0	87.6
1971	John Passmore	5	0	64.0
1972	John Passmore	7	0	71.1
1973	John Passmore	7	0	70.6

Indiana—Junior Girls

1967	Carolyn Wright	5	0	
1969	T. Bussard			
1972	Janice Passmore	3	0	16.4

PITCHING CHAMPIONSHIP HORSESHOES 336

IOWA

1957	Ernie Danielson			
1959	Neil Vandergriff	7	0	
1960	Marvin James	3	0	
1962	Neil Vandergriff	9	0	
1963	Neil Vandergriff	11	1	
1964	Ronnie Burgess	5	0	
1965	Bill Michael	11	0	
1967	Doug Edwards	8	0	
1968	J. Braumochweiz	2	0	47.1
1970	Randy Fite			39.9
1973	Paul Roberts	5	1	

KANSAS

1973	R. Potts	5	0	

KENTUCKY

1969	Rickey Curran	5	0	31.9
1970	Rickey Curran	7	0	32.7
1971	Jack Elliott	7	0	39.9
1972	Tony Wash	7	0	46.7
1973	Clyde Bell	7	0	47.7

Kentucky—Junior Girls

1970	Donna Blakeman	5	0	4.5
1971	Donna Blakeman	4	1	18.6
1972	Carol Glass	2	1	27.1
1973	Carol Glass			

MAINE

1965	Rene Sirois	7	1	44.0
1966	Larry Roux	6	0	56.4
1967	Larry Roux	3	0	44.8
1968	Larry Roux	4	1	58.0
1969	Marc Pepin	6	0	50.9
1970	Doug Keinia	5	0	53.0
1971	Doug Keinia	4	1	73.5
1972	Doug Keinia	5	1	73.0
1973	Doug Keinia	8	2	71.4

THE JUNIORS 337

Maine Junior Girls

1973	Bobbie Verrill	4	0	28.4

MASSACHUSETTS

1964	Bob Gore	4	0	30.9
1966	B. Renfro	2	0	32.3
1967	Joel Kaddy	2	0	
1968	Joel Kaddy	5	0	36.8
1969	Robert Progen	3	0	35.0
1970	Robert Progen	Retained title—Unchallenged		
1971	Robert Progen	Retained title—Unchallenged		
1972	Robert Progen	5	0	50.4
1973	Chris Erikson	6	0	63.3

Junior Girls—Massachusetts

1973	Mary Ellen Riordan	3	0	22.0

MICHIGAN

1960	Jim Ostrander			
1961	Bill Malvitz	3	1	
1962	Tommy Smith			
1965	Tommy Smith	5	0	42.4
1966	Fred Smith, Jr.			
1967	Fred Smith, Jr.	5	0	
1968	Fred Smith, Jr.			
1969	Fred Smith, Jr.			81.1

MICHIGAN WOLVERINE

1970	Norman Smith	10	0	56.7
1971	Carl Smith	6	0	
1972	Fred Smith	4	0	46.3
1973	James Smith	3	1	47.9

MICHIGAN UPPER PENINSULA

1970	Don Kangas	3	0	34.0
1971	Don Kangas	6	0	49.0

PITCHING CHAMPIONSHIP HORSESHOES 338

| 1972 | Ray Paquette | 5 | 0 | | 22.9 |
| 1973 | Jeff Oinas | 3 | 0 | | 25.0 |

Michigan Upper Peninsula—Girls

1971	Tammy Huotari	4	0		21.0
1972	Tammy Huotari	2	0		31.3
1973	Tammy Huotari	2	0		36.0

MINNESOTA

1922	Stanley Harlan				
1923	Frank Stinson, Sr.			Forty feet	
	Ralph Rasmussen			Thirty feet	
1924	Frank Stinson, Sr.			Forty feet	
	Ralph Rasmussen			Thirty feet	
1925	Ralph Rasmussen				
1926	Andy Paglarini				
1927–1969	No Junior tournaments held				
1961	Dick Bussey				
1962	Dick Bussey	9	0	Thirty feet	
	Frank Stinson, Jr.			Forty feet	
1963	Allen Lindquist	6	0	Forty feet	
	Billy LaBrosse			Thirty feet	
1964	Frank Stinson, Jr.			Forty feet	
	Billy LaBrosse			Thirty feet	
1965	Jeff Hill	4	1		47.4
1966	Tom Ronchetti				
1967	Billy LaBrosse	5	0		
1968	Steve West	6	0		
1969	Jerry LaBrosse				
1970	Jerry LaBrosse	5	0		59.8
1971	Jerry LaBrosse	4	1		40.0
1972	Mark Rosenthal	7	0		60.0
1973	Mark Rosenthal	4	1		67.5

MISSOURI

1968	Melvin McNeal	2	1		
1969	Dan Plute	5	0		25.8
1970	Dan Plute	5	0		34.9
1971	Rick Gibson	5	0		35.4
1972	Dan Plute	5	0		40.0
1973	Dan Plute	5	0		59.3

THE JUNIORS 339

STATE RECORDS

High ringer percentage, tournament	Dan Plute	1973	59.3
High ringer percentage, game	Dan Plute	1973	73.3

NEBRASKA

1971	Kent McCance	5	0	30.8
1972	Joe Krajicek III	4	0	40.5
1973	Kent McCance	4	1	41.3

NEVADA

1969	Byron Cork	2	0	
1970	Rick Hammond			
1971	Rick Hammond	7	0	28.0
1972	Dave Talent	7	0	35.0
1973	Dana Moler	7	0	22.0

Nevada—Junior Girls

1969	Karen Swanson	3	0	
1972	Ann Nappa	4	1	5.0

NEW HAMPSHIRE

1966	Mike Pickering	5	0	33.4
1967	R. McIlvene	5	0	31.3
1969	Mike Pickering	5	0	42.3
1970	G. Castor	5	0	44.5
1971	Bobby Barlow	5	1	48.3
1972	K. Lacoille	6	0	50.6

New Hampshire Girls

1971	Cheryl Belville	4	0	13.1

NEW JERSEY

1966	Len LaBance	6	0

PITCHING CHAMPIONSHIP HORSESHOES 340

Year	Name	Won	Lost	Ringer %
1966	Len LaBance	6	0	
1972	Alan Apgar	3	0	
1973	Alan Apgar	3	0	36.3

NEW MEXICO

Year	Name	Won	Lost	Ringer %
1969	Paul Martin, Jr.	5½	1½	23.1
1970	Dan Martin	3	0	20.0
1971	Robert Buckingham	7	0	30.9
1972	Pat Pyle	5	0	28.0
1973	Wes Wood	5	0	26.4

STATE RECORD

Highest ringer percentage, tournament — Pat Pyle — 1973 — 34.4

NEW YORK

Year	Name	Won	Lost	Ringer %
1965	Ricky Crandall			
1966	Ricky Crandall	5	0	59.3
1967	Ricky Crandall	3	0	33.3
1968	Ricky Crandall	5	0	50.0
1969	Richard Crandall			
1970				
1971	R. Astrab			38.7
1972	D. Astrab	3	0	53.0
1973	T. Powers	3	0	53.1

New York—Junior Girls

Year	Name	Won	Lost	Ringer %
1967	Pat Thomas	3	1	14.3
1970	Pat Thomas	5	0	42.8

NORTH DAKOTA

Year	Name	Won	Lost	Ringer %
1968	Dennis Wiger			
1969	C. Sabin	3	0	28.8

OHIO

Year	Name of Champion	Won	Lost	Shoes Pitched	Ringers	Ringer Percentage
1958	Gary Roberts	6	0	280	104	37.2

THE JUNIORS 341

Year	Name	W	L			%
1959	Gary Roberts	5	0	250	130	52.0
1960	Jerry Webb	5	0	164	83	50.6
1961	Gary Roberts	5	0	202	110	54.5
1962	Gary Roberts	6	0	180	118	65.5
1963	Danny Marcum	9	0	334	171	51.2
1964	Dennis Riffle	5	0	234	133	56.8
1965	Dennis Riffle	5	0	312	163	52.0
1966	Dennis Riffle	5	0	158	115	72.7
1967	Dennis Riffle	5	0	226	131	57.9
1968	Dennis Riffle	4	1	284	161	56.6
1969	Bobby Chappel	3	0	196	132	67.3
1970	Jerry Anthony	5	0			67.5
1971	Doug Riffle	5	0			53.0
1972	Dale Riffle	5	0			56.9
1973	Doug Anthony	3	0			58.1

Ohio—Junior Girls

Year	Name	W	L	%
1969	Connie Cool	4	1	16.6
1970	Connie Cool	4	1	33.1
1971	Jennifer Reno	5	0	42.9
1972	Connie Cool	5	0	48.1
1973	Lynne Harrison	3	0	38.7

STATE RECORDS

High ringer percentage, tournament	Connie Cool	1972	48.1
High ringer percentage, game	Jennifer Reno	1972	77.2

OREGON

Year	Name of Champion	Won	Lost	Percentage
1963	Glen Hollin			32.4
1964	Glen Hollin	5	0	33.1
1965	Glen Hollin	4	0	36.3
1966	Jack LaVoie			26.1
1967	Jack LaVoie			45.2
1968	Jack LaVoie	3	0	50.0
1969	Randy Burke			23.8
1970	Blake Sarff			17.6
1971	Blake Sarff			22.4
1972	Randy Burke			59.9
1973	George Schuster			46.9

PITCHING CHAMPIONSHIP HORSESHOES 342

PENNSYLVANIA

| 1963 | Larry Thompson | 3 | 0 | |

SOUTH DAKOTA

1970	Kim Nagel	3	0	18.3
1971	Dean Kai	3	0	21.2
1972	Kirk Schaunaman	3	0	17.3
1973	Duane Moe	3	0	21.0

TENNESSEE

1969	Jerry Kirkpatrick			
1972	Bill Hatmaker			
1973	Bill Ward			64.0

TEXAS

1957	John Bowers	2	0	
1967	Brian Burgess			
1969	Jonathan Burgess	6	1	48.2
1970	Tommy Self	5	1	
1971	T. Haslett	6	0	
1972	Gabriel Zuniga	6	0	
1973	Jolynn Minnich			

VIRGINIA

1968	J. Cooper	3	0			
1970	Cecil Monday, Jr.	2	0			50.0
1971	Ronald Walker	5	0			
1972	Ronald Walker	3	0			64.9
1973	Ronald Walker	4	0	206	125	60.6

VERMONT

| 1972 | Kevin Hollister | 5 | 0 | 51.0 |
| 1973 | Kevin Hollister | 4 | 0 | 73.5 |

WASHINGTON

| 1957 | Jim Saari | | | |
| 1963 | Gary Batcheller | 4 | 0 | |

THE JUNIORS

1964	Steve Jackson				
1965	Steve Jackson				
1966	C. Martindale	6	0		28.2
1967	Jim Malvern	5	0		64.2
1968	Earl Ketterson				
1969	Mike Weber	5	0		74.8
1970	Mike Weber	6	0	172 136	79.8
1971	Lonnie Griggs	5	1	316 163	51.6
1972	Sam Woodman	7	1	512 264	51.6
1973	Glen Walker	7	0	434 281	64.7

Washington—Junior Girls

1967	Wilma VanEgdom					
1972	Kelly O'Brien	6	0	416	122	29.3
1973	Kelly O'Brien	4	0	170	88	51.8

STATE RECORDS

High percentage, tournament	Mike Weber	1970	79.8
High percentage, game	Mike Weber	1970	88.5
Most consecutive doubles	Mike Weber	1969	9
Most doubles, game	Mike Weber	1969	31
Most ringers, game	Mike Weber	1969	76

WYOMING

1961	Max Miller					
1962	Terry Anderson	4	2			23.3
1963	Terry Anderson	6	5			
1966	Farron Eisemann	6	0			53.5
1967	Farron Eisemann	10	0	356	271	76.1
1968	Farron Eisemann	12	0	440	351	79.8
1969	Mike Marlatt	9	3	610	196	32.1
1970	No Junior tournament held in Wyoming.					
1971	James Hughes	5	1	266	28	10.5
1972	Miles Holiday	4	1	330	77	23.3
1973	Beverlee Holliday	5	1	504	140	27.8

STATE RECORDS

High ringer percentage, tournament	Farron Eisemann	1968	79.8

PITCHING CHAMPIONSHIP HORSESHOES

High ringer percentage, game	Farron Eisemann	1968	96.4
Most shoes, tournament	Mike Marlatt	1969	610
Most shoes, game	Rod Holliday & Leo Hinkle	1967	94
Most state titles	Farron Eisemann	1966–68	3

17

Advantages of Horseshoe Pitching

Horseshoe pitching is one of the least expensive hobbies. For ten dollars one man can acquire shoes, drive stakes in his back yard and pitch ten thousand games with his friends without spending another dime.

Leagues and tournaments involve a small entry fee but less than most participation sports. The greatest savings comes in practice. Practicing golf or bowling costs about the same as does league play, whereas one can play endless hours on the horseshoe court without charge.

Access to a playing area is more readily available. Construction of a playing court is a job one man can do in a small area and at a minimum cost. This would be more difficult if not impossible were the same man to take up baseball, basketball, golf or bowling. A home court eliminates driving.

The game is suited to all ages and both sexes. Little Gungie Strauss pitched some ringers from 20 feet in a special attraction at the 1969 World Tournament at the tender age of 3½ years. W. O. Maxwell was still pitching 70 percent tournaments at the age of 81.

A great deal of walking and bending is involved which makes the sport a good one for getting some daily exercise.

PITCHING CHAMPIONSHIP HORSESHOES 346

With the advent of indoor courts horseshoes has become a year round sport in all types of weather.

If you are looking for a challenge it is here. The game is simple enough that anyone can play it and yet so complicated that no man has ever mastered it. The man has not come along who can throw all ringers. Nor has the man come along who can't be beat. It can be a pleasant game for idle moments or a deadly serious and scientific one which will beat you before you beat it.

The Williams Family of California

All nine members of the Williams family play tournament horseshoes. Kneeling are Walter Ray, Jr., Jeffrey; in the middle row, Deborah, Nathan, Cynthia, Jonathan, and Barbara; back row, mother Esther and father Walter Ray, Sr. Walter Ray, Sr., is the Secretary of the NHPA and horseshoe pitching is very much a part of their family life. Every member of the family has won some class or event.

This family illustrate the aspect that a family that plays together stays together. Here is a sport where both sexes and all ages can compete against each other on an equal basis.

ADVANTAGES OF HORSESHOE PITCHING

Health

Dale Carson of Baltimore, who is 69 years old as of this writing, has been the Maryland State Champion since 1942 with only one exception. Dale says that:

"I would not have my good health today if it were not for horseshoe pitching. My doctor recommends it."

Floyd Toole of Little Rock, who has been recognized as the Arkansas State Champion since 1958, tied with Ray

DALE CARSON
Maryland State Champion since 1947 except for 1961 and 1973

PITCHING CHAMPIONSHIP HORSESHOES 348

FLOYD TOOLE
Arkansas Champion
Consistently in eighties.

Martin of Philo, Illinois, for second place in the World Tournament in 1965. He constantly averages between 80 and 85 percent ringers.

Toole has had a running fight with arthritis for many years and says, "Horseshoe pitching is all that keeps me going. I would be a bed patient today were it not for this game. The type of exercise involved in pitching is suited perfectly to fighting the kind of pain which accompanies arthritis."

DR. SOL BERMAN
New Jersey State Champion
1955-1957-1965-1969-1970-1973

Convenience

Dr. Sol Berman of Elizabeth, New Jersey, a medical doctor whose wife, Rita, is a psychiatrist, pitches horseshoes for convenience. He is the New Jersey State Champion, averaging in the mid-sixties.

Says Dr. Berman, "I have a court in my back yard. Any time I have a few moments I can get out to the court and back in a hurry. During the period between my afternoon and evening hours I would not have time to go to a bowling alley or golf course. But I can pitch horseshoes for an hour, take a shower and be back in my office refreshed and relaxed in time for the evening's work.

18

Horseshoe Pitching Goes to South Africa

When Robert G. Pence, then Secretary of the NHPA, first learned about a game called jukskei, which was played in the Republic of South Africa and which was reputed to be a game much like horseshoe pitching, Pence began a correspondence with the South African Jukskei Board. The result was an invitation from D. A. Kruger, Secretary of the SAJB, for an exchange of representatives of the two games.

The exchange of representatives became a reality in 1972 and the games proved to be sister games indeed. Annual trips are now being made to South Africa by American horseshoe pitchers and to America by South African jukskei players. Each nation is slowly but surely trying out the other's game.

The first Americans to go to South Africa were Robert Pence and Lois Pence, Ottie Reno, Janet Reno, and Jennifer Reno. As guests of the South Africans they were both ambassadors and exhibition pitchers speaking to many groups throughout the Republic and pitching for five days at the National Jukskei Tournament in April of 1972 at Kroonstad.

The South Africans who returned the visit in August 1972 were M. P. Prinsloo, member of Parliament, Mrs. Prinsloo, Hermanus LeRoux, a grape farmer, Coen Brand, a lawyer from Southwest Africa, Susan Brand, Charel Uys, and Bertie Venter, a prison warden. They, too, were ambassadors of good will as well as demonstration pitchers.

In 1973 Peter Shepard made the trip to South Africa. In 1974 Mr. and Mrs. Glen Henton, Mr. and Mrs. William Cessna, Jim Knisley, and Tommy Brownell made the trip. Coming to the 1974 horseshoe championship in Keene, New Hampshire, will be another group of South Africans including Louis Hollender, George Hambidge, and Peter Erasmus.

Horseshoe pitching seems to be more popular in the United States and Canada than anywhere else, but England, Mexico, and several other countries play quite a lot. The entry of the game into South Africa not only widens the scope of the game but encourages the notion that international competition will increase and that horseshoe pitching will be recognized as a major sport.

Jukskei and horseshoe pitching have much in common. Each tosses an object at a stake with the same style and motion. The origin of the games, the scoring systems, and the orientation around the family unit have much in common. The use of horseshoes originated with shoes discarded from the horses that pulled the wagons of our ancestors; jukskei from the "yoke skeys" of skey pins from the yokes of the oxen that pulled the wagons of the South African's ancestors. A horseshoe encircles a stake for three points; a skey knocks a stake down for three points. A horseshoe within 6 inches is one point; a skey within 18 inches is one point—each one length of the

HORSESHOE PITCHING GOES TO SOUTH AFRICA 353

object thrown for the convenience of measuring.

The fact that jukskei players took readily to horseshoe pitching is a hopeful indication that South Africa will become a serious contender. Only time will tell but at least the trial has begun.

First South Africans—1972

This group from the Republic of South Africa was the first to visit the United States under the present exchanges between jukskei and horseshoe pitching. They came to the World Horseshoe Tournament at Greenville, Ohio to observe and to demonstrate their own game. The first raising of the South African flag and the singing of their national anthem was quite a stirring moment.

From the left they are: Bertie Venter, a prison warden, who became the first South African player to qualify in the World Horseshoe tournament; M. P. Prinsloo, a member of the South African Parliament; Charel Uys, who operates a milk bottling plant; Susan Brand, one of the finest women jukskei players in South Africa; Coen Brand, a lawyer from Southwest Africa; Hermanus LeRoux, a grape farmer from Boland.

LeRoux is the most decorated jukskei player for a career and Venter the most valuable player in the 1972 National Championships.

Hospitality Started at the Top

The hospitality shown to the American visitors started at the top. In this picture Ottie Reno, left, and Bob Pence are greeted by Prime Minister B. J. Vorster, center, and Mr. and Mrs. M. P. Prinsloo, member of Parliament.

The Women Play Jukskei

Two women's teams competing in the 1972 National Jukskei Championships at Kroonstad are looking over the count. This scene gives a good view of a playing court. Behind them can be seen several men's teams in action.

The 1974 Visitors from South Africa
These five South African jukskei players will visit the National Horseshoe Championships at Keene, New Hampshire in 1974. From left to right the players are: The Johan Kapp, Louis Hollender, George Hambidge and Peter Erasmus. They will compete against a United States jukskei team at Heritage House in Sutton, Massachusetts and in Keene, New Hampshire.

Americans Receive Medals
This picture is from the stage of a school in Kroonstad where some 600 people gathered for a concert and awards night. From the left Mr. D. A. Kruger, Secretary of the South African Jukskei Board, presents medals to the Americans, Ottie Reno, Jennifer Reno, Janet Reno, Robert Pence and Lois Pence. Joining them on stage were the South Africans chosen to return the visit, Coen Brand, Susan Brand, Charel Uys, Bertie Venter and Hermanus LeRoux.

First Horseshoe Match Between United States and South Africa
On the last day of the Kroonstad tournament the first match between the nations was held with Willie Botha and Trecia Grobler pitching for South Africa, left, and Janet Reno and Ottie Reno, right, pitching for the United States. The U. S. won 53-16.

Pence and Reno Exhibition Game

During the first four days of the Kroonstad tournament the Americans competed against each other and pitched demonstrations. Here Ottie Reno, left, and Bob Pence, right, play each other for a throng of interested South Africans. In this one Reno hit 70% ringers, Pence 56% in a game won by Reno 51-30.

Mother vs Daughter at Kroonstad

The South Africans enjoyed this match between Jennifer Reno, left, World Junior Girls Champion, and her mother Janet.

Index

Addressing the stake, 70
Advantages of horseshoe pitching, 345
Allen pitching shoe, 40
Allen, Ted, 78, 194
American pitching shoe, 40

Backstops, 28
Backswing, 72
Batteries of courts, 33
Beller, Elmer, 197
Bradenton Herald, 24
Brust, Fred, 201
By-laws, 42

Canadian Horseshoe Pitchers' Association, 22
Canadian records, 290
Cancellation scoring, 59, 173
Care of playing courts, 25
Charts and tables, 144
Clay, care of, 28
Club activities, 122
Cobb, F. Ellis, Editor, 23, 199
Concentration, 86, 93
Confidence, 82
Constitution and By-Laws, 42, 126
Construction of playing courts, 25, 56
Correcting mistakes, 82, 116
Cottrell, David D., 195
Count-all scoring, 173
Courts, construction and care, 25, 56

Davis, C. C., 197
Day, Curt, pitching tips, 93, 198
Dean, Cindy, pitching tips, 314

Detroit Flyer pitching shoe, 40
Diamond pitching shoe, 40
Distance, court construction, 27
Distance, pitching, 27, 98
Dixon, Dale, 203
Dixon pitching shoe, 40
Doubles play, 61
Dykes, Ralph, 203

Elimination charts, 155
Emotion, 77
England, 16
Equipment, 17, 38
Executive Committee, 61

Fargo Forum, 24
First local club, Meadville, Pa., 17
Focht, Paul, pitching tips, 101
Follow through, 74
Forsstrom, Ralph, 202
Foul lines, 58

Goals, 83
Gordon, John, 201
Gordon pitching shoe, 40
Governing body started, 17
Grand League formed, 19
Gregson, Archie, 195
Grip, 65

Hall of Fame, 191
Handicap system, 174
Hangen, Ruth, pitching tips, 313
Heritage Recreation Center, 36
History of the game, 15
Hohl, Elmer, pitching tips, 106, 198

INDEX 359

Horseshoe court layout, 27, 56
Horseshoe Pitchers' News Digest, 23, 199
Horseshoe World Magazine, 23
Howard, Raymond B., 23, 196
How to pitch, 63
How to practice, 89

Imperial pitching shoe, 40
Indoor courts, 30, 31, 35
Indoor pitching, 35, 57
Instructions, court construction, 25
Instructions, playing, 58, 63
Intermediate division, 269, 275
Isais, Fernando, 194

Jackson, Frank, 194
Johnny Carson show, 24, 119
Jones, Casey, 197
Julskei in South Africa, 10, 350
Juniors, 326
Jurisdiction, 61

Kamman, Art, pitching tips, 86
Knisley, Jim pitching tips, 89
Kuchcinski, Dan, pitching tips, 112
Kuchcinski, Sue Gillespie, pitching tips, 310

Lanham, Mrs. C. A., 201
Leagues, how to run, 129
Lee pitching shoe, 40
Lighting of courts, 30
Local clubs, 122

McLaughlin, Dean, pitching tips, 297
Manners on court, 77
Martz, Clyde, 110
May, George W., 21, 202
Model constitution, 126
Monasmith, John, pitching tips, 104
Mortenson, Leland, 200
Mossman, Putt, 196

National Horseshoe Pitchers' Association, 22, 187

Nunamaker, Blair, 200

Officers' duties, 46, 126
Officers of the NHPA, 46, 189
Official playing rules, 46
Ohio pitching shoes, 40
Open shoe development, 17, 20, 98
Organization meeting, 123
Origin of the game, 15

Pence, Robert G., 12, 199, 350
Pitchers' box, 57
Pitching instructions, 63
Pitching shoes, 40
Playing rules, 56
Practice, 76, 83, 89, 90
Preface, 9
Pressure, 82, 96, 105
Prize money, 265
Program of local clubs, 125

Quoits, 15, 16, 39

Record keeping, 81
Release, 74
Reno, Harold, pitching tips, 116
Reno, Jennifer, 24, 330, 350
Reno, Ottie W., pitching tips, 63, 350
Rhythm, 80, 94, 97
Ringer defined, 60
Ringer percentage chart, 160
Risk, Jimmie, 200
Roberts, Donnie, 135
Roland, Ernolf, "Red," pitching tips, 90
Round Robin schedules, 146, 172
Rules, 18, 42, 56

St. Pierre Mfg. Co., 40
Scoring, 59, 173, 184
Senior division, 275
Shoe size and weight, 59
Smith, Roy, pitching tips, 118
Solomon, Jim, pitching tips, 75, 91
South African jukskei, 10, 350
Stakes, 57
Stance, 68

Standardized rules, 17
State champions, 204 317
Steinfeldt, Carl, pitching tips, 86, 202
Step, 72
Stinson, Frank, 203
Stokes, Arch, 195
Sutton, Sam, pitching tips, 111

Tables and charts, 144
Team matches, how to run, 129
Three-handed game, 61
Timing, 76, 94
Titcomb, Don, pitching tips, 96
Tools, 38
Tournament, how to run, 129
Turn, 65, 76, 86

Turning the shoe, 65, 76, 86

Uniform rules, 18, 42, 56

Wearing apparel, 34, 64, 77
Williams, W. Ray, 12
Winston, Vicki Chappelle, pitching tips, 199, 304
Women, 298
Woodfield, Harry, 198
World Champions, 271, 299, 327, 330
World Tournament Records, 262, 301, 328, 331

Zadroga, Al, pitching tips, 100
Zimmerman, Guy, 196